fast girl

Don't Brake Until You See the Face of God
and Other Good Advice from the Racetrack

INGRID STEFFENSEN

SEAL PRESS

FAST GIRL
*Don't Brake Until You See the Face of God
and Other Good Advice from the Racetrack*

Brick House
Words and Music by Lionel Richie, Ronald LaPread, Walter Orange, Milan Williams, Thomas
    McClary and William King
© 1977 (Renewed 2005) JOBETE MUSIC CO., INC., LIBREN MUSIC, CAMBRAE MUSIC,
    WALTER ORANGE MUSIC, OLD FASHION PUBLISHING, MACAWRITE MUSIC and
    HANNA MUSIC
All Rights Controlled and Administered by EMI APRIL MUSIC INC.
All Rights Reserved   International Copyright Secured   Used by Permission
Reprinted by Permission of Hal Leonard Corporation

Library of Congress Cataloging-in-Publication Data

Steffensen, Ingrid.
  Fast girl : don't brake until you see the face of God and other good
advice from the racetrack / Ingrid Steffensen. — 1st ed.
    p. cm.
  ISBN 978-1-58005-412-6 (pbk.)
  1. Steffensen, Ingrid. 2. Automobile racing drivers—United States. 3.
Women automobile racing drivers—United States. 4. Automobile
racing—Anecdotes. I. Title.
  GV1032.S736A3 2012
  796.72092—dc23
  [B]
                            2012012282

9 8 7 6 5 4 3 2 1

Cover design by Debbie Berne Design
Interior design by Domini Dragoone
Printed in the United States of America
Distributed by Publishers Group West

To Mr. B

Table of Contents

CHAPTER ONE

Finding Wonder Woman

Let's start *in medias race:* I'm sitting in the hot grid. I'm waiting patiently to get onto the racetrack in an orderly double row of about twenty other rumbling sports cars. First I do a mental check: crash helmet on and chinstrap securely fastened. Neck brace underneath. Driving gloves on. Wraparound sunglasses firmly seated on my nose. Lip gloss accurately applied. Six-point harness pulled so tight my boobs and thighs are smooshed. Air conditioner off. Windows down. Plenty of gas. All gauges reading well. I'm good to go.

So then I start to sing.

"She's a brick (pause, pause, pause) *HOWSE.*

Mighty, mighty, just lettin' it all hang out."

I beat my flame-retardant gloved hands on the steering wheel to emphasize the pauses.

"She's a brick (baow, baow, baow) *HOWSE.*

She's the one, the only one, who's built like an Amazon."

It helps to settle my stomach and my nerves, all buzzing with anxiety in anticipation of the signal to go. Since I'm the only girl in the group, the lyrics help wind me up. Plus, I've always wanted to be built like a brick house, despite my modest 34Bs.

"Shake it down, shake it down, shake it *down* now.

Shake it down, shake it down, shake it *down* now."

I sound like the audio track to a cheap porno flick from the seventies, but nobody can hear you if you have a sport exhaust.

Now I can see the previous group of cars obediently parading off the track. That means we're up. My heart starts to beat even faster. After they've all filed off and the walkie-talkies confirm that the track is clear, the guy at the front of the line starts waving us into the chute. *You!*—he points at a driver—*go!*—and his finger swoops toward the chute. *You—go. You—go.* And so on down the line until it's my turn. I give him a smile and a thumbs-up, turn into the chute, accelerate modestly, and gently shift into second as I approach the flagger at the end of the chute. He waves me on, I give a little wave back, and I settle my hands on the wheel. I put my game face on, press the accelerator pedal down, hear the engine shriek into life, the force pressing my back into my seat, and—*hoo-ahh*, I'm off, baby! Down the track I rocket, heading for another twenty-five precious minutes of sphincter-clenching wrestling with a ton of squirrely machinery and the non-negotiable outer limits of physics. Dude.

I PRACTICE GOOD periodontal hygiene. I sort and I recycle and I bring reusable shopping bags to the grocery store. I'm the kind of gal who cleans the lint trap after every load. I wear sunscreen, get regular exercise, and eat plenty of fiber. I live in a nice three-bedroom house with central air in a charming New Jersey suburb [insert snarky Jersey snub of choice here] with a husband, a preteen daughter, a fluffy little embarrassment of a dog, and a few sadly struggling houseplants. What in the name of all that's sane, sensible, and low fat is someone like me doing on a racetrack?

This is the story of a nice, conservative, cultured woman who led a nice, conservative, cultured life in a nice, conservative, cultured suburban enclave—hey, *wake up!* I'm not done yet—who had her life turned upside down and her expectations of herself utterly transformed through the unlikeliest of means: high-performance driving on closed racetrack circuits. This was a woman who thought her story was written, her path mapped out, her self-image well defined, until one day—thinking she'd be a good sport and maybe learn something about what made her car-crazed husband tick—she wodged a helmet on her head, took her tiny car to the racetrack, and learned how to drive it really, really fast. What began as a companionable lark became a full-blown obsession, and in the course of an eventful year, she discovered high-performance sports car driving to be an exhilarating antidote to the shackles of post-feminist suburban conformity. That woman is—and this still comes as a surprise every time—*me*.

AND WHO AM I? I grew up in small-town Pennsylvania with a father who designed traditional, colonial-style furniture for a local furniture company, and a mother who was born in northern Germany. I had a younger brother, and we all lived the American dream in a brick house with a piebald dog named Perry and a succession of ill-fated guinea pigs. The backyard of my house backed up to the deep backyard of another family's house, and that's where my boy-next-door lived. His name was Charlie, and I was going to marry him. We spent hours and hours playing together, alternating backyards. His Carolina-raised mom would make us fresh lemonade or iced tea, and the best thing about that was the special silver stirring spoons that had long hollow handles attached to their bowls: They were simultaneously stirring spoons and straws in one, and I thought they were brilliant. We'd dump several spoonfuls of sugar in the bottom of our glasses, and then we'd slurp up the sugary sludge through those special spoon-straws. Why the spork caught on and the stroon did not is beyond me. Drinking sweet iced tea through a silver stroon on a hot summer afternoon: Life doesn't get any better than that.

Except maybe when we'd go up to Charlie's bedroom and read his comics. Lucky Charlie had a big bed with a patterned chenille bedspread, and we'd lounge around on it and read his DC and Marvel comic books

superfriends!

while the knobby chenille dug red runnels into the skin of our elbows. Charlie and I would play superheroes, too. He was still pretty attached to a threadbare, tattered green baby blanket, and it was often tied around his neck as a cape, endowing him with superpowers. Many afternoons were spent flying off the swing set, making spittle-filled gunfire noises, and saving the planet from evil.

Charlie, being a boy, could be any one of a pantheon of superheroes. "Look at me, I'm *SUPER*man!" he'd yell, launching himself from the armrest of the hideous rust-colored brocade sofa that had been banished to the basement playroom. His green cape fluttered behind him, and despite the thick, prismatic glasses he had to wear for his wandering eye, to me he was completely believable as the Man of Steel.

The next play session had Charlie, with his stocky little seven-year-old frame, recreating the pectoral-flexing posturing familiar to bodybuilders the world over.

"*Raaaaargh,* I'm the *HULK*," he'd pipe in his childish alto, and I could just see him grow larger and start to turn green.

The gleeful declaration, "It's *clobberin'* time," announced Charlie's transformation into the grinning, granite-clad and fissured Thing, ready to tackle any Skrull that came our way.

He could be Batman or Spider-Man, Flash Gordon, the Green Arrow, or Shaggy from Scooby-Doo for that matter, but as a girl in the seventies, my options were much more limited. I dabbled occasionally with the Invisible Woman, but being invisible just wasn't all that seductive. As a freckled little girl with a homemade haircut, I was already mostly invisible to the world anyway. Supergirl was also pretty unsatisfying. Like Robin, she was just a sidekick, and sidekicks never get the glory, the bad guy, or any respect. They're eternally stuck in Ed McMahon Limbo, wearing dorky glasses and guffawing at other people's jokes.

No, for me there was really only one superhero, and that, of course, was Wonder Woman. She was the only powerful female character who regularly appeared in the comic books, and she also starred in *Super Friends* on Saturday morning cartoons, the one glorious time each week that my brother and I were allowed total dominion over the single family television with its staggering array of four different channels.

If Superman could fly, well, so could I: I could leap tall buildings, and if I had to go further, there was always the invisible plane. If The Thing was impervious to gunfire, I could also deflect bullets with my quick-acting, gold-cuffed wrists. If the Flash was fast, I could run at eighty miles per hour, too. When I was Wonder Woman, I was strong and brave, and I could take anything that Charlie and our combined overactive imaginations could dish out in the great backyard battle of good and evil.

WHEN I HIT the impressionable age of nine, the live-action Wonder Woman series starring Lynda Carter had its moment on TV.

I was completely in love with the television version of *Wonder Woman*. By then I was a geeky kid who already needed glasses, always won the class spelling bees, and was almost completely inept at reading the social coding of fourth-grade fashions and peer group interactions. I continued to carry my Holly Hobbie lunchbox far too long after all the cool kids switched to paper bags.

I could just immerse myself, though, in the character of Diana Prince, Wonder Woman's everyday alter ego. Carter's Diana was competent, prim, and brainy, and wore oversized glasses that looked a lot like the ones I had chosen for myself in a fit of misguided youthful exuberance. I may have been only nine, but her quiet smarts and buttoned-up public persona resonated with me. She looked like she had won all her fourth-grade class spelling bees, too.

But when evil plots were afoot or gunfire could be heard in the distance, she dashed to an unobserved corner, pulled off her glasses, stretched out her arms, and started to spin. As she spun, her hair shook free of its confining bun, and amidst a dazzling explosion of light and a sonic *boom,* she became bullet-deflecting, invisible plane–piloting Wonder Woman. She was strong, she was smart, and she was incredibly sexy in her killer red boots and pointy-tipped gold corseted top. And she always saved the day.

How I longed to transform myself from an awkward, glasses-wearing, straight-A student to someone so sexy, so tall, so glamorous, so confident. If that transformation was ever going to happen to me, it certainly wasn't going to occur in a blinding television flash lasting a couple of seconds. I had years of growing up to do, and I could be pretty certain that with my genetic inheritance, I was never going to grow Lynda Carter's gazelle-like legs. But I could dream—and dream I did—of filling out a corseted top the way Wonder Woman did, and saving the world while doing it.

MY CAPE-WEARING SUPERHERO Charlie is now Charles, a fully adult engineer with Intel, married, with a daughter and a mortgage and all the trappings of an ordinary human. As far as I know he has ditched that green blankie, and with it all his superpowers—except for the kind that transforms silicon into computer innards, which is sci-fi enough when you think about it. Like Charlie, I grew up and discarded superhero role models a long time ago, as adolescence, with its pimples and bras, pushed out those sorts of childish fantasies. Little did I suspect then that Wonder Woman would make her reappearance in the well-ordered life I spent building in the subsequent years.

Even if I tried, I doubt I could come up with a less exciting story than the one that comprises my actual life in its post-superhero phase. Best just to hit the fast-forward button. I graduate as high school salutatorian (damn that B in freshman biology). I major in English in college, the bookworm's default. Ultimately, I pursue a PhD in that guaranteed-career-builder of academic fields, art history. I marry my high school sweetheart—Mr. B—in a move that surprises us both. He becomes a New York banker (stifle yawn). We buy a house in the 'burbs. We are procreational slackers, but manage to produce one little hamster—the Divine Miss M. I bounce around academic jobs, but ultimately land a cushy, part-time position at an elite women's college, where I bask in the presence of smart young students and a campus so postcard pretty, so idyllic, it's been in the movies (my orbit briefly touched Luke Wilson's, and let me tell you, that got my orbit all pink and shiny). So I teach, I parent; I am a whirlwind of domestic efficiency. And it's all as dull as that *thud* you hear when you wake up and find you are forty years old and there's no chance you'll be discovered by Hollywood while shopping at the mall anymore.

But I was happy with this state of affairs. I was not one of those eternally discontented seekers, always on the hunt for something more. My life, I thought, was good. No—not just good—*great*. I reached the horror of my fortieth birthday thinking that I pretty much had it all—the job, the house, the husband, the kid—add a couple of mid-level designer handbags, and who could ask for anything more? It was a safe, conventional, predictable life. If it was Monday, it was yoga night. If it was the third Thursday of the month, then it was book club. Saturday was date night. Each summer we took a nice vacation, and over time we managed to knock off Rome, Madrid, Paris, Edinburgh, Prague. In mid-October we mothballed our summer clothes and pulled out our woolens. And every January we toasted another year of wedded bliss. If there was anything missing, I was completely unaware of it.

SO THIS IS not a story that begins with a crisis. I was not compelled to embark on a quest to find spiritual enlightenment or a better relationship or the sleek thighs that no amount of time on the treadmill seems to be able to produce. In this Martha Stewart Age, I figured I had already achieved Wonder Woman status by managing, Xanax-free, to juggle a husband, a house, a kid, and a more-or-less career. I didn't think any superhero-type transformations were necessary. Those DNA-altering gamma rays came at me out of nowhere, as they so often do, and wrought their surprise transformation anyway.

That transformation came about because of a freak exposure to high-speed driving and high-octane race fuel. One day, I was mild-mannered mommy and tweed-jacketed—true!—college professor, and the next, irradiated with the go-fast isotopes, I was Track Girl, able to negotiate high-G turns on squealing rubber and slay Corvettes in a single lap.

Okay: not true. It may have taken only one weekend to be bitten by the radioactive spider, but it took over a year (and counting) to cultivate all my superpowers. This is the chronicle of that year and of the transformations it wrought. Just as Diana Prince went from the quietly efficient First Class Petty Officer Yeoman in the Navy to spy-catching, plot-foiling, bad-guy trouncing Wonder Woman, so, too, did I tread the path of the superhero, finding speed, strength, courage, and mastery of the torque wrench along the way. The outfits aren't nearly as flashy, much to my dismay, but I've got my crash helmet in lieu of the golden tiara and my sports bra in place of that spectacular eagle-cupped corset. More importantly, I've discovered the fierce joy of biting into life like a juicy steak, tearing at it with my teeth and tossing it down my throat with the red juices dripping down my chin.

Nothing could be further from my tofu-based alter ego, who blends in among the unsuspecting residents of her New Jersey suburb with seamless realism.

THERE WAS ONE thing that, as a reasonably intelligent nine-year-old, I simply couldn't understand about Wonder Woman: How come nobody ever recognized her? Unlike the Hulk, who on TV was played by two different actors, and, after all, turned green, or Spider-Man, who had his full-body costume complete with balaclava, the only differences between Diana Prince and Wonder Woman were hairdo, glasses, and the star-spangled, abbreviated jumpsuit. Maybe it was because no one looked her in the eyes when she was wearing that strapless number, but I was always outraged, as only a moral fourth-grader can be, by the apparent idiocy of the otherwise competent, magnificently haired Steve Trevor. How could the resemblance between Diana and Wonder Woman elude him so completely? But that's the way it so often is with superheroes. Even those who are closest to you aren't able to recognize you. Screaming down the straight at 135 miles per hour, dogging the tail of a Porsche, I don't even recognize myself.

And in my quiet suburban enclave, I can visit the grocery store with total anonymity. I fully understand now the double life that Diana Prince lived. I move among my fellow suburbanites—the mommies in their SUVs, the daddies with their lawn mowers, the sullen, overprivileged adolescents trudging home from the middle school—and no one gives the slight, jeans-clad, middle-aged mom with the kooky haircut a second glance. I continue to teach architectural history to my unsuspecting students. I pilot my beloved Mini along the curving, tree-lined streets of my pretty neighborhood, practicing my heel-toe downshifting and nursing my pleasurable little secret behind an unremarkable façade.

Even those closest to me are often unable to come to grips with my superpowers. My friends who are in the know are utterly dumfounded by my choice of hobbies and seem to regard me with some of the same horror-struck fascination that they bestow upon the latest report of celebrity infidelity or natural disaster in a far-off land. A racecar-driving suburban mommy is probably about as common as a tsunami, and almost as scary.

"Come join me at the racetrack for a weekend," I urge my excitable and fabulous Argentinean girlfriend, no slouch with the accelerator pedal herself. "You're a good driver, and I think you'd like it. There's an extra bed in my hotel room, and I'd love to have the company."

"That would be fun," she replies, with her enviable Latin accent and a flip of her thick dark hair.

But what with children and husbands and in-laws and jobs, somehow it never works out—though I think she and my other friends relish my exploits in a vicarious sort of way, and at the very safe distance of a book club confab with a nice glass of Shiraz in hand.

My own mother wasn't so sure she recognized the Wonder Woman within her daughter. At first she regarded the whole business with semi-tolerant skepticism. As it became clear that Track Girl had become an in-extricable part of my life, she became more openly hostile.

"You don't want your daughter to become an orphan, do you?" was the guilt-and-cringe-inducing query I received from her one day.

Ooph, I thought, *Wonder Woman never caught that sort of flak.*

"No, Mom," I answered, "I don't. But I swear it's a whole lot safer than the daily free-for-all that is my commute on the Garden State Parkway."

Since then, she's come to the racetrack to watch me in action, with the result that she has in fact transferred her maternal fears from the track to my commute—a zero-sum gain, but one that still nets me occasional babysitting for a weekend at the track with the inimitable Mr. B.

MR. B, WHO, like the crack dealer trying to make a permanent customer, offered the heady experience to me in the first place, is fortunately more per-ceptive than the purblind Steve Trevor. Not only has he supplied me with all the heavy artillery one needs to be a track warrior, but he's also been fully behind a transformation that has affected all areas of our lives. He's watched me become more adventurous, more assertive, more demanding, and—curiously—he seems to like the new Wonder Woman in his life.

A year into my adventures in driving, Mr. B and I found ourselves celebrating our anniversary most elegantly at that grande dame of French restaurants in America, Le Bec-Fin in Philadelphia. So romantic! What a treat. The perennially suave Mr. B, all gussied up for the occasion in tailored suit and silk tie, ordered the escargots as his appetizer.

"Want to try one of my snails?" he offered, ever the gentleman.

Now, I have to admit that up to that point, despite having entered my fifth decade of life, I had never, not once, tasted a snail. *Nasty little shriveled-up black things*, I always thought; they resemble animal droppings far too closely for my peace of mind. But then I caught myself and thought: *Dammit, woman, if you can enter a 180-degree banked curve at eighty miles an hour and rocket out the other end at ninety-five, then sure as shootin', you can eat a snail.*

Besides, I realized, looking askance at the little critters luxuriating in their garlicky bath, *cardboard* would taste good with that much white wine and butter ladled on top.

"Okay," I said, doing my best rendition of the nonchalant sophisticate while still squirming a bit queasily on the inside, "sure. I'll try one." And I leaned in across the table, opened wide, and allowed Mr. B to pop one of those bad boys right in. "Umm, good," I allowed, chewing on the little garden pest I'd voluntarily allowed in my mouth. Bring it on.

As it goes with snails, so it goes with cars, and the rest of my life, too. A year at the racetrack has taught me a whole new take on myself—I now look at life, and myself, through an entirely different lens. From my first encounter with the racetrack, quivering with terror, to the triumphant moment I passed a flame-spitting Porsche Turbo, I discovered an inner Wonder Woman who has been waiting for me, tapping her red-booted toes, since elementary school. When at long last I earned the solo-driver's checkered wristband, I felt like I'd been awarded the golden cuffs that render Wonder Woman invincible.

For years I'd been following a script that was in every respect exactly what I wanted out of life. Then I got my own invisible plane in the form of a little car I took to the racetrack, and suddenly, I began to stretch my arms out, and I started to spin, and sparks of light started to come off me, and a sonic *boom* invaded my life. This is a tale about finding my own Wonder Woman again, after many years of having neglected her. To my tremendous surprise, she came back into my life and exposed the self-imposed psychological boundaries I'd erected. She reintroduced me to the terror and the joy that comes when you pump your legs and push the swing as high as it will go—and then you close your eyes, hold your breath, let go of the chains, and go sailing high over the neighbor boy's lawn, far away into another planet where your superpowers make you masterly, invincible, and—well—*fast*.

I NEAR THE end of the sweeping turn that leads onto the front straight. To my left menaces the blue Armco that seems only inches away from my vulnerable side door panels. Yet I know that what is called for at this moment is not—as every sane, reasonable neuron in my head is screaming—to let up on the gas, but to press it firmly down. Coming out of the turn, acceleration is my friend, pinning down the rear end of the car and shooting it out of the turn and onto the long straight.

Ahead of me, a quarter-mile ribbon of asphalt unfurls itself seductively before coming to an abrupt end at a ninety-degree turn. I take a deep breath. I exhale. I wriggle my fingers along the edge of the steering wheel a couple of times to loosen them up.

Somewhere offscreen, over the whine of the super-charged engine, my theme music is playing:

Wonder Woman, Wonder Woman.
All the world's waiting for you,
and the power you possess.

A smile briefly flickers across my face, but then I quickly refocus as I press the accelerator firmly all the way down to the floor. I watch as the needle on the speedometer noses upwards. Past 95 to 100, then 110—115—120, before the brake zone ahead approaches, and all my attention must be focused on slowing my car down again for Turn One.

Change their minds, and change the world.

I laugh at the five-hundred-foot marker, foot still to the floor. *Much too soon to brake.*

I smile at the four-hundred-foot marker, but regretfully lift my foot off the gas.

I hesitate a split second longer, and then just after the three-hundred-foot marker flashes by, I press down on the brake pedal firmly, decisively, but not too sharply. The car shudders a little, as if in protest of this request, but just as it's time to dial into Turn One, we're slowed down enough that we'll make this turn, one more time.

Wonder Woman, Wonder Woman.

You're a wonder, Wonder Woman.

CHAPTER TWO

So You Think You Can Drive?

icture, if you please, someone born and raised in a hot, dry, dusty, landlocked sort of place. She needn't be a Bedouin; Oklahoma City, say, or Wichita will do. Her relationship with water is appreciative but not passionate: She drinks it gratefully, likes to shower, maybe waters her plants and enjoys seeing them thrive. She knows how to swim and takes her children to splash around in the local pool. She is vaguely aware that there are people who swear allegiance to the sea, and that elsewhere there exist deep-sea divers and Olympic swimmers and all sorts of competitive water sports participants, but as these have no relevance to her life she does not follow them, and could not, if asked, name the most recent Olympic medalists. Then, after four decades of this comfortable, if distant, relationship to water, she decides one day to take up platform diving, joins the American Association of Amateur Platform Divers (a purely fictional invention), and specializes in handstand dives from the ten-meter platform. As there are no ten-meter platform pools in her hometown, she must travel for hours and hours and go to great expense in order to indulge her passion. Her friends might look at her askance, but she finds she is addicted to the nose-searing aroma of chlorine and the heady moment when she stares down a thirty-foot drop to the water below and decides one more time to take the plunge.

If you got that, you pretty much got me. My relationship to driving was like my hypothetical Kansan's to water: I accepted it as part of my daily routine, but didn't think a whole lot about it beyond that. I had no prior interest or experience in driving beyond what most any American can claim as his or her birthright from the age of sixteen on. I'm not Janet Guthrie or Danica Patrick and there are no Andrettis dangling from my family tree. I never had even the remotest interest in Formula One or NASCAR, would not have recognized Richard Petty if he had showed up on my doorstep with a Domino's Pizza box in his hands, and would not have cared all that much if the subterfuge had been pointed out to me. I'm sure he's a great guy and I'd thank him for the pizza, but it would not have been one of the crowning moments of glory in my life if we'd shared a medium sausage with the works and maybe a nice cold brew or two. No—other than basically liking to drive and being relatively competent to bring myself to work and my child to school, to get to the grocery store and to play dates, I had no particular interest, knowledge, or talent in cars and driving, nor was I on the lookout for an expensive way to endanger and complicate my already jam-packed life. That life, though, was filled from morning to night with time spent behind the wheel of a car, and in that, I am no different from any of the millions of women who populate the suburbs of America from Baltimore to Los Angeles, Minneapolis to Dallas.

The fantastic women in my suburban world are all fiercely smart and frighteningly well educated. They attended international universities and ivy leagues and top-tier colleges, and they possess advanced degrees in finance, the arts, law—you name it. All of us thought, when we proudly framed our minty-fresh degrees and nailed them to our walls some twenty years ago, that we'd accomplish profound, world-changing things with those credentials. Which is not to say we haven't. We're a talented bunch, we suburban mommies, and we have the résumés to prove it. What none of us fully realized when we signed up for the husband-house-offspring value meal, though, was all the extra credit work we'd have to do on the home front. It kind of creeps up on you: the grocery shopping, the errand-running, the maintenance of the social calendar— the whole Mommy CEO role. And have you ever noticed how just about every one of those things starts with the key turning in the ignition and the car backing out of the driveway? If there's one thing we all have in common, it would have to be the incredible, soul-sucking, planet-killing amount of time spent behind the wheel.

When, in the 1950s and 1960s, women started getting their own cars and the two-car garage began to be a real-estate standard, it looked, I imagine, a whole lot like liberation. Women could work outside the home as easily as men could, and it meant that there was nothing stopping them from pursuing their own agendas with equal geographic freedom. When my dad bought my mom a used Corvair in 1966, she thought it was the most exciting, wonderful gift she'd ever been given. Never mind that Ralph Nader singled out the Corvair in the opening chapter of his scathing indictment of Detroit, *Unsafe at Any Speed*, for its tendency to over-steer, spin out, and even—alarmingly—flip over. Pioneering TV comedian Ernie Kovacs died—his famous, signature cigar found just inches from his body—after losing control of his Corvair in 1962. What my mother saw was, however, not a death trap but the glittering freedom to come and go as she pleased and the realization of the American dream, heady and limit-less for a young woman raised in rubble-filled, post-war Germany. To this day she remembers the Corvair, her first car, as a gift of almost unimaginable promise and excitement. Forty-plus years later, having our own car still represents independence and freedom to most of us, but I'm not so sure that it doesn't also come at a cost: for we suburban women are practically slaves to our vehicles. We live an indecent amount of our lives consuming fossil fuel, ferrying children and shuttling goods back and forth between schools, stores, outings, sports, and base camp. Many mommy mobile units are highly specialized combat vehicles equipped with DVD players, Bluetooth, child seats, luggage nets, roof racks, wardrobe changes, snacks, drinks, and enough cup holders for a soccer team. I suspect the U.S. Army could learn a thing or two about strategic maneuvering and troop logistics by observing the tactics of a mommy mobile unit in suburban New Jersey for a week. I'd like to see an Army general get, say, three average school-age children to all their respective gymnastics, tennis, swimming, tutoring, haircuts, playdates, and chess clubs, with said children properly attired, equipped, and on time, along with the right carpool companions to the right events. My personal belief is that if you put an elementary school's worth of suburban mothers onto the front lines, we'd have Afghanistan put to rights before the spring break trip to Disneyland.

WHEN YOU WERE in your premarital twenties, a pickup line was something you heard in a bar, and it went something like this: *If you were a laser, you'd be set on stunning.* Not anymore. If you have traded the bar scene for the Parent-Teacher Organization, one of the greatest horrors of your life is the elementary school pickup line. If Dante were composing the "Inferno" today, he would have to introduce the elementary school pickup line as an extra level in the architecture of hell. The minivans start bellying up to the curb as much as half an hour before the inmates are released, because the choice is either to be early and wait at the front end, or arrive at three o'clock and wait at the rear end, where all the bad mommies (wave at me back there) live.

When a baby emperor penguin hatches, it imprints on its mother, and even though she goes on a months-long journey to nourish herself, mama and chick can still find each other upon her return amidst a sea of seemingly identical tuxedo-clad penguins. Mother Nature is a wondrous thing. So is Mother Detroit. When the bell rings and the children are disgorged from the school, complete chaos ensues as hundreds of children are matched up with seemingly identical minivans (there are but two varieties:

COURTESY OF THE AUTHOR

the Corvair, my brother, and me in 1971

beige, or gray-blue) and sent back to the nest again. Remarkably, each child almost always goes home in the correct mommy mobile unit.

After pickup, an after-school activity regimen unfolds that could give a logistics specialist a nervous breakdown. The minivans and SUVs bounce around from rec center to dance studio to dentist's office in a precise and urgent ballet that often lasts from the close of school until hours later when all troops return to the mess hall in search of rations to power them through another round of maneuvers tomorrow. Add to that the seemingly endless quest for food, toilet paper, birthday cards, tampons, and toothpaste, and it's a wonder that we don't need our buttocks to be surgically removed from the driver's seat, or that we haven't yet sprouted headlights where our breasts used to be.

Did Paul McCartney have us suburban chauffeuses in mind when he wrote "Drive My Car"? When my husband proposed to me, this is what he should have said: Baby you can drive my car, and maybe I'll love you. Oh, sure, he's a star and I do love him. But if I had entered into the matrimonial and matriarchal contract with full disclosure, I would have had to be notified about my implicit contractual agreement to be owner-operator of Mom's Taxi Service, Inc.

WITH SO MUCH practice, we're all pretty good at this driving thing. Collectively we manage thousands of hours and hundreds of thousands of miles behind the wheel with a very low body count—squirrels possibly excepted. I, for one, sure didn't need to learn how to drive. I got my driver's license at the standard age of sixteen, so that means I've been on the roads for longer than Lindsay Lohan has been alive—and my record remains far cleaner than hers. I got my first car when I was in college. Since then, if you count up all the cars I've owned and tally their odometer readings, I figure the total comes to roughly 375,000 miles, or (at around 25,000 miles per round trip) about fifteen times around the planet. It's an astonishing amount of driving when you add it all up, but probably nothing exceptional in our car-happy society. I drove all those miles, too, without one serious accident—no bodily harm, no major crashes, just a couple of piss-on-your-weekend fenderbenders.

So I thought I was a pretty good driver, and by all measurable, insurance-company standards, I was, too. Who's safer than a middle-aged mommy behind the wheel? Once I entered the realm of high-performance driving, though, I quickly found out that like any beginner in any endeavor, *I didn't know how much I didn't know.* I had absolutely no idea—for the simple reason that I had absolutely no experience with it—what happens at the limits of automotive physics. How many of us really know the maximum stopping power of our car's brakes? We rarely ever push them that hard. Do you even know what it feels like when your antilock brakes activate? I didn't. I'd never been in a situation extreme enough to need them. What do you do when your front end won't turn in as sharply as you are asking it to? How about if the rear end kicks out? Or if two wheels go off the pavement? What's the tightest turning radius your car can negotiate at seventy miles per hour? You could maybe come up with some of these answers if you thought really hard, but could your hands and feet come up with the right answer in the split second that something begins to go wrong? For just about all of us, the answer to all of these questions is no, because we don't ever practice pushing our cars to their limits.

On the whole this is probably a good thing. If everybody started taking their Jeep Cherokees and Honda Odysseys and Ford Focuses onto the roads and careened around trying to ascertain the limits of their brakes and cornering capabilities, our nation's highways and byways would quickly be littered with the failures. On the upside, this might solve the slump in U.S. automakers' sales. But it would be an expensive lesson. It's fortunate for us that our cars come with so many standard safety features that they can do most of the tough thinking for us, and should we make a mistake, our cars are now so stuffed full of airbags that they can outdo a political convention.

And speaking of thinking: How much brainpower was I really giving to the everyday act of driving? Truth be told, not much. I was a good, solid, safe driver. So good, in fact, that I could drive around with most of my brain occupied with other things. My car isn't just a way to get from one place to another; it's an edited version of my entire house. The living room is the front passenger seat, where I throw my purse and jacket and umbrella and bags and packages. No big-screen TV, maybe, but certainly the entertainment unit is there, with radio, CD, and MP3 hookup. My telephone, calendar, and notepads serve as my home office. The kitchen is represented by the water bottle, thermal cup, energy bar, potato chips (when I'm in a devil-take-the-diet mood), mints, gum—whatever I need to power through the next shift behind the wheel. The bathroom is represented by the mirror and makeup kit. The trunk, like the basement, is where all the ugly stuff goes. And the closet, as it often is at home, is strewn all over the place: puffy coat in the back, extra pair of shoes in the passenger footwell, and sometimes, when my feet have just had a long day, the shoes even come off in the driver's footwell. (Is it against the law to drive barefoot? Can't be any worse than driving with stilettos.) I'm a hermit crab on wheels. I'm so busy in my little house that sometimes I've arrived at my destination with no recollection whatsoever of how I got there. But I've always trusted my instinctive driving senses to get me there in one piece.

The act of driving is so mundane, so automatic, that we really don't *need* to pay that much attention to it. Point it where you want it to go, push down the accelerator, brake gently at the stop sign. It simply isn't that difficult. Because we use so little of our cars' capacity, they forgive us our inattention. Steer with one hand, sing along with Rihanna, let the dog sit on your lap (guilty, guilty, guilty), and still you can get by with nearly perfect safety. Many's the time I fished for lost binkies, went spelunking for dropped sippy cups, or substituted a new book or CD for the old one, all while navigating my own mommy mobile on the back lanes and divided highways of New Jersey.

I know I am not alone in this. About every mommy I know will admit to a divided attention between what is on the other side of the windshield versus what is going on in the backseat. In addition to driving, the mommy behind the wheel is usually multitasking to a frightening degree. One girlfriend with a toddler admitted: "I know I probably shouldn't be driving with my right arm stretched behind the passenger seat so much, but the DVD player's buttons are difficult to find, and it sometimes takes me a dozen tries to fast-forward past the 'scary' parts of *Curious George.*"

SO BETWEEN NOT really knowing what I was doing, and not really paying attention to what I was doing, it turned out that I wasn't really as good at driving as I thought I was. I learned very quickly that I did not know much about what happens as you begin to approach the physical limits of your car's ability to adhere to the surface of the road. It turns out that your ordinary car is an amazing piece of equipment that can handle way more than we dish out on a daily basis. Even more exciting to discover was the fact that the computer behind the wheel—the multitasking Mommy Mind—is capable of even more extraordinary gymnastics than I had given it credit for, and that the experience of mastering this complicated ballet between car, track, and physics would open my mind and my life to a whole new turbocharged world.

Do I drive any differently on the streets because of this newfound knowledge? Mostly, the answer is no. It's more than a little scary out there on the track, and believe it or not, what the experience has given me is not the urge to drive fast all the time nor the over-confidence to blithely ignore the process of around-town driving. I don't go zooming around my leafy suburb as if I were going around the racetrack. I don't even drive especially fast on the highway—why bother, when you can floor it with impunity at the track?

Nope. Instead, my experiences on the track have caused me to focus more attention on what I am doing and to appreciate the process of driving for its own sake. I'm actually stricter with myself than I used to be: Hold the wheel properly at three and nine o'clock; unhook your thumb from inside the wheel; don't rest your hand on the gearshift knob; sit up straight and keep your eyes on the road. It's a little bit Zen, and a little bit self-preservation, but I now pay even more attention while I am driving to the driving itself, even when I am going on those deadly-dull, familiar paths that I have trod hundreds and hundreds of times before. I won't claim that I never covertly pick up my cell phone or fiddle with my radio dial while underway, but I know I have changed how alert I am behind the wheel. Dealing with the high-speed context at the racetrack has attuned me much more finely to all the circumstances around me: the topography of the road itself, the traffic, and my place in it. So now do I think I can drive? As with so many things in life, the more you learn, the less you realize you know. As a result of the practice at the racetrack, I just might be better in a pinch than your average mommy behind the wheel. But I also appreciate how much more there is to know. Like the perfect golf swing or the best path down a black diamond slope, it's a skill with an infinite capacity for refinement.

What the experience has given me above all else, however, is a new-found respect for what both car and driver are capable of. It is without doubt both eye-openingly instructive and rip-snortingly fun to discover the deep bank account of performance that even an unmodified commuter car draws upon. But the even greater head-smacker was the discovery of the untapped wells of reserved brainpower, skill, bravery, and out-and-out guts that a mild-mannered full-time mommy and part-time college professor had hidden deep within her. I thought I knew myself pretty well, and I was pleasurably comfortable with that knowledge. I thought: I'm pretty smart, I have a good life, I take excellent care of myself, my family, my friends, and I'm happy. None of this was actually wrong. But I discovered in addition to all this that I am quicker, stronger, gutsier, freer—more ambitious, more powerful, more aggressive—than I had ever realized I was capable of being. It's not just that I can push a car harder than I thought. It's that I can push myself to places that it had never occurred to me to even *want* to go. It is not too much to say that the experience has upended everything I thought I knew about myself and wanted from my life. Suddenly, I expect more from myself and from what the world has to offer me.

So my story isn't so much about the cars and the driving as it is about the driver. But the two do go together, so it's the perfect opportunity to introduce you to the cars of my life, from the cars I grew up with to my beloved Mini, the car that took me beyond the orthodontist's office, beyond the toll booths on the Garden State, and into the adventure of a lifetime.

CHAPTER THREE

An Auto Biography

The year I was born—it was 1967, the year of the Summer of Love in San Francisco—my granddaddy bought my grandmama a brand new Ford Thunderbird. This was not the sporty little two-door convertible of "daddy took the T-bird away" fame, but a car that represented a shift in Ford's thinking about the Thunderbird. Ford had introduced the Mustang in 1964, and its huge success ate into the Thunderbird's own market. So they decided to make the Thunderbird larger and more luxurious, poised to ride the coattails of the highly successful Lincoln Continental.

I called my German-speaking grandmother Oma, and my Oma's car was "da bomb." At over seventeen feet long and close to two and a quarter tons, this was a late-sixties gas-guzzling land yacht in a glorious shade of metallic Brittany Blue. From the front, the car had a grille the size and shape of Tennessee, scooping out to gulp the air it traveled through like the gaping mouth of a manta ray. It was filled with a chromed grid that hid the headlights. They emerged from behind secret trapdoors only when directed to do so from Command Central behind the wheel.

It was the era of the Cold War, and I suspect that it was no coincidence that the Thunderbird's silhouette resembled a submarine or torpedo, with

COURTESY OF THE AUTHOR

T-bird and me, both vintage 1967.

its thrusting snout in front and a trunk that a Mafioso would love. You could fit, oh, probably three bodies in that trunk, cement galoshes included. It looked nearly the same going as coming, with a rear end as wide and bechromed as the front. It sported the lettered Thunderbird logo as well as the most sensational detail of all: three-part rear directional indicators that blinked in succession as you made your turn. Blink-blink-*blink*, blink-blink-*blink*, blink-blink-*blink*, to signal your way through life like a neon-lighted movie marquee.

Inside, the car coddled you in padded-cell softness. The two front seats and the bench seat in the rear were divided by an ocean of carpeting. Everything was upholstered in off-white vinyl and an elegant satiny taupe-colored cloth reminiscent of silken pantyhose. As kids, my little brother and I floated like baby jellyfish in a warm Caribbean sea, riding in the back of that Thunderbird as our Oma took us on special outings for grilled cheese sandwiches and Shirley Temples at the Horn & Horn restaurant in the shopping plaza in Hershey, Pennsylvania. I loved that car almost as much as I loved my Oma; my memories of her are inextricably linked with that vehicle. I will forever associate it with her, as it is the only car she drove for my entire life.

The Thunderbird plays a vital role in my own romantic history. Oma still owned and drove the T-bird when I turned eighteen and convinced Mr. B to make a sojourn home from college and take me to my senior prom. Oma came for that weekend in the T-bird, and in exchange for an entire afternoon of washing and waxing and polishing of its acres and acres of chrome, she allowed us to take it to my prom. I hope she will forgive us posthumously when I reveal that Mr. B decided he needed to see what this baby could do on the back roads of central Pennsylvania, and on a clear, straight stretch with no cops in sight, he mashed down the accelerator and brought it up to over one hundred miles per hour, which it ate up greedily like it was something it was born to do, eighteen years too late. We hooted like the teenagers that we were, and if I didn't lose my virginity in the backseat that night (kind of wish I had), it wasn't for lack of my beau's trying.

My Opa was a bona fide car nut. A mining engineer for Bethlehem Steel, he loved gadgets and widgets of every stripe—cameras, stereos, televisions, he loved them all. He set up a studio in his basement so he could do time-lapse photography of growing plants and butterflies emerging from their cocoons. He built himself an underwater camera and took pictures of sea turtles on a trip to pre-Castro Cuba. And when he hurt his back and had trouble getting in and out of his easy chair, he created a remote control for his TV well before they were commercially available. How clever was he? But most of all, he loved his cars. He came by this affection naturally: In 1908, my great-grandfather bought the first car in the tiny hamlet of Poy Sippi, Wisconsin (a real place!—you can't make this stuff up). It was the year the Model T was introduced. Family lore has it that as Great-Granddad approached the homestead and attempted to bring the horseless carriage to a stop, he pulled up on the steering wheel and yelled, "Whoa, *whoa, WHOA!!*" My Opa learned to drive at the tender age of nine years old, and his love affair with cars lasted until he died at the age of eighty in 1985.

The first in his family to attend high school, Opa went on to college and even in the Great Depression managed to do well enough that his first big promotion with Bethlehem Steel came in 1937. He was rewarded with the stupendous annual salary of $12,000, and his first big purchase was a Lincoln-Zephyr that cost $1,550—a tremendous indulgence, though perhaps not as reckless as it seems when one realizes that income taxes were nearly nil at that point in history and he lived in what amounted to company housing in those patriarchal corporate days. The Zephyr had twelve—count 'em, twelve—cylinders, but not one of them put out as much as ten horsepower, for all combined the Zephyr could only boast 110 horses under its hood. From there on out, Opa was a rolling stone—not with his women, for he was a faithful man—but with his cars, which he churned through on a ritualistic annual basis. He loved them big, he loved them luxurious, he loved them top of the line.

His son, my father, did not take after his pa. I did not grow up in a carburetor-crazed home. Perhaps knowing he could never keep up with his father's automotive acquisitiveness, my own father chose the

Zephyr

cars-as-useful-tools route. Though he would perversely and gleefully re-
ject the Environmentally Conscious label, my dad adopted a frugal practicality that led to his choice of small, economical, fuel-efficient cars well
before their time. The first cars I can clearly remember in my own family are the 1974 Volkswagen Super Beetle and the 1975 mustard-yellow
Volkswagen Rabbit that my dad owned in tandem for many years. The
forty-six-horsepower Super Beetle was distinguished by its curving front
windshield, and it was as cute as a button with a red exterior and off-white
waffle-textured vinyl that would leave its pattern imprinted in reverse on
the backs of children's thighs in the summertime. The People's Car was
small, economical to purchase, cheap to maintain, and positively puritani-
cal in its demands at the pump. But neither my brother nor I cared about
any of that. What we loved above all else was the small well behind the rear
seats, where one of us could crawl and ride in a space just big enough for a
seven-year-old. Lamentably, I grew out of that well long before my three-
years-younger brother did.

My dad, my brother, and the Super Beetle

COURTESY OF THE AUTHOR

THE RABBIT CAME and left, followed by inexpensive American knock-offs—a two-tone brown Plymouth Horizon, succeeded unimaginatively by a silver one. You couldn't kill the Beetle, though, and I think it was the only car my father was ever really nostalgic about, because he just couldn't seem to get rid of it. I think the only time I ever felt jilted by my parents' playing favorites was when my brother, instead of me, got to take the Beetle to college. I can still hear the music of the Beetle's air-cooled engine, chirruping away as my brother drove off down the road. Bastard.

When I turned sixteen, and the beneficent state of Pennsylvania bestowed upon me the longed-for learner's permit, I learned to drive in that Beetle. Since both cars in the family at that point possessed manual transmissions, I had no choice but to learn to drive a stick. (Was my dad a closet automotive purist? Did he value the extra performance a manual transmission imparts? Nope. It was just cheaper.) I remember vividly the session in the middle school parking lot when I jolted and jounced and stalled out all over the asphalt as I attempted to master the complicated samba of coaxing the Beetle into first gear. My mom and dad are a restrained, highly cultured pair. It was the first time I ever said *shit* in front of them. It was very embarrassing, and I remember feeling my ears turn hot and apologizing profusely. I'm still a fairly big believer in keeping your four-letter words in reserve for really special occasions, like when you slam your finger in the car door.

I passed the test for my driver's license on my second try. The first time I went the wrong way through the orange-coned slalom course because I misread where the DMV official was pointing his meaty finger. That's my excuse, and I'm sticking with it. Is there any more glorious day than the one on which your teenaged self secures the Holy Grail of independent locomotion? When you finally, finally, get the keys to the car and get to drive someplace all by yourself? You're only sixteen, you can't vote, you can't drink (legally), you can't get married, though you sure could get pregnant, and suddenly you can go out and get into all sorts of trouble because you are free, gloriously free from the tethers of parents and home. Sure, you have to whine and beg for the use of the car, and okay, maybe you've got curfews and you'll have to take your little brother with you some of the time, but boy, oh, boy, is that freedom a heady feeling. I wish I could go back to my teenaged self and tell her to enjoy it more, because it won't be long before driving becomes more of a burden than a joy, and getting in a car in the near future will almost always mean going to work, running errands, or visiting in-laws. I don't think I'd tell her about going to the racetrack after she turns forty. That would probably scare her needlessly.

POSSIBLY THE NEXT best thing to the thrill of getting your driver's license is getting your first car. Like your first love, you never forget it. I was nineteen, nearing the end of my first year of college, and my parents were quickly tiring of figuring out how to transport me the three hundred miles between Charlottesville, Virginia, and central Pennsylvania on an ongoing basis. Ever-practical Dad, who loved his small, fuel-efficient hatchbacks, found a small, fuel-efficient hatchback for me, my beloved 1984 Honda Civic. In what was surely a good omen, it was painted a shade of metallic baby blue that was very close to my Oma's Brittany Blue Thunderbird. It was also somewhat smaller but in my proud eyes no less stylish. It was used but in excellent condition, and from the time I got it in 1986 to the time I traded it in in 1992 with over one hundred thousand miles on it, the Putterbug, as I christened it, ran like a top and never let me down. It saw me through my undergraduate degree, two more graduate degrees, my marriage, and my dissertation. The little hatchback could hold all my earthly belongings in those days, and it was my steady, square-backed companion as I shuttled back and forth between one campus or another and the regular assignations with Mr. B that eventually ended in our legal union. To this day he declares that the reason he married me was because I had a car and he did not. Works for me. Though you'd think a guy as hot as my Mr. B could hold out for a much better car—an Accord at the very least.

The Putterbug and me: perfect together

For years after we sold it, Mr. B and I played our own variation on the Punch buggy game, which was spotting Honda Civics of that specific vintage and color while on the road. "Putterbug blue!" one of us would yell, and then deliver the obligatory punch to the shoulder. It was a testament to the legendary Honda reliability that it has only been in the last few years that we have ceased to spot them anymore. Since then I have owned many nicer cars but none ever came as close to my heart. God bless you, little Putterbug, wherever you are. I hope you are sipping a dry gasoline martini in a Castrol-filled Jacuzzi and dreaming about overtaking Lamborghinis somewhere in automotive heaven.

YOU CAN PRETTY much chart the course of your life's stages via the cars that went along with them. Though none of the individual cars may be that unusual, the succession is as unique as a fingerprint. The Putterbug was succeeded by a Milano Red Acura Integra hatchback—the first car Mr. B and I purchased together, shortly after getting hitched. Sleek and sporty, the Integra reflected the fact that we were young, childless, and upwardly aspirational. I loved that car. It made me feel like we'd arrived. As we started to settle into our careers and moved toward buying a house and thinking about contributing to the global overpopulation problem, we bought the first of a series of wagons, which made us card-carrying suburbanites. The parade of wagons, too, indicated our increasingly satisfactory financial situation—first a VW, then a Saab, then a Mercedes C-class. But you have to come full circle, back to the two-door hatchback, to find a car as near and dear to me as the Civic. Cuter, sportier, and adorably attired in red and white, the Mini Cooper Mr. B acquired for me as I started that vicious slide toward forty was like coming home again.

For a gal with one child too big for a baby seat and a very long commute, the Mini was the perfect match, especially because I was suckled on little cars—the smaller the car, the happier I am. In the land of Enormolades and Jumburbans, I know this makes me a little strange, but since I was a terminally uncool teenager who spoke German and joined the

COURTESY OF THE AUTHOR

my beloved Mini

marching band, I am pretty comfortable with being just a little skewed. The moment I first drove the Mini, I was in love. I loved its peppy handling, its responsiveness, and its maneuverability. The Mini and I made a very happy couple, tootling back and forth on the New Jersey Turnpike for work and plying the curvy suburban roads of Essex County for household errands, and there our story might have ended, were it not for the involvement of Mr. B in our lives. After many years of gentle persuasion, Mr. B at long last lured us to the racetrack, and there the Mini and I embarked on the adventure of a lifetime. Thus begins the story of a gal, her itty-bitty car, and an unlikely romance with the stomach-lurching twists and face-flattening speeds of high-performance driving.

CHAPTER FOUR

Learning the Line

So was it like Clark Kent dashing into the phone booth to emerge as Superman? Mild-mannered Mommy jumps into Mini and becomes Track Girl? Where along the way did the radioactive spider bite me and turn me into my super-alter-ego, RaceMama? Rather than a single epiphanic moment, it was more a series of steps that brought me to the racetrack in the first place.

One of my bedrock principles for marital bliss is simple if deeply unoriginal: If you can't beat him, join him. I fell in love at age sixteen with the high school track star. He didn't seem to mind dating an actual cover girl for nerds: I once graced the front page of a local newspaper's weekly insert—in full living color, no less—holding my French horn in front of me like the badge of geekiness that it was.

This is the social outcast I was in high school, and to this day, I'm not sure what possessed the cool guy, the popular athlete with the sun-kissed blond mop and those stylish aviator glasses to ask me out. But his lean physical grace entranced me, and suddenly it seemed like a good idea to match my intellectual and artistic accomplishments with some physical ones. So I laced up my brand-new running shoes, hit the asphalt, and gradually got into shape, and found I liked being that way.

When that boyfriend ran for Princeton, got injured, and couldn't run anymore, he took up bicycling, so I took up bicycling, too. Why not? I was in pretty good shape, what with all that running, so I bought my own road bike and we cycled on our weekends together while he was living in New York and I was in grad school in Delaware. He expanded his repertoire to mountain biking, and our relationship got more serious, so he bought me a mountain bike for a Christ-

FREE With SUNDAY GRIT

INSIDE "SCENE"
Television, Concerts, Films, Plays,
Festivals, Artists — What's Happening!

April 3-9, 1983

An actual cover girl for nerds

mas present after we got engaged. I gamely hit the trails, bumping along behind him, hoping like hell I wouldn't wipe out and leave all my teeth on the handlebar. Seven years after we first met, he proposed, I accepted, we got married, and soon we bought a tandem bike. How's that for a metaphor of togetherness? We rode a Century (one hundred miles), I got pregnant, and we bicycled together until I was eight months along.

OUR ADVENTURES ON the road came to a screeching halt with the arrival of the Divine Miss M, who absorbed a lot of the time and energy that I used to expend keeping up with her daddy. He still biked when he could find the time, but wife, house, baby, and career was a lot to pull along behind him. There are, however, some advantages to getting older and more established, and one of them was that Mr. B started earning enough money to begin to indulge one of his more expensive tastes—the kind that comes with four wheels and a bottomless thirst for fossil fuel. Over the years, he scaled up automotively as the paychecks permitted. Then, when the toddling Miss M turned three, he purchased a BMW M3, a kind of stealth Mustang. Unless you look really closely, or you are one of those guys who can play Name That Car by the sound of the engine, the BMW M3 doesn't look like the kind of beast it is—which is to say, the kind that could blow by a standard Mustang in the time it takes to say *gesundheit.* Mr. B decided that he needed to "learn" how to drive this monstrous machine, so he signed up for a BMW driving school at the manufacturer's facility in South Carolina. After that, he was hooked, and soon I became the wife of a track addict, silently gnashing my teeth [note from Mr. B: sometimes not so silently] as he left me to fend for hearth and home, child and dog—not to mention my own lonely self—while he roared off to the New Jersey Motorsports Park in Millville; Lime Rock in Connecticut; Pocono Raceway in Pennsylvania; Watkins Glen, New York; and Summit Point, West Virginia, and learned the techniques that are the bread and motor oil of Formula One racecar drivers. He eventually got so good at it that he became an instructor himself.

Props to Mr. B: Now and then over these years he would gently suggest that I should try going with him some time. I didn't take him very seriously. I had a house, a languishing career, and a small child to maintain—who was going to take care of all that if I went along with him to the track? Besides, it sounded silly. Going around in circles, really fast, and at great expense, sounded like a stupendous waste of time and energy. Embarrassingly, I didn't make much of a secret of my contempt for the whole idea, which meant a lot of crow-eating later on. More props to Mr. B: He never rubbed my nose in that, as I so richly deserved.

Then, suddenly, the Divine Miss M was no longer a small child. Any parent can tell you this, but you never really believe it until you have your own baby: One day that baby is potty training, and the next she is sporting a training bra. When you are immersed in the care of a small child, you somehow think that she will always need your help tying her shoes and helping her blow her boogers. It comes as a shock when you realize she doesn't need your constant attention and hovering presence all the time anymore. There might be a certain attendant sadness in this—she's not your baby anymore—but it is also very liberating. You can have your life back. Not entirely, and perhaps not ever, but the invisible umbilicus starts to stretch and thin, and you realize, hey, I can go back to doing my own stuff now and then.

SO, ONE RECENT August when the aquatic Miss M was going to be stashed at her grandmother's house by the lake, there was no longer any reason why I could not go along with Mr. B on a track weekend to famed Watkins Glen International Raceway in the Finger Lakes region in upstate New York. Here's a place where Grand Prix races were run in the heyday of the sport in the fifties, and where NASCAR and IndyCar still run. And I thought, hell, why not see what it is that has been luring Mr. B away from his devoted wife all these years? What, exactly, does the competition look like? And then I thought how boring it would be just to sit on the sidelines and watch. I took up running for this guy; I took up biking; both of those turned out okay, so why not give his latest obsession a try? At long last I gave Mr. B the green light and said, "Sign me up; the Mini and I will give it a go."

Was I *nuts*? As the big day loomed, I got really, really anxious. Unlike running or biking, driving at the track sounded seriously, limb-manglingly dangerous. I also thought, *What if I make an utter fool of myself*? Will they make me go faster than I feel comfortable with? Will I be pathetically awful? Will I embarrass Mr. B so badly that he will disavow me as his lawfully wedded wife? *Nope*, I could imagine him saying, *that slow chick is no wife of mine; she must belong to some other guy.* I even had bad dreams about it. When I shared some of my anxiety with Mr. B, he said, very reasonably, in an anti-Nike sort of way, "Just don't do it."

"No way," I said, "I've expended far too much anxiety on this to back out now."

So off I puttered, misgivings and all. There are quite a number of brand, or "marque," specific car clubs across the U.S.: the BMW Club, the Audi Club, the Porsche Club, the Corvette Club. Regional chapters organize what are euphemistically termed "High Performance Driver's Education" (HPDE in the lingo, or even, simply, DE) events at area racetracks a few times a year. These Driver's Ed events are not races but instead provide both classroom and in-car instruction to teach you how to get the most out of your car. In many cases, you don't actually need to drive a particular brand of car to join the club, and generally they will let you drive most anything serviceable with four wheels (though you can't drive a minivan or an SUV on the track). I followed Mr. B to a BMW club-sponsored HPDE that was a two-day event, structured in what I learned was a standard setup. The drivers are divided into "run groups" from novice to advanced, and while one group is out speeding around the track, the others, especially the beginners, are in classroom sessions, learning driving theory.

After the morning greeting in the big garage, I went to the classroom and tried to wrap my head around what I was shortly going to be doing. After covering some basic safety issues—like the meaning of the flags we'd be seeing—I learned that the first thing I needed to understand was what was termed, with great reverence, The Line.

The Line is God at the racetrack. It is, quite simply, the most efficient way to drive through a turn in the road, and the most efficient way is by definition the fastest way. And the fastest way is always the best way. Instinctively, everyone on the road already knows this. I watched The Line in action the other day, riding shotgun with one of my girlfriends as she guided her car through a particularly twisty section of road near her home. As the road bent sharply to the left, she started drifting in towards the left, into the opposite lane. Since there was someone coming at us in that other lane, this caused the oncoming driver some consternation, which I could divine from some angry gesticulating behind the other windshield. Though I am not a lip-reader, I suspect some Jerseyisms were deployed. But as the turn began to straighten out, she drifted back into her own lane, and all was well again.

What my oblivious girlfriend had just done was let her car drive The Line because that is actually what it likes to do best. Cars don't like to turn. The most elementary Newtonian physics tells us that they much prefer a straight line. The less they have to turn, the more they like it, and the faster they will go. So The Line simply maximizes the turning radius around any given corner. On a right-hand turn, you start out as far as possible to the left, go in as far as possible to the right, then out again as far as possible to the left. The Most Holy Spot on a turn is that very inside point, The Apex. If you look at it on paper, you can see that if you do all this, you in-scribe a turning radius that is far larger than the turn itself. Brilliant. Easy. But a total revelation to someone who had never really given it any thought before. In fact, it had always been a pet peeve of mine when people were sloppy about sticking to their lane when going around corners. Now, suddenly, I knew why they did that.

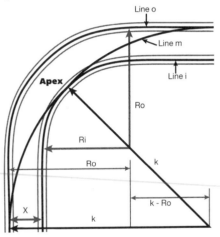

Enriched with one single, yet precious nugget of driving wisdom, I apprehensively clambered into my beloved little Mini, strapped on my helmet—an older model Mr. B had recently replaced—and drove over to the hot grid. This is where the cars about to go onto the track queue up, engines revving and ready to run. I was almost a blur, I was shaking so hard. I hadn't been able to eat anything since lunch the previous day, and

I was feeling almost empty enough to float away after a number of urgent trips to the ladies' room. Imagine my further dismay when my instructor jogged up to my car wearing a full racing suit, bright blue booties, and a mirror-visored helmet. He looked like something out of a low-budget sci-fi movie, and I steeled myself for the anal probes to come.

Luckily for me, instead of being an inquisitive alien, E.T. turned out to be a really nice and patient guy who offered to pilot the car around the track a few times so that I could start to learn The Line without having to drive it at the same time. With a tremendous sense of relief, I turned the car over to him and watched from the passenger's seat as I experienced for the first time the dynamics of a racetrack through my very own windshield. E.T. didn't drive my Mini very hard, so I never felt that we were going dangerously fast. He just took it turn by turn, describing where he was taking the car through each turn, where he was positioning it as it entered, where it should hit at the very inside—The Most Holy Apex—of the turn, where it should spool out as it exited. I watched him as if my life depended on it, which in a sense I suppose it did. It was with some reluctance that, after three laps around, I meekly answered "yes" to his suggestion that perhaps I should start driving my own car.

The big moment had arrived. We pulled into pit lane, the lane off to the side of the track where cars can safely and smoothly enter or exit the track, and swapped seats. Nervously I adjusted everything back to my size, fastened the seat belt, gripped the wheel, and thought, *Okay, chica, now's the time to look this monster in the face and jump right into its gaping maw.* Before I could cripple myself by thinking about it any further, I took a deep breath, engaged the clutch, and slid into the flow already in progress at Watkins Glen International Raceway.

All my energy became focused on doing one thing: attempting to replicate what my instructor had just done by driving The Line just as he had. This turned out to be shockingly difficult. I had only the vaguest ideas about car racing before this, and—to the extent that I had ever given it any thought at all—I presumed that racecars went around more or less in big circles like the Indy cars at Indianapolis or the NASCAR vehicles at Daytona. I also figured that, sure, okay, they go fast in a straight line. When you are behind the wheel, though, I can tell you that it's not speed in a straight line that is terribly daunting. The real knuckle-biter is approaching a turn at high speed and staring straight ahead at imminent doom in the form of a cement barrier and knowing you have to coax your car to turn before it hits that barrier.

Here's what the track at the Daytona International Speedway looks like:

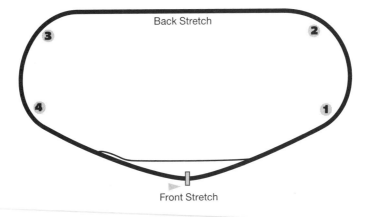

It's basically a big, flat oval: two long, curving, 180-degree turns, banked for safety and maximum speed, connected by straights. The additional bellied-out turn at the front stretch technically makes it a "tri-oval," but you get the idea. It would be kind of dull to drive for its own sake. This is not to say that the NASCAR drivers aren't doing anything difficult when they race the Daytona 500. It's just that the dynamic of the race has more to do with strategy and the interaction of the cars—drafting, passing, pit stops, male egos, and so forth—than it does with any inherent complexity of the course itself.

Now take a look at the layout of the track at Watkins Glen International, which by comparison resembles an amoeba on Viagra:

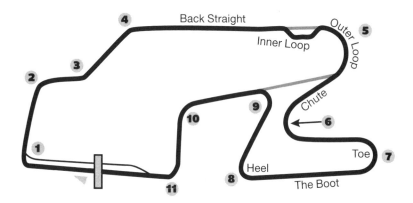

This kind of track is designated a "road racing" track, though there are no actual public roads involved (once upon a time they were, though, and these closed circuits solved the whole mowing-down-of-innocent-bystanders thing). Its layout is as twisty and complicated as a Swedish thriller. In a 3.4-mile stretch of asphalt, the circuit comprises eleven different turns and over 100 feet of elevation changes. This means that the longest distance you're going in a straight line is 1800 feet (on the back straight, between turns four and the little sideways jog called the Inner Loop or Bus Stop before turn five), which at a walk-in-the-park speed of 100 miles an hour lasts for all of about twelve seconds. Even my little Mini can be coaxed up to 120; Mr. B gets up to about 150 on this stretch, in which case it lasts for a blinding eight seconds. It's important, incidentally, to know that in track-rat lingo, a speed over 100 miles per hour is referred to as a *buck*, as in: *I got it over a buck-thirty-five on the straightaway*. But these high-speed straights are only connectors joining one turn to the next. Consequently, negotiating The Line is a complicated dance of ups and downs, twists and turns, all coming at you way faster than any trip to the mall ever did. The only way to master The Line is by memorizing it. The track is helpfully marked with clear indicators of braking zones, turn-in points, and shrines (orange cones) dedicated to The Most Holy Apex. Nevertheless, you have to know when they are coming in order to make the most of them. And although it is easy to understand the geometrical theory behind The Line, the challenge comes in linking the many turns together—turns that vary in size, angle, sharpness, direction, and even sideways cant (called camber).

So I tried, really hard, to find and follow The Line. In the course of eight twenty-five-minute driving sessions spread out over two days' time, I can't claim to have mastered The Line at Watkins Glen. That would be presumptuous. But I did begin to understand the satisfaction found in the geometrical perfection of The Line. As I exited the car for the last time on the afternoon of the second day, my legs were still wobbly and my brain was in a speed-benumbed fog. My first thought was, *I don't have to go back out there again*, and then my second was, *Hot damn, I'm still alive.* Mr. B and I packed up for the long drive home and headed out, he in his car, I in mine. And as we covered the long miles between the Finger Lakes and our home in New Jersey's sprawling exurbia, a peculiar thing happened to me. I found I couldn't stop thinking about what I had just done. The curves of the track kept running through my head. The sharp ninety degrees of Turn One—the uphill Esses—the Back Straight—the Chute, the Boot, and so on down to the Front Straight to start all over again. In my head, the Mini did exactly what it was supposed to do at every turn. We nailed The Line every time, and it was a beautiful thing. And to Mr. B I said, "I must do this again."

LIFE IS FILLED with twists and turns. We never get to practice them. The Line of Life is always variable, never clear or mathematically symmetrical. We blunder through from one moment to the next, and sometimes you sail right through it, and sometimes you go right off the road. That's the way it is, since life is shot in a single take. You never get to go back to try to do it better the next time. The beauty of The Line of the track is that there is a Platonic, perfect way to drive it, and you can practice and practice and practice until you can nearly nail it every time. And when you do, you rejoice in the elegant simplicity, the pure, perfect precision of The Line. Nothing surpasseth the beauty of The Line. And so, I was hooked.

CHAPTER FIVE

Embracing (in) the Rain

I have an ambivalent attitude toward the sun. Sure, after a long, dreary gray week in late February I relish a sunny day as much as the next person, but because of its deleterious effect on my fair, freckle-prone skin and my sun-sensitive blue eyes, I am a bit the vampire. I've always worn sunglasses on all but the darkest of days, and if I go out in bright sun, I don a hat, slather on the thick white goo that is supposed to protect me, and seek out shady spots wherever possible. I am easy to spot at the beach: I'll be the one huddled under the umbrella, tracking and following its shade as the sun makes its way across the sky.

This also means I've developed a slightly perverse enjoyment of overcast, rainy days: handy if you live in the Northeast. Perhaps it's also the melancholy Dane in me, or my depressive Teutonic background, but I rather relish the somber and reflective mood of a cloud-darkened sky. A gentle rain is okay by me, as long as I don't have to go much of anywhere, but I nevertheless used to hate driving in the rain. Hydroplaning is a real and frightening danger—who hasn't felt the ominous lifting up of the car as it starts to skim on an invisible sheet of water coating the road? And one thing I am almost maniacally finicky about is the speed of the wind-shield wipers. I cannot say why, but a sound I find as sanity-threatening as teeth grinding or squeaky balloons is the sound of windshield wipers running on dry glass. I shudder just thinking about it. Getting the windshield wiper speed just right in spotty rain is a major challenge, and usually I end up initiating the human-activated wipers, pushing the button by hand to get the interval just right. I know there are medications that could help. But I've decided it's a neurosis I can live with.

Eventually anyone who takes up driving at the racetrack will have to come to terms with rain. Rain, of course, is a tremendous challenge to high-performance driving, because it compromises grip. Among professional racecar drivers, those who excel at racing in the rain are considered the real lords and gods of the sport. Those who come to the racetrack as a hobby are generally less than enthusiastic about driving in the rain. Rain makes the freewheeling sport of driving fast considerably less fun for most, and without a doubt more dangerous for all. Often, if the rain starts to fall in earnest, particularly toward the end of the day, many of the drivers will pack up their things and go home. Who can blame them? Your stuff, sitting out on the asphalt, gets wet, you get wet, the inside of your car gets wet (the standing rule about open windows does not relent for falling rain), and you run the very real risk of sliding off the track if you are not very, very careful. You really have to slow down, and that isn't, after all, what you came for.

MY VERY FIRST time out at the racetrack, though, colored the way I view adverse conditions both on and off the track. Losing my automotive maidenhead at Watkins Glen was all around one of the most intimidating experiences of my life. The first day was a blur of new sensations and impressions as I tried my very best simply not to make a fool of myself. All I was doing was desperately trying to learn The Line and stay in one piece. Since I was in my Mini and surrounded by much more athletic automobiles, I was completely unsurprised by the fact that I was slower than—truth be told—all my fellow novices. As I crawled around the track that first day, with my left hand permanently dedicated to waving everybody by, I had to make a mental shrug: *Oh, well, guess I'd better get used to being the slow one.* I may have been—unbeknownst to myself—eating up the learning curve, but so was everybody else, and they seemed to be in a much bigger hurry to get wherever it was they were going. I figured that was the way it was going to be: them, fast—me, slow. Not a whole lot of fun in that. In fact, it was a little depressing.

And then, midway through the second day, it started to rain—a drizzle at first, then slowly increasing to a steady soaker. My instructor assured me that there was no reason we couldn't continue, and that he would tell me what to do in order to stay safe. During our first session in the rain, he encouraged me to discover that, with my normally treaded street tires, braking and accelerating in a straight line in the rain is not that much compromised. As long as I did it in a straight line, I could brake and accelerate pretty much as hard as I wanted. Turning corners, however, was very different. Sideways grip is seriously affected by wet surfaces, and this means that you have to take the turns slower, and with greater care, working hard to keep most changes in speed to the straights. When grip is reduced, asking your car to do only one thing (turning) rather than two (braking and turning) is a way to use what grip you have more efficiently. My instructor also showed me The Rain Line, which is different from The Dry Line chiefly by locating the road surfaces that have more grip and avoiding the slicker areas of the track. I worked hard to memorize The Rain Line and was slowly becoming interested in the challenge of dancing around in the rain.

I still didn't feel I was getting much faster or making any gains on my fellow drivers until we came to the very last session. The rain had been getting steadily harder, and maybe—just maybe—I was getting a little bit braver. We went out on the streaming-wet track, wipers going like mad, windows wide open, and he took me through my paces one last time, telling me I was nailing The Rain Line and doing very well. I frankly didn't believe him. But suddenly, a lap or two in, I started to gain on a BMW M3—a real powerhouse of a car, as I knew from Mr. B's early ownership of such a beast. *What's this,* I wondered. *That's funny,* I thought. *I'm going to catch up to him.* Suddenly there I was, on his back bumper, with my instructor commanding me to *stay on him, stay on him, stay right on his ass*—and exhorting the driver in front of me to *come on, come on, give it to the lady.* And, wonder of wonders, miracle of miracles, at the next straight, out popped the driver's left arm—he raised it over the roof—and he pointed me by on the right-hand side. I uttered a disbelieving expletive under my breath (a really deserving occasion for *shit,* I thought), pushed down the accelerator, and . . . I . . . *passed him. Whoa,* I thought. *So this is what it feels like. Woo-hoo!*

"He's got two hundred more horses under his hood than you do," my instructor explained, "but he can't use all that horsepower in the rain, or he will just power himself right off the track. You," he maintained, "are the better driver."

Sure, I thought. *Right.*

But then it happened again. And again. I kept passing cars, all more powerful than mine, as I sloshed through the sodden track during that last session in the rain. Better still: No one passed me, except for one sure-footed four-wheel-drive Subaru that was born for nasty conditions. As the checkered flag waved and the session came to a reluctant close, my instructor turned to me and announced, "We won!"

For the first time that weekend, I had a silly smile plastered on my face.

"Caught you," he teased. "Admit it," he demanded, "you had a good time."

"I guess so," I responded, still slightly stunned by what I had just done. For the first time I realized: This is a skill, which can be learned like any other, and I can take up that gauntlet if I so choose. And it was, perversely, thanks to the rain that I saw I might even be okay at it.

SO ALTHOUGH THERE is no doubt that you can go faster and stay much more comfortable both on and off the road if it's a sunny, picture-perfect day, because the scene of my first driving triumph—my first pass!—occurred in the rain, I have developed an odd liking for driving in the rain. I suppose it fits in fine with my general enjoyment of Scandinavian gloom and my anti-freckling policy of sun-avoidance. Every time the heavens have opened up and many of the more soluble (or perhaps less foolhardy) drivers start packing up to go, I am always among the diehards who are lining up to drive in the rain. I will proclaim my love for the rain to anyone who will listen, and though I am partly trying to convince myself, it is also true because it allows me to relive that first moment of triumph. (Hey, when you've mated for life by age sixteen, you don't get a lot of passes: I have a lot of catching up to do.) But I also really do like driving on wet tracks because the enforced slower pace and more hazardous conditions mean I really, really have to pay attention, be precise, and focus not on the yee-haw fun of the speed, but on being very smooth and very skilled.

Later on when I switched from the rock-solid, sure-footed Mini to the much more squirrely, tail-happy Lotus (more on the Lotus later), driving in the rain became even more of a challenge. The Lotus is so light it will start to skate if it hits a slippery dance-floor section of track, so I have to be even sharper when conditions start to deteriorate.

The first time I had to run her in the rain, we were at the historic track at Lime Rock, Connecticut, for a driving event run by the family of a retired racecar driver. He was a real former pro who was personally acquainted with the racer Jackie Stewart—the "Flying Scotsman"—a Formula One star of the late sixties and early seventies. In between sessions I gently flirted with the gentleman, who has the ebullient personality suited to a retired racer. He told me where to buy kilts in Edinburgh (certainly very useful information), and he performed a hilarious Scottish-accented imitation of Jackie Stewart. He clearly enjoyed making a bit of a pet out of me in pit lane, since there are not that many women who drive at the track, and I did not mind exchanging a little light banter with him.

I'd had a fine instructor for the first half of the day, but after lunch, it started to rain, and as my session approached, the rain was falling steadily. When I lined up in pit lane for my chance to drive in the rain, my instructor was nowhere to be found. A mischievous impulse seized me by the short hairs, and I suddenly found myself asking this retired racer to ride with me. "Wait a sec," he commanded, "I'll go grab a helmet." *Oh boy,* I thought, *I get to ride with a real racer! What,* I wondered, *will* that *be like?*

Off we charged, into the torrential breach, the rain now streaming over the surface of the track. As I gingerly picked my way around the track, desperately hoping to keep my wiggly diva from shimmying right off the road, Retired Gentleman Racer dropped the flirtatious façade and turned into dashboard-thumping Old Yeller—and by this I do not mean the color, but the volume control. "WHAT ARE YOU DOING?!" he boomed when I made a secondary turn-in adjustment to the steering wheel. "COMMIT TO YOUR TURN AND KEEP YOUR HANDS SMOOTH!" Turning in a bit soon earned me another reprimand. "YOU KEEP DRIVING LIKE THAT AND YOUR HUSBAND WILL TAKE YOUR NICE CAR AWAY AND YOU WILL NO LONGER GET TO BE THE HOT CHICK IN THE LOTUS!" I finally executed a turn the way he wanted me to, and he gave my pink and quivering dashboard a resounding spank. "THAT'S IT! THAT'S IT! GO, GO, GO!" he hollered at the top of his lungs.

In all my life no one has ever yelled at me like that. I come from a highly restrained, not to say repressed (on second thought, yes, I guess I do say repressed), family not given to emotional outbursts. Neither are fist-pounding pep talks delivered at maximum volume the pedagogical method of choice for music teachers and art historians. If Mr. B and I were to argue—not that we *ever* argue, darlings—we'd do so in measured, if perhaps slightly acidic, tones. Being harangued like a bush league baseball team at the bottom of the rankings was an entirely novel experience for refined and ladylike me. Surprised and a bit taken aback at first, I decided to roll with it as part of the situation, which I had, after all, invited upon myself. Certainly the seriousness with which he took the driving emphasized the importance of doing this dangerous thing well, and I will never, ever, forget to be as smooth as I possibly can, both in the rain and in the dry. Oddly, I loved that he cared enough to get so excited by both my mistakes and my little successes, although I'm kind of relieved that not all of my instructors teach with such unrestrained gusto. I thanked him heartily when the session was over. When the cold, heartless rain changed over to sleet (welcome to April in Connecticut), the last session of the day was canceled. Even lunatics have their limit.

LEATHER-LUNGED EX-RACERS ASIDE, certainly the most informative rainy-day session I ever had was with my first female instructor. She was the polar opposite of Old Yeller in terms of instructional delivery, low-key in the extreme and both analytical and informative. When the rain started to fall, instead of dictating a Rain Line (or bellowing preemptive instructions), she drew my attention to the surface of the road and began to describe what she saw. I was reminded of the persistent urban legend of the one hundred different Eskimo words for snow or the infinite linguistic variations that *Vogue* can employ to describe a choice pair of stilettos.

"Notice the sheen on the road surface here," she said. "It's starting to get moist, but you should still have plenty of grip." "See how the surface over there is reflective," she pointed out. "That means that it's now totally covered with water." And: "Here we can see that the water is actually rippling across the track, and here there is some standing water, which is very dangerous, so you want to tippy-toe around that."

Would a male instructor ever have told me to "tippy-toe"? I think not; but it remains an indelible description of what you want to do when the grip is less than CEO-handshake solid. Then she asked me to describe what I saw, and this forced me to examine the road surfaces—and draw on my bank of asphalt-related adjectives—more thoroughly than I'd ever done before. By the time we had finished with the session, I felt like Sacagawea tracking the spoor of an elusive prey. I imagined myself crouching down and sampling the earth between my fingers.

"Here the panther comes for a drink, Kemosabe, and there he crouches in the bushes, ready to pounce on the deer that comes when the sun goes down."

Or, in my case, the unwitting Porsche that lets its guard down when the rain starts to fall.

But at my next event, to my dismay, came the ultimate test of aquatic fortitude: the skid pad. You know those car commercials in which achingly beautiful, glimmering cars slide sideways in slow-motion majesty across your liquid-crystal screen? I have always wondered: Why do they do that? Is showing a car that is clearly careening out of control actually supposed to be an incentive to buy? And you know how at the bottom of the screen, fleetingly displayed in an eye-straining font, is an illegible line of text? It's lawyer fodder, and what it says is: PROFESSIONAL DRIVER ON CLOSED CIRCUIT. DO NOT ATTEMPT. That closed circuit is a skid pad, and I have flouted all the lawyers by attempting it anyway. Look at me, ma: no grip! The skid pad is a stretch of asphalt—usually doughnut-shaped—that gets hosed down so that it's good and wet and slick as infomercial patter on purpose. When a driving event has a skid-pad component, there will be specially trained instructors who climb into the car and direct the driver in a series of exercises designed to allow the experience of what happens when the car loses control, but at low speeds and with little risk to the car and passengers. Because grip is lost the fastest when the turn is tight and the surface is slippery, driving circles on a small wet doughnut creates an almost total lack of control at speeds of little over twenty or twenty-five miles per hour—though it feels much, much faster.

It was a full year into my driving escapades before I encountered a skid pad. Good thing, too. I was depressingly awful at it. Although I was

on the skid pad

pretty good at modulating my speed by easing off the accelerator pedal as soon as I felt the grip loosening, I had great difficulty moving the wheel around fast enough once the tail started to step out and the car started to spin. The trick to this is the one that you hear about but never really believe or are able to practice on the New Jersey Turnpike: To gain control over a spinout, first you steer *into* the skid, and then once you've regained grip and control, you steer back. The difficulty is twofold: First, steering into a skid is so counterintuitive that both head and hands rebel. "Wrong, wrong, *wrong*," yammer all the instincts of decades on the roads: "If I don't want to go that way, I don't want to steer that way, either, *idiot*." The second problem is that even at very low speeds this all happens so quickly that even if you triumph over the instinct that really dislikes steering into a spin, as soon as you do regain that grip, you have to turn the wheel back again. Really, really fast.

Obeying my instructor, I drove around and around in circles like I was spreading cream cheese on the giant Bagel of Insanity. I got so good at feeling when the car wanted to drift out from the center, and gently lifting off the throttle until I was just at the edge of control, that I started to think I was all Mario Andretti. But when my passenger asked me to stab at the accelerator with the deliberate intention of inducing spin—well: That is exactly what the car obediently did. It spun. And it spun. Again and again I tried, and again and again I was unable to rescue it by first steering into the spin and then immediately turning the wheel back again. I wanted either to cry, or throw up. As for the former: Like baseball, there's no crying at the racetrack. And as for the latter: I managed to keep my lunch down—just. I exited my session thoroughly disheartened and ready to crown myself Queen of the Spinout, Dunce of the Skid Pad. It was a glorious, sunny mid-September afternoon in West Virginia, and I felt as glum as a monsoon forecast.

"How'd it go?" asked Mr. B, greeting me in the paddock afterward.

"Terrible," I grumped. "I stunk."

I thought I'd be able to carve perfect sideways drifts around the skid pad like a Cadillac commercial. That, at least, is what I *wanted* to be able to do. I stood on the sidelines for a while, watching some of the other hapless drivers lose it out there on the skid pad, and as I watched them spin out, too, I realized I was by no means the only one struggling with this picky-tricky skill. If I wanted to conquer it, I would have to reengage that masochistic Teutonic enjoyment of rain and deliberately created adversity, and redouble my own determination to defeat it. *Right,* I said to myself. *Woman up.* Next time, it's me against the skid pad, and I will work even harder to get this thing right. After all, I *like* driving in the rain. Don't I?

TELLING MYSELF I like driving in the rain makes me feel more confident about it and has prompted me also to try simply telling myself that other adverse conditions at the track and in life are things I embrace. If you tell yourself often enough that you like something that you really shouldn't (or don't), it has the habit of more or less coming true. I say that I like driving in the rain, and I actually believe it. It makes me feel kind of brave just to say it. "I rock in the rain," I will say, and I've convinced myself of it far enough that I take every opportunity to practice driving in the rain. It certainly is true that practicing in the rain pushes your skills harder than when everything is nice and dry and grippy. Eventually I may actually be Mistress of All Precipitation. Just like life, I suppose, you find what you're made of when things become challenging. It's easy to be fast—and happy and successful—when the road is straight and dry and clear. It's harder to maintain your equilibrium when life throws cold water in your face.

AFTER MANY YEARS of promising ourselves we would venture to Scotland to see the land of Mr. B's ancestors, we finally made our way to that country of haggis and bagpipes: The former, incidentally, is not as awful as it sounds—the latter, however, is worse. Despite distant ancestors of Scottish nobility, Mr. B declined to buy a kilt in his family's plaid, thus rendering the helpful advice from my favorite ex-racer useless. Discretion in this case is probably the better part of valor, given that the clan plaid in question is quite simply hideous. No elegant Black Watch or understated Royal Stewart but a Christmas-bright red and green for Mr. B's ancestral kilts. We'd been warned that Scotland in August can be cold and rainy, but nothing could have prepared us for our adventure to the ancient island of Iona, just off the coast of the Isle of Mull in the Inner Hebrides. We wanted to see the famous abbey where Christianity spread throughout Europe and where the real King Macbeth is buried. The island is rumored to be stunning in its beauty, but we will never know because the day we were there was so windy and rainy that the rain was hurling itself at us sideways. Gamely Mr. B and I took the vomit-inducing ferry ride across to Iona and battled our way to the abbey, umbrella borne horizontally like a shield against the pummeling rain.

I like the rain, I like the rain, I repeated to myself as I hunched deeper into Mr. B's warm and protective embrace. As we completed a circuit around the small group of ancient stone buildings while huddled against the extremist Scottish weather, a gust of wind nearly knocked us over. Helplessly giving up, we reversed our steps and hightailed it back to the ferry and our hotel, where a fire roared in the lobby and a hot bath waited upstairs. Our jeans were soaked from the knees on down, and our feet squished inside our shoes. We made tea in our room, liberally fortifying it with the samples of Scotch we had bought on our boozy Islay distillery tour a few days earlier. Warm and dry, with a whiskey-laced tea spreading its warmth through my system, I watched as the seagulls flew backward past our window. I do like the rain, really I do. But sometimes it's better from a distance.

CHAPTER SIX

A Day at the Races

Once I'd attended a couple of High Performance Driver's Education events with the intrepid Mr. B, it became clear that there was a standard structure that governed these gatherings reverently known as "track days" by their ardent followers. In fact, at the track, few things are as important as your Number. Your Number is not the jealously guarded secret that is your age, or your weight, or even the number of sexual partners you have enjoyed, but something far, far more significant: the Number of track days you can claim. It is not at all considered rude if one of the first things a new track acquaintance asks you is, "How many track days do you have?"

Most events are two days long, but some are only one and others are as many as three, so you simply tot up the number of days for your Number. Twenty days per season is an enviable record; a career total of forty or higher makes you pretty experienced. As with sexual partners, it might be tempting to inflate your Number, but this is inadvisable since once you are out on the track, you'll have to back up your claim with know-how. I quickly became accustomed to the rhythms and rituals of these days. A typical one might go like this:

6:20 AM

In the predawn gloom, the alarm shrieks into life. I moan. I am not a morning person. Stupid hobby. Why didn't I go in for, I don't know, skunk hunting or celebrity stalking, something reliably nocturnal? Every night before a track day, Mr. B and I do the same little dance. He is a morning person. Getting up at six is sleeping in for him. He likes to wake painfully early so he can stop at Dunkin' Donuts for some breakfast, arrive at the track with the dedicated gearheads, and have plenty of time to putter and prep and visit the gents. I just want to sleep for as long as I can and get there at the last possible moment. So we negotiate alarm settings as avidly as a farmer bargaining for a prize heifer at a big agricultural auction. He offers 6:00 AM, I counter with 6:35. He offers 6:15, I settle for 6:20. It doesn't really matter. In my opinion anything requiring the alarm to be set with a "6" before the colon ought to come with a pay stub.

I blearily pull on my long johns if it is mid-May in upstate New York, or my tank top if it is July in southern New Jersey. I brush my teeth and ignore much else. For better or for worse, there's not much need to fuss with hair or makeup or accessories, so I pull on my baseball cap, grab my cute little Kate Spade black nylon backpack, and head for the motel door.

7:10 AM

We pull up to the track gate. The same thing happens at every one: An attendant at the little gatehouse comes out to greet me with a clipboard, and in exchange for a fibrous plastic-coated wristband, I sign my life away should anything happen to me here, and pledge not to hold the owners of the track responsible. I shrug, I sign, and once again, I laugh bravely in the face of death. Onward.

7:15 AM

Arrival in the paddock: This is the large paved area inside the track perimeter where you park and unpack and set up for the day. Parking here is like looking for a picnic spot at an open-air concert in Central Park. No matter how early you arrive, there's always a crowd that has beaten you to the really good spots. You prowl up and down the aisles, carefully eyeing the remaining empty spaces. You look for the optimal spot that allows easy access to the toilets yet is not too close to the mayhem at pit lane and the staging area nearby. After settling on your real estate of choice, you proceed to make the squatter's claim: You unpack everything from your car and lay it out carefully on the asphalt around you. This serves two purposes. The first is the emptying of the car, which is required in order to drive on the track. If you administer this emetic, you will be astounded to see how much stuff you think you need in the car in order to drive it. Everything from the trunk, everything from the glove box, everything from all the little nooks and crannies of your car has to be purged. Spare change, maps, user's manuals, sunglasses, umbrellas, and electronic toll readers—all of it must go. Even the floor mats have to come out. It's all for the very sensible reason that you don't want things flying around loose inside your car while you are pulling major G's in a corner. The second reason for doing all this unpacking is to delineate your own little space to prevent unscrupulous hunters from poaching your territory when you and your car are away. Once you have done this, the space is yours for the weekend. Change spaces at your own peril.

Picnickers in Central Park maintain a hierarchy according to the seriousness with which they take their plein-air dining. There is the majority of the picnicking populace who bring an old sleeping bag and a plastic bag filled with nachos and subs, a six-pack of beer or a bottle of wine with a screw cap and some plastic cups to drink it out of. The midlevel picnicker ups the ante somewhat by bringing a nicer ground cover, a plastic cooler, and some fancy deli food—maybe even wine with a cork. And then there are the Rockefellers of the picnic set. They are the ones who bring beautiful wicker hampers filled with pâté and strawberries and Dom Pérignon and elegant champagne flutes. They spread out sumptuous plaid blankets with plastic liners on the lawn-contact side, real corkscrew bottle openers, flatware, and sometimes even a candelabrum. They are the ones whose excess you make fun of but secretly envy because you wish you had the dedication and the panache to pull it off.

There's a similar hierarchy of the paddock. Mr. B and I belong to the sleeping-bag and screw-cap set. We park our cars and unload some basic mechanical equipment and a little swing-top cooler with drinks and energy bars onto a blue tarp in case it rains. The majority of the track rats belong to this clan. Most of us in this category bring folding chairs; those on the edge may bring a collapsible four-poster awning for shade. The midlevel track devotee has invested in a trailer. This generally means that the car is no longer legal to drive on the road and so must be hauled to the track. In this case its owner usually drives a big American pickup truck, and the upside to this is riding in far greater comfort while on the highway and having the ability to pack much more stuff. The downside would be that you get about seven miles to the gallon. There are hierarchies within hierarchies—no-name deli versus Dean & DeLuca—and at the track it is open trailer (lighter, cheaper, easier to pull) versus closed trailer (lots of interior space, ability to decorate, a place to retreat from heat or cold). Mr. B has been ogling trailers with a lustful eye for a while now. I suspect it is only a matter of time.

There are the Rockefellers of the paddock set, too. Their wicker hampers are massive RVs or even tractor-trailers outfitted with space for the cars and living quarters, which come equipped with beds and showers and gas grills. With their coterie they enjoy cookouts right there in the paddock. Their rigs are as big as houses, and probably cost nearly as much. But, as the bumper stickers available at the track state: You can sleep in your car, but you can't drive your house. We make a little fun of these elaborate setups, but not without a certain amount of awe and envy. The only thing they're missing is the string quartet, as far as I know.

Before I can proceed with the business of the day, I also have to apply my race numbers. This is the number by which you are known to the authorities at the track. Applying your race number is a key psychological moment when your car goes from ordinary, road-ready vehicle to superhero track star. It is like pulling on the Spanx before a big party. You are now gird(l)ed for action. As much thought goes into choosing your race number as goes into naming your own child. Maybe more. Some guys have laid claim to certain numbers; they are longstanding members of the club and the number belongs to them. Many of them have their numbers permanently appended to their cars (these are almost always trailered cars, since a car driving with numbers on the highway is an engraved invitation to the state highway patrol). You have to respect this—seniority has its privileges. You want your own number to be easy to remember, so you can put it on your forms, and you want it to be easy to fashion out of electrical tape, the number-making material of choice (ones, sevens, and fours are popular; twos, threes, and fives less so). Mr. B likes 808 because, he says, it will read the same if the car is upside down. I like 101 for its ease of application and academic sound.

7:30 AM

An announcement booms over the PA system. It is time for the ritual of the tech line. This is much like the receiving line at a wedding. I wait politely in a line of very well-dressed fellow guests, enjoying and assessing the unaccustomed finery—the rented tuxes, the fancy hats, the blingy jewelry. When I get to the head of the line, the wedding party greets me with oft-rehearsed small talk and comforting, familiar gestures. "So nice to see you." "Thank you for coming." "Wasn't it lovely?" At the tech line, the members of the bridal party are the ranking members of the club, and their job is to ascertain that your vehicle is track-ready. They make sure that your helmet is properly certified and that your car is completely empty. They check the torque on your wheels' lug nuts. They look under the hood and give a grunt of satisfaction. What do they see there? I've

© KLAUS SCHNITZER

affixing race numbers

never been entirely certain. "Make sure you take that coffee cup out before you go onto the track," they joke. "Beautiful day for a drive," they say. Or a big favorite, "Shiny side up!" They affix my stickers, give my hood a pat, and wave me on. My car is now officially ready to race.

After tech line, I complete registration. Here I acquire another piece of jewelry in the form of a plastic-coated wristband, and again I carelessly sign away another release of my life. Easy come, easy go.

8:00 AM

The driver's meeting in the garage ensues. Everyone shuffles in, cooling coffee cups in hand, to hear the exact same introductory talk they heard last time and the time before that. Rehearse the flags. Thank you to the workers. If you need mechanical help, see Bob of Bob's Things & Parts there in the back. There were some incidents last time, let's keep it clean today. The track is a little slippery this morning, take it easy 'til it dries. The *Hill Street Blues* admonition: Let's be careful out there. Attention is wandering and eyes are a bit glazed, since by now everybody's been up for hours and we're dying to get out there on the track.

8:30 AM

It is time for the eagerly anticipated first session. The air is thick with the deep-throated rumbling of barely-muffled engines, which have been warming up and idling for some time now. First one fires, then another, like jungle drums pounding out their ominous messages of battle. The call and response gathers volume, and the decibel levels rise as the time for the first skirmish on the track approaches. The avant-garde is usually the instructors, who get to reconnoiter the track and report on conditions. Plus, they are the tribal leaders and therefore have first rights to the kill. Since they are also the most experienced and dedicated warriors here, their steeds are by far the most battle-ready. Interiors stripped down to metal body panels. Full roll cages. Massive wheels with tread-free racing slicks. Spoilers so big no one would ever bother going to see the movie. They come decorated with badges of honor—stripes, numbers, decals galore—and, often, the battle scars to prove their fearlessness. When the instructors roll out onto the hot grid, ready for combat, it is a sight to behold. *Morituri te salutamus*: We who are about to die salute you.

When their engines roar into life and they stream out onto the track, we in the ranks know that the day has truly begun. Admiringly we will watch them for a time before dispersing to our various tasks. From here, the day stretches out in an orderly and predictable fashion. Foot soldiers are divided by experience and seniority into novice, intermediate, and advanced "run groups." Each run group is allotted its time in twenty-five-minute increments so every driver gets a chance to go out twice in the morning and twice in the afternoon. The color of your sticker—which run group you belong to—constitutes the most important signifier of your identity and place in the pecking order. Confusingly, a novice may be green (for greenhorn?) in one club and red (for hazardous?) in another, but at any given event, you are quickly sorted by your skill level and experience, and the tendency is for the members of the same run group to stick together, although fraternizing with members of other run groups is not necessarily frowned upon.

8:45 AM

In between on-track sessions, novice and intermediate drivers also attend classroom sessions dedicated to driving theory and track-specific tips and pointers. It is these classes—and the in-car instruction—that presumably help to designate these entire events as DE, or Driver's Education. Your high school Driver's Ed this ain't. My high school Driver's Ed class was a state-mandated course taught by the bottom-most member of the high school faculty totem pole. The aptly-named Mr. Dohman was also, ironically, the high school athletic director. (This was really his name. Sometimes God is good to the writer of nonfiction.) His shape resembled a bell curve, the result of many frequently consumed calories clustered thickly around the middle.

Driver's Ed with Mr. Dohman was the very epitome of the public-school lowest-common-denominator educational experience. To be fair, this was not entirely his fault, as it was a required class that every sophomore in the school had to take, and the curriculum was predetermined and unimaginative in the extreme. In the democratic world of the high school Driver's Ed class, the shop rejects sat together with the cheerleaders, the math nerds together with the guys whose jeans had a circular wear pattern in the back pocket where they stashed their cans of chewing tobacco. Glassy-eyed and fleetingly united in our contemptuous teenaged boredom, we absorbed such ageless pearls of wisdom as Aim High in Steering, Leave Yourself an Out, and, the favorite of taxicab drivers the world over, A Friendly Toot on the Horn.

The magnanimous State of Pennsylvania also declared that if you completed a certain number of outings behind the wheel of an actual car with the Driver's Ed teacher in the passenger seat, you would qualify for a reduction in car insurance premiums. Thus, although it was optional, every single one of us went for numerous rides with the redoubtable Mr. Dohman. He captained a specially equipped vehicle with emergency controls on the passenger side so that the imperiled instructor could save his own hide if necessary. If Mr. Dohman turned to deep-fried comfort foods as consolation for this life, it is no less than he deserved for taking out an entire town's population of sixteen-year-olds, year after year, for their first driving lessons on the road. Poor Mr. Dohman. Not too many years later, a predictable heart attack sent him to the Great Parking Lot in the Sky, where he is doubtlessly enjoying mowing down teenagers with a Zamboni and utter impunity.

Driver's Ed classes at the racetrack are a little bit different—although it turns out that Aim High in Steering is quite possibly the best piece of advice you ever got in high school, at least as it pertains to driving. Classroom instruction varies widely in delivery, from no-kidding old-school overhead projectors (alert the archaeologists!) to erasable markers on white board and high-tech PowerPoint presentations with video. Novices learn the safety essentials—what the flags mean, how and when to pass—and then such basics as The Line and the Traction Circle. More advanced drivers will encounter more advanced automotive physics and complicated techniques, like heel-toe downshifting, throttle steering or trail braking, and the quirks of the track you are presently driving. Just as in high school, there are the bored macho know-it-alls who sit in the back with their arms crossed, and there are the nerdy, brainy suck-ups like me, who always raise their hands and like to show off how smart they are. Some things never change.

9:24 AM, or thereabouts

At last it is time for my own first session of the day. I have been working up to this moment since the alarm went off hours ago. I have been checking the schedule with the same religious intensity that I once devoted to feeding sessions, naptimes, and poopy diapers. A good fifteen minutes before my run group is scheduled to go out, I get myself and my car ready. I go over the car once again—tire pressure, lug nuts, gas gauge. I fire it up and let it get warm. I climb in, get my gear on—helmet, neck brace, sunglasses, gloves—strap myself in, and make my way over to the hot grid. All the cars are lined up and ready to go out on the track, and if there are drivers who claim they can sit here without their stomach doing flip-flops and their bowels feeling on the loose-ish side, I don't believe them. My instructor meets me here if he has not found me earlier in the paddock. We exchange greetings, and he too climbs in and ascertains everything is secure. And then we wait. The final few minutes I spend on the hot grid before it's my turn seem to stretch out into eternity until at last I am waved out onto the track.

And finally we're off! The cars take turns, obediently following the signals from the hot grid and alternately entering the chute, the entry lane to the track. At the end of the chute is a flagger who waves the orderly line onto the track proper. The warm-up lap ensues, usually under a yellow flag that forbids passing until engines and tires have warmed up and brains and reflexes are firing on all cylinders. Once the yellow flag is lifted, though, all hell breaks loose. What follows is about twenty-five minutes of the most intense activity you are likely to experience outside of a trauma room in a heavily armed city like, say, Miami. (No offense to Floridians intended.)

My fellow drivers and I rage around a two-to-three mile circuit of devilishly complicated twists and turns, attempting to push ourselves and our cars to their respective limits while looking out for those passing from behind and hoping to do a little passing ourselves. All nerves are on high alert, and my entire body is in combat mode. Any little mistake could send me plowing into the surrounding landscaping if I'm lucky, or into a concrete barrier if I'm not. The danger hones a serious edge into what is otherwise breathtakingly wild and fast and, in a weird sort of way, beautiful.

Twenty-five minutes passes in a blinding blur that has the contradictory effect of simultaneously telescoping and compressing time, so that I am always surprised and disappointed when the ride is over, but also a bit relieved. That endurance racers do this for hours on end is mind-boggling.

A flagger inscribes swooping figure eights in the air with the checkered flag. The first session of the day is over. I ease up on the accelerator as I complete the last lap, letting car and heart rate settle down to more normal speeds. I pull off the track, feeling triumphant despite the fact that I have won nothing more than a fully intact car, which will allow me to do it all one more time before lunch.

10:15 AM

In between on-track sessions and classroom sessions, what occupies the driver's time? Once I'm done fiddling with the machinery—and there is a ridiculous amount of such fiddling—there is not a great deal to do. Down time is largely filled with—you guessed it—car talk. Being part of the small female population present at these events—typically no more than 5 percent of the participants are women—I find it is a great deal of fun, and highly educational, to watch and listen to the gentlemen in their natural habitat. I imagine myself transported back to those family evenings in front of the television watching *Mutual of Omaha's Wild Kingdom*. I swear I can hear Marlin Perkins doing the voiceover:

"Observe the male of the Gearhead Species, as small roving bands of them prowl the garages and the paddock, eyeing and assessing the sleek and brilliantly colored prey. Slowly, patiently, they circle their prey, drawing closer and closer, until they are ready to pounce upon a particularly plump and juicy specimen. This predatory behavior may seem violent to us, but it is nature at its wildest, and the evolutionary process in its rawest form."

Their tendency is to pair up—they need someone to share their insightful observations with—and then stroll around until they happen upon a vehicle whose lovely lines or purring engine possess particular appeal, and then they stop and admire and comment knowingly to one another. If the owner if present, they will strike up a conversation; if not, no matter, they will discuss the beauties and flaws of the vehicle without him or her. It is a ceaselessly entertaining game of which they never tire.

11:35 AM

The second on-track session is usually better than the first. The first session reminds me of the configuration and the peculiarities of the track, reacquaints me with my car's personality and feel, and sharpens my brain and reflexes. By the second session, the track has warmed up, the car has warmed up, and the human has warmed up. I begin to feel more confident, and I start to push a little harder. My instructor may give me new tips and new things to try—turn a little earlier here, brake a little later there, straighten out the wheel or upshift in a particular stretch. To the outsider the track may look like an endlessly repeating loop, but to the driver there are infinite variations that can be experimented with, honed, and polished until each turn is a thing of finely crafted precision. I become greedy for another session, another opportunity to wrestle that perfection out of the car and myself.

Noon to 1:00 PM

Lunchtime. Relative quiet descends on the paddock as the track clears out for an hour that is chiefly dedicated to refueling—both human and automotive. You might think that hanging out in a parking lot all morning and driving for a grand total of fifty minutes if you're lucky wouldn't burn a lot of energy beyond a tank of high octane fuel, but it does. Brain and body work in overdrive during those on-track sessions, and the adrenaline dumped into your system is enormously depleting. If you haven't munched on a mid-morning energy bar or other snack, you will be shaking with hunger. I know because I've been there.

Lunch is rather like high school, too. The food is just as bad. Possibly worse. These days everyone is so concerned with childhood obesity and the wretched food choices that have dominated school cafeterias for generations that my own daughter now has school lunch options that are gourmet compared to the racetrack all-you-can-fry-for-$5.95 food concessions. The Divine Miss M may be able to choose between grilled chicken wraps or the salad bar, but at the track it comes in a bun, or it is fried, or it is both. Once, a vegetarian fellow driver ordered the token veggie burger that was on the menu board (comes in a bun, so it's okay). It took the entire lunch break for him to come into possession of the cow-free burger, so confounded were the poor fry cooks by the unexpected order. One is under no illusions of just-picked freshness here. Presumably they had to excavate mounds of burgers, hot dogs, and chicken fingers (and just when did chickens grow fingers anyway?) to locate the poor lonely veggie burgers at the back of the freezer. He ate the questionable puck regardless, so starved was he. As a woman cautious of her waistline and hostage to her slowing metabolism, I usually circumvent this whole predicament by judiciously packing apples, gorp, and energy bars.

Also much like high school is the seeking of tables. There is never enough room to sit, and you cruise, tray in hand, the pressure-treated lumber picnic tables hoping that there is a table occupied by a group you are cool enough to sit with. It helps that I am often in the company of Mr. B, whose instructor status makes him cool enough to sit with anybody. Just as in high school, I am the geeky girl lucky enough to be dating a varsity letter athlete, so I get a free pass to sit with my social betters. Fortunately I am slightly less self-conscious now than I was then. And nobody here knows about the whole marching-band and high-school-musical thing or the perm-gone-bad episode of junior year.

Part of the lunchtime ritual involves the scramble to refuel your vehicle, and here you have two basic choices: leave the self-contained haven of the paddock, drive into town, and pay real-world prices for your gas but have little to no time for your own lunch; or stay on the compound where you have plenty of time to eat the fried food but will pay in the neighborhood of eight bucks per gallon of *grand cru* gasoline. If you opt for the latter, it helps to imagine that you are in France, where, because of the hefty taxes, this is the normal price for gasoline. If only the food were as good. In France you can purchase roasted-chicken-and-thyme potato chips and blood-orange-flavored Diet Coke at a highway refueling station. Why is it that even their industrial snack foods are better than ours?

1:55 PM

I am in the middle of my first postprandial session when the flaggers suddenly throw the black flag. This means that something dangerous has happened, and everyone is required to clear the track and exit into pit lane as soon as they have completed their circuit. If we are lucky, all that has happened is that someone has gone off the track, or spilled some oil, and the incident is quickly cleared: The off-roader is pulled out of the rough, or some kitty litter is shaken onto the spill, and the group can proceed back out again to try our hand at avoiding being the next source of an on-track incident. If the run group is unlucky, we'll lose the rest of the session while a car is peeled off a wall and spare parts are swept off the track, or—worst of all—the ambulance and/or the fire truck is called in to deal with vehicular or personal injury. Although that last one is fortunately rare, there is *always* something that goes wrong sometime during the day. Drivers are constantly flinging themselves off the track, and parts are always exploding or falling off of the cars. It's the nature of the beast, and being black-flagged is as certain as taxes. On a human scale, these events are really very safe. Cars are not so lucky. In a short time I've seen a distressingly large number of cars shuffle off their mortal coils to go meet the Great Mechanic Above. I've always thought that if there were a God, He would look like the Michelin Man: snow-white and bouncy and good-natured.

3:10 PM

A certain listlessness begins to descend onto the spirit of the track. I believe that around 3:00 PM there occurs a spiritual and psychic low point that knows no national or cultural boundaries. It is a time that belongs not to the energizing outset of the day, when all things are fresh and fuel tanks are full and anything is possible. It belongs not to the end of the day, when things begin to wind down and we can see the light beer at the end of the tunnel. Three o'clock is an evil time that in my opinion ought to be avoided altogether. The Italians treat it with an espresso and a cigarette, the British with tea and crumpets, the Spanish with a siesta. The clever Brazilians, I believe, are just starting their day. Stupid Americans do nothing about it except for maybe pounding a Mountain Dew. Why do we refuse to acknowledge this essential human fact when we should be encouraging everyone to take a nap or have some cake? We just don't like to stop. But caution is critical when undertaking a hazardous hobby like driving a fast car around a challenging course at this time of day.

4:35 PM

Dire warnings are always imparted before the last session of the day. Brain fade is typical, and mistakes proliferate. The day takes a great deal more out of you than you might ever think possible, and the brain has only a finite capacity to maintain its attention and focus. I'm not entirely sure why, but this is often my very best session. Perhaps I'm a little tightly wound (you think?), and the knowledge that the end of the day is nearing allows me to relax my mental death grip ever so slightly? Relieved that I'm still alive and intact and I'm only twenty minutes away from my first beer, I often find that beautiful connectivity, that flow and oneness with the car and the road surface that is part of what makes this sport so utterly addictive. It is therefore with a certain amount of reluctance that I pull off the track for the last time that day. Parting is such sweet sorrow.

5:00 PM

The driving day is over. The last road warrior trundles off the track. Those whose last sessions were over earlier have already packed it in and headed for their hotels, if this is a two-day event. Gradually the paddock empties out, the noise and exhaust fumes begin to dissipate. The day began before dawn and now, eleven hours later, I count myself exceedingly lucky if I have enjoyed a grand total of one hour and forty minutes of driving in the day. Strung like precious pearls at twenty-five-minute intervals throughout the day, this may not seem like a lot, but to the hopelessly addicted gearhead it is: So. Totally. Worth it. I feel as if I've just planted my flag atop K2, and I'm physically and mentally wrung out and almost stupefied with happiness.

5:45 PM

In our everyday lives, Mr. B and I are fortunate to enjoy the luxury of being fairly discriminating diners and travelers. We are borderline foodies who love to seek out the latest bistro or try out the kooky new molecular gastronomy (fried mayonnaise cubes, anyone?). When we vacation we put in a fair amount of research to hunt down charming small inns or historic hotels that are just dripping personality onto the sidewalks. We seek out the interesting, unusual, and authentic local experiences so that we really feel like we have been somewhere other than home. We figure: There's a Hilton two miles down the road—if we stay in one of those, we might as well stay in New Jersey, and isn't the whole point of a vacation to leave New Jersey? Since, however, most racetracks are located in exurban and often slightly depressed areas, the authentic local experience usually comprises a modest motel or national hotel chain. Why would we look for ambience anyway when we are spending every waking minute in the paddock? And as for the culinary experience, we always, always bring two vital, life-giving ingredients: a six-pack of beer and a bag of potato chips. So much for gastronomy. But here's the thing—no foie gras or free-range organic chicken can outshine the incomparable deliciousness of the first cold beer after the driving is over. And a crispy, greasy potato chip—plenty salty and preferably coated with that terra-cotta powder called BBQ—is the only possible accompaniment, even for the junk-food-phobic, eat-your-vegetables, food-obsessive that I am. I swoon.

The only sensual experience that might possibly rival the beer and the chips is the shower I take after stewing in my helmet all day. Mr. B, who drives with an intensity that is fearsome to behold, gets extremely ripe by the end of the day. As big a fan as I am of smoked fish and funky cheeses, I send him to hit the showers first. Yours truly is also no longer the dew-bedecked meadow flower that she (almost) was at the start of the day. Even the meager flow and plastic shower curtain of the family-run motel cannot squelch the heavenly delight of the post-race-day shower. Clean and fluffy, with the first beer under our belts, we head out to score dinner off one of the chains on the strip. Chi-Chi's, here we come.

Back at the racetrack, darkness and stillness descend, the crickets chirp; the asphalt cools in the sweet respite of night. A day at the races is the best day ever.

CHAPTER SEVEN

Life Is
93 Percent Maintenance

After an adrenaline-packed couple of days at the track, coming back home can be a bit of a letdown. I've just spent two days as Track Girl, Queen of the Petrolheads, and now I have to return to my humdrum Clark Kent existence of teaching, mothering, and keeping the home fires burning? What a thumping anticlimax. I often spend the following day in a kind of petroleum-induced hangover. My mind is blurred around the edges from the high-speed mayhem, my body is dragging from the physical intensity of the driving (not to mention the usual repeated sorties to the ladies' room), and who the hell wants to be bothered with peeling carrots, peeling paint, or facial peels once one has shot over 130 miles per hour on the back straight at Watkins Glen?

But there it is: Wonder Woman is forced to shimmy out of her golden corset, pack away the tiara and the golden cuffs and lariat, park the invisible jet in the invisible hangar after refueling it with invisible gas, and wait for the next far-off clarion call to action when once again bad guys and Porsches will need a good solid thwacking from the forces of righteousness. If, in one April-to-October season, I have managed a total of eighteen days at the racetrack, then I have had by all track-rat standards a very good year. That leaves, excluding leap years, 347 days in which my suburban alter ego, mild-mannered mommy and college professor, has to maintain her façade of normalcy while the invisible jet languishes, unloved and unattended, in the two-jet garage (every Wonder Woman needs a spare jet in case of emergencies, right?). I have learned that it is necessary to be philosophical about this, and I have formulated a set of principles to deal with it, which developed in the following way:

I host a great party—ask any of my stuffed and hungover friends. My favorite kind involves ten to twelve congenial guests, food on which I have spent as much time and energy as Dr. Frankenstein in his laboratory, and lots and lots of wine. The oenological ideal, in my philosophy, features pink champagne for the nibbly hour, white wine for the opening salad, red wine for the main, and dessert wine for the afters. Each type of wine deserves—and in my house, gets—its own kind of glass. There are tall, thin, elegant champagne flutes, the supermodels of the crystal set. Then there are the shapely whites, the blowsy reds, and the petite yet voluptuous tulip-shaped dessert wineglasses. I used to think having a different type of glass for every type of wine was rampant snobbery (and I am not above using my wash-and-wear fifty-cent IKEA glasses for both red and white when nobody is looking), but I have become a convert. The stuff really does look, smell, and taste better when it's in the right receptacle: Nothing beats the luxurious feel of those velvety bubbles cascading over the eggshell edge of a proper champagne flute. When the wine flows and the company is as sparkling as the bubbly, there can be nothing more gratifying in my book.

Until, that is, the evening is over and cleanup begins. Glass after glass lines up on the kitchen counter, exhausted little soldiers queuing up for their R & R after dispensing their life's blood for the greater good of the groaning board. One dozen diners, four glasses per diner, and there are just shy of fifty glasses that cannot go into the dishwasher because they will break, they will spot, or they just plain won't fit. Mr. B and I are a fearfully efficient kitchen S.W.A.T. team (Soap, Water, And Towel), and we will usually have the whole demilitarized zone clean before we go to bed after a big party—all except for the battalion of empty wineglasses that will need to be hand washed in the morning. Now, you might think that nothing could be more daunting or more tedious than hand washing and drying fifty delicate wineglasses. On the contrary, it is a task I perversely like. The following morning, I put on some music, fill up a little plastic tub like a Jacuzzi with hot water and detergent, slather on some thick hand lotion, don my dorky yellow latex gloves, and enter the Wineglass Washing Zone. This is a kind of meditative state based on the slow rhythm of dunk, swish, swipe, rinse, and dry, and when the sharp, shining glasses are all lined up on the other side of the counter, I feel a small proud throb of satisfaction knowing my little soldiers are all ready to do battle again the next time they are called upon to serve their Commander in Chief.

There are chores I like and chores I don't like, and there are chores I simply detest. I like doing the laundry, for instance. This is nothing to be inordinately proud of: The labor itself is, let's face it, laughably minimal if there's a washer-dryer in your home. It's not as if I have to go down to the river and beat my linens against the stones. Sorting through and folding a warm, fresh-smelling pile of clean laundry, especially on a cold, wintry Sunday, is actually pretty gratifying. Popping the neat stacks back into their drawers feels a bit, I imagine, like the pioneer woman's pleasure in knowing she's canned enough food to last the winter—all those glossy rows of peaches and pickles stored up for future consumption. In my case I have the comfort of knowing that my family and I can dip all week into the sock drawer and find a fresh pair to wear each day. Slipping later that evening into a newly-made bed with soft, clean sheets still redolent of Tide and the scent of lightly cooked cotton is reward enough for the only moderately tedious chore of stripping, washing, and remaking the beds. Would I rather be sipping mai tais on the beach at Waikiki? Sure. But as chores go, laundry gets pretty high marks. Ironing, on the other hand, is something

I have organized my entire wardrobe, and that of my family's, to avoid. I will do almost anything not to iron. Mr. B's beautiful Gatsby-esque work shirts go to a cleaner: I could iron all day and never get them crisp and smooth enough to pass muster anyway. Every other wearable item in the house needs to be capable of emerging from the dryer or the drying rack presentable for immediate use. You will find a great deal of jersey in my house, but you could scour my closet east to west and back again searching for broadcloth, and you would come up empty-handed.

Since I like my food so much, food-related chores are also not so bad. The list-making, the grocery shopping, the cooking, the cleanup: It's all for a good cause. The more energy I put into it, the better I eat, and the process is kind of a detox period for me each day. Mincing garlic, stirring sauce, whipping up a little salad dressing are all chores that I use to wind down at the end of the day, and, what's even better, there's a genuine reward in being able to eat well afterward. Not so with house cleaning. I know there are some people who enter a cleaning zone, who find running the vacuum cleaner therapeutic and derive great satisfaction from knowing the blinds are thoroughly dusted. I'm not one of them. I have always detested house cleaning more than any other chore out there, ironing included, and the moment I secured my own paying job, I outsourced that albatross.

You know how when you are about to go to the dentist for a regular checkup and teeth cleaning, you absolutely have to give your teeth a good going-over beforehand, even though the hygienist is about to do that for you? It's the dirty-underwear-in-a-car-accident scenario. If you went to the dentist with spinach between your teeth, you would be exposing your intimate, slovenly habits to a complete stranger. Like holey panties: humiliating. This is the downside to having someone else come to your house to clean it. It is a weekly ritual of mine to go around tidying up before the housekeeper gets there, making sure everything is put away and straightened up and looking guiltlessly neat in preparation for her arrival. You can't have your housekeeper come to a messy house now, can you? It is partially an act of self-defense, too, for if it is out, it will get put away, and then I have to go hunting for that particular missing item because invariably she will put it in a place it does not usually live. Vegetable parers and small useful knives have gone MIA for weeks this way.

Fortunately, the house is never in a hopeless state of dishabille before the housekeeper arrives, because I am married to a neatnik *par excellence*. In this respect I found someone just like Dear Old Dad, and it was not all that difficult for me to adjust to connubial bliss with the passionately tidy Mr. B. There are upsides and downsides to living with someone who absent-mindedly straightens pencils on the barren, windswept tundra that is his desk blotter while he talks on the phone. Nothing, but nothing, can enter the house without the dreaded question being asked within the first five minutes: Where are we going to put this? And all life comes to a screeching halt if a lightbulb has the chutzpah to burn out. It would not matter if a bikini-clad Charlize Theron herself were standing in the foyer with a margarita on offer if a lightbulb needed replacing.

"Hang on a sec," the man of the house would say to the beauteous Ms. Theron, "while I go get a new bulb. Then we can get you a jacket, 'cuz you look really cold."

The upside is that I have never in all my years as the missus had to pick up a pair of socks off the floor, nor even ask for the garbage to be taken out. Thus it is that every week after the housekeeper has been through and done her magical thing to the abode, Mr. B's compulsory obligation is to prowl around the house and straighten all the picture frames. His theory is that she skews them a little bit so we will know that she has passed through. They may or may not be dust-free, but having each one of them just a little bit crooked makes us think that they are.

Here emerges the theory we have developed: Life on this earth is a constant battle against entropy. Nothing in our human environment improves—or even maintains—its status without our constant energy and oversight. The spaces we inhabit and the machines we fill them with can only tend in one direction: towards disintegration and chaos. The plumbing, the heating, the major and minor appliances can never, *ever*, improve their limited capacities. Take the refrigerator, that most useful workhorse of any functioning household. It can do precisely one thing: make cold air. This is all it can ever do. It can't ever get better at it. There will never—sadly—arrive a day when the refrigerator will suddenly go from making cold air to making cold air *and* mixing perfect martinis or producing fluffy Belgian waffles. It does what it does until it can't do it anymore, and then it breaks down. This is as true of the toaster oven as it is of the toilet. The remaining non-mechanical objects and the surrounding spaces are just the same. The house can only go—of its own volition—from clean and tidy to dirty and disorderly. Pantries only empty; they never fill. Clothes never become clean, only dirty. Grass only grows and never cuts itself. And so on. Every aspect of life tends only towards needing maintenance, and you are the one who has to do it. Even our own bodies need constant maintenance—we breathe and think and play on the Wii, so we need fuel. We sweat, so we need cleaning. We run the human treadmill of life, so we need sleep. All of it is maintenance, a bulwark against our own dilapidation.

It was Woody Allen who claimed that 80 percent of success is showing up. Mr. B and I have a correlated theory about life and maintenance. We believe that life, on average, is about 93 percent maintenance. Here's how we figure it:

Life is 93 Percent Maintenance: A Mathematical Proof

1. Monday through Friday, we get up, shower, eat, get to work, do our jobs, return from work, ferry child to and from activities, run errands, help with homework; fix, eat, and clean up dinner; get child to bed; pay bills; phone a family member; pack a lunch. All of this is maintenance. At the end of a typical day, we are left

with about forty-three minutes—the length of a one-hour television show stored on a DVR minus the time it takes to fast-forward through the commercials—in which to do absolutely nothing related to home, self, or family maintenance. Then it's off to brush teeth, wash faces, undress, climb into bed, and commune with the pillow, for sleep is maintenance, too. Hence during the week:

$$24 \text{ hours x } 60 \text{ minutes} = 1440 \text{ minutes per day}$$
$$1440 \text{ minutes per day} - 43 \text{ minutes for } CSI = 1397 \text{ minutes}$$
$$1397 \text{ of } 1440 \text{ minutes} = 97\% \text{ maintenance}$$

2. Saturday and Sunday are clearly a little more variable, but in our home there is a great deal of weekend maintenance, including, but not limited to, laundry, grocery shopping, lawn and garden care, automotive care (obviously a biggie), and home improvement projects large and small. Certainly we have some fun on weekends, meeting with friends, going to movies, attending concerts, and the like. A rough but I believe fair estimate is to permit about eight and a half hours of unencumbered, purely maintenance-free time over the weekend. Some weekends it may be more, some weekends less, but on average that's about right. Ergo:

$$1440 \text{ minutes x } 2 \text{ weekend days} = 2880 \text{ minutes per weekend}$$
$$8.5 \text{ pleasure hours x } 60 \text{ minutes} = 510 \text{ pleasure minutes}$$
$$2880 \text{ weekend minutes} - 510 \text{ free minutes} = 2370 \text{ minutes}$$
$$2370 \text{ of } 2880 \text{ weekend minutes} = 82\% \text{ maintenance}$$

3. Thus, if we average the percentage of maintenance during the week together with the percentage of maintenance during the weekend, weighted at a ratio of 5:2, we arrive at:

1440 minutes per day x 7 days per week = 10080 minutes per week

10080 – (43 x 5 = 215 free weekday minutes)

– 510 free weekend minutes = 9355

9355 of 10080 minutes per week = 93% maintenance

QED

There are days when we arrive at the end of a long day dedicated to upkeep of myriad kinds, and we pour ourselves a finger or two of Scotch, and we clink our glasses together, and we note, in passing: For now, for the next forty-three minutes, *we are fully maintained.* Perhaps the moment is all the sweeter for its evanescence. Eat, drink, and fiddle with the remote, for tomorrow we rise and do it all over again.

ONE BASIS FOR any successful long-term relationship has to be the amenable division of household chores and maintenance. Mr. B and I don't split them fifty-fifty so much as divvy them each according to his or her preferences and talents. I spend the money, he pays the bills. I like to cook, he likes to eat. And to be fair, he always does the dishes, although he seems to have an inexplicable mental block when it comes to leftovers management. I do the laundry, partly because I like it, and partly because fiber content appears to represent a mystery as deep as cold nuclear fusion to my mate, who will toss—gasp—Lycra-containing garments into the dryer if I don't intervene. Whereas I am goddess of the fluff-and-fold, I am hopeless in the garden. I possess a shriveled, brown, aphid-infested thumb, and, shamefully, I just don't like getting dirt under my fingernails. Yecch. So our small plot of manicured suburban paradise is chiefly managed by Himself, with occasional begonia-planting stints grudgingly undertaken by yours truly, wearing gloves. As you might imagine, car maintenance was always Mr. B's realm. Combine a finicky neatnik with a certifiable car

nut, and you get someone with a near obsession with optimal car maintenance. I was more than happy to let him be in charge of this chore, which
interested me not in the least. I like my car neat on the inside, and a clean
exterior sure looks nice, but it never particularly bothered me if it was
dirty on the outside. I always figured that was part of living an outdoor
existence in the temperate climate of the mid-Atlantic region.

There are essentially two basic attitudes towards the exterior cleanli-
ness of one's car, and they can be gauged by one's reaction to a forecast
for rain. Mr. B regards a threatened period of rain with glum resignation,
because it means the car is about to get dirty. Although there is absolutely
nothing he can do about it, the rain will spoil the gleaming perfection he
regards as the car's natural state.

"Damn," he mutters, "it's going to rain. I'm going to have to wash the
car again."

At the other end of the spectrum is a girlfriend of mine, a single gal who
is not especially interested in her car beyond its capacity to get her to work
and back home again. She is always cheerful about an imminent rainstorm.

"Oh good," she says, "it's going to rain. My car will get a good washing."

I veer more towards the rain-splashed freshness than to the artificial mirrored shininess of a just-washed car more from practicality than
anything else. There is so much entropy threatening my life that screams
louder for attention than a dirty car—from hungry dogs to unmade beds
to the funny smell emanating from the downstairs bathroom—the house
clamors for so much of my maintenance-devoted energy that I don't have a
lot left over for cars. I was always happy to let that be Mr. B's realm.

I was, however, forced to revise my position once I entered the auto-
centric world of the racetrack. Vehicular maintenance reigns supreme
here. There are two basic kinds—the functional and the superficial. I
immediately recognized the vital, hide-saving importance of maintaining
brakes, tires, and engines in top working order. When you are screaming
along at 120 miles per hour and suddenly need to make a ninety-degree

turn, you really, really want your brakes working well. I am actually rather proud of having become both knowledgeable and conversant in brake pads, tire compounds, lug nut torque, and so forth. It isn't anything a reasonably smart, college-educated woman can't comprehend. If you are capable of maintaining the mental inventory of a fully stocked diaper bag, you can keep on top of vehicular maintenance, too. I mean, come on, men can do it, right?

But then there's the more superficial maintenance that I did not exactly warm to right away. Mr. B says that a clean car is a fast car. Your car gets wicked dirty after a couple of days at the track. The most obvious offenders are the little peas of black rubber that peel off hot tires and then bounce off the lower parts of your car, weaving a lacy pattern of black streaks along the front and side panels. No ordinary car wash will remove this evil stuff. The only way to get it off is to use powerful citrus degreasers and Bengay-worthy amounts of elbow grease. Then there are the wheels. It had never before in my life occurred to me that wheels needed cleaning at all, beyond what they got when the soapy water runs past them when you are washing the rest of the car. Kind of like your feet in the shower. Maybe I am a podiatric slob, but I simply cannot be bothered to soap and scrub between each individual toe on anything like a regular basis. I've always figured that all that shampoo and facial foaming scrub and shower gel goes past them on the way down the drain, and they get pretty clean in an incidental sort of way. Well: not so with wheels after you have been to the track. Heavy brake usage generates thick layers of corrosive black brake dust, which must be removed from all the surfaces of the wheels. You even have to go in between the spokes to get that gunk out. Finally, you can imagine how dirty the inside of the car gets after many laps of three-digit speed with the windows rolled down.

The very first time we returned from the track together, Mr. B engaged in his usual post-track car-cleansing ritual while I busied myself with other household maintenance tasks indoors. After he'd finished with his car, he came inside and offered, "I'll wash your car for you, but you have to come out and clean your wheels."

I'm not sure if I actually rolled my eyes, but inwardly I huffed like my preadolescent daughter being told to go make her bed. Her attitude towards this hateful chore goes something like this: Why should I bother making my bed when I am just going to unmake it again at the end of the day? We have explained our position that this is what one does in a civilized house and that a made bed is a sign of an orderly mind and respect for oneself and one's cohabitants. This impresses her not at all. In the end it always devolves into the thing you promised yourself you would never say: "Because I said so." It is true: You *do* turn into your own mother.

Aware that I could not, without seriously embarrassing myself, stamp my feet and stalk out while moaning and groaning about the unfairness of it all, I donned my ridiculous yellow dishwashing gloves and did as I was told. It was just as awful as I had feared. In some misguided earlier fit of automotive accessorizing, I had picked—get this—*white* wheels. Not just white ones, but white ones with about a thousand spokes per wheel.

torquing the nuts on the great white wheels

"Stupid, stupid, *stupid*," I berated myself as I labored over the removal of brake dust like toe jam from between every spoke. Note to self: Next time, get *black* wheels. With as few spokes as possible. Maybe just a big black Teflon-coated Frisbee design. Sigh. I persevered, and the wheels came clean and white and ready for their next outing, when they would once again go black with the abuse I was going to dish out to them.

I realized that an attitude adjustment was in order, and that the post-racetrack scrubbing of the car would be a piece of maintenance I was just going to have to live with. Like the wineglasses, once the party was over, I might as well view it as part of the fun of the night before and part of the preparation for the next party to come. Now, every time after I return from an excursion to the track, I enter the Rubber Removal Zone much the same way as I do the Wineglass Washing Zone. I pull on my rubber gloves, mix up a nice soapy bath, and allow myself to become enveloped in the Karate Kid rhythm of spray on, wipe off—soap on, rinse off—and, yes, wax on, wax off. For here is a frighteningly off-putting disclosure: The car requires a protective layer of wax after *every* track event. If you skip it, the rubber will be all the harder to remove the next time. So I've resigned myself to making friends with the random orbital buffer that is Mr. B's most beloved weapon in his car-cleaning arsenal.

Still, my standards remain somewhat lower than his. Sometimes he helps me out with the purification process, which surely makes it jollier if not exactly a romantic candlelit dinner for two. In Mr. B's view, the waxing process goes like this:

1) Apply wax.

2) Remove wax by hand with towel.

3) Buff once with terry cloth buffer cover.

4) Buff a second time with sheepskin buffer cover.

5) Buff anything else within reach just in case.

The last time we undertook this routine, I had my car buffed to a blinding shine by step 3 above. I made ready to put the buffer away, unplugging it from the extension cord and winding the cord around the grip.

"Aren't you going to run over it again with the sheepskin?" asked the appalled Mr. B-San.

"Nope," I said, "she looks pretty shiny to me; I'm packing it in for the day."

"Sounds like a go-slow attitude to me," chided my perfectionist Mr. Miyagi. "How are you going to slay Corvettes with an attitude like that?"

But I was already on my way inside, ready to shower, change, and pour myself the longed-for glass of bone-chilled sauvignon blanc that would signal my arrival at that all-too-elusive, remote desert oasis that is the Dominion of the Fully Maintained.

CHAPTER EIGHT

The Care and Feeding of the Speed Demon

The relative urgency of maintenance issues can be represented by the different levels of the Hierarchy of Needs. The Hierarchy of Needs resembles that old-style FDA food pyramid that used to have my all-time faves, the carbs, at the base. The Hierarchy of Needs pyramid was created by a mid-century psychologist to help people visualize the way we prioritize our lives. At the bottom level are the basic human necessities: breathing, eating, sleeping, and pooping (he said "excretion," but a rose by any other name . . .). In the middle are things like physical safety, then love and belonging, then esteem—both self-esteem and the esteem of others. At the very top of the pyramid was the loftiest of human goals: self-actualization.

Now, I have to admit that while I'm definitely on the prowl for self-actualization, I'm pretty keen on one key aspect of the bottom of that pyramid of the Hierarchy of Needs, and that's food. It's true that when you're hungry, other more esoteric goals of love, esteem, or self-actualization really do take a backseat. If you're ravenous, which are you going to choose: the burrito, or Bachelor Number 3? No contest. But food is so much more than just sustenance, isn't it? And hunger, metaphorically, can run the entire spectrum from the bottom-most level of the Hierarchy of Needs to the very top. I started to think a lot about hunger when I went to the racetrack. For one, it was because the food was so Alka-Seltzer awful. But it was also because I began to be fueled by a deeper hunger that soared all the way to the top of the Hierarchy of Needs to the level of self-actualization. Let me explain.

Food isn't just about calories alone. I'm thinking of that moment I call the Hunger Slam. It strikes without warning, and I am utterly powerless to resist it. I'm puttering around the house, say, doing chores, tidying up, sorting through the mail, and suddenly, I'll be gripped by a single, uncontrollable urge that, if articulated, would be: *I WANT SOMETHING.*

Now, I'm perfectly well fed, I had a nice lunch, my stomach is not growling, I don't actually *need* anything, and didn't I want to shed a couple of pounds anyway? All of this is entirely irrelevant. The Snack Lizard skulking in the shameful back corners of the brain comes out of hiding and slinks up to the Uncontrollable Desire Sector and hijacks the uptight captain of Impulse Control, and quicker than you can say "Cool Ranch Doritos," I'm off to the cupboards to find that one perfect nibble that will satisfy the unnameable desire.

Why, oh why, can't that desire ever consist of a longing to attack the nice fat bunch of broccoli that is patiently waiting its turn in the fridge? Wouldn't it be great if all the Snack Lizard wanted was a handful of grapes or baby carrots or any of the other innocent, fiber-filled, vitamin-packed, good-for-you comestibles I've so sensibly stocked the kitchen with? But *no-o-o-o*, it has to be something that satisfies the wicked black soul of the Snack Lizard, and celery sticks will never, ever cut it. For some of us, the craving takes the form of a yen for something sweet, and we'll rummage through the shelves and the drawers, desperate to uncover some long-forgotten packet of Oreos or M&Ms that we hope—without any rational basis whatsoever—we'd somehow overlooked before. If you're not a sweets-junkie, then you are a salt-seeker. The salt fiends are the ones who pathetically contemplate the crumbs at the bottom of the potato chip bag, deciding which will be the less demeaning: shaking the crumbs into the folded edge of the bag and channeling them towards the gaping maw, or pinching the crumbs with fingers and then using the spit-sucked fingers to get the last little bits of salt and barbecue flavoring adhered to the grease-coated interior of the bag.

Me, I'm in the salty camp. When that moment hits, you will find me guiltily reaching for the Wheat Thins. I have a longstanding and completely untreatable addiction to those little square spawn of the devil. I love the moment when the first salt crystals hit my tongue, dissolving on contact with the crunch into the slightly nutty counterpoint of wheaty sweetness that is enhanced by the evil high-fructose corn syrup. Ah, Satan, Nabisco is thy name. I love my Wheat Thins beyond all measure of reason, and they are my Hunger Slam snack of choice that I return to again and again. Maybe it's just the name, with its dual implication of health on the one hand (hey, they're *Wheat!*) and slimness on the other (and they're *Thin!*). I try to ration them out, and can usually make a box last a week, which I think demonstrates my really superior reserve of self-control. I've tried simply not buying them, but unfortunately that doesn't really work, as I will just seek to substitute my longing for my true love with pale imitations, which I often need in even greater quantities. In the end I've decided that the only thing to do is just to keep a supply on hand and try to maintain a little dignity by keeping it all out in the open. But I warn you: Don't ever come between me and the little pile of salt that lingers at the bottom of the bag. When I approach that salty nirvana, all semblance of dignity flies out the window, though I do somehow manage to restrain myself from actually licking the inside of the bag. Mostly.

The Hunger Slam comes to everybody, I think, and though sometimes it's as benign as a craving for Cheetos or Chips Ahoy, it comes to us all sooner or later as a deeper hunger that can't be sated with food alone.

Hunger comes in many forms that have nothing to do with the animal need for sustenance. Isn't the Hunger Slam, after all, not about nourishing the body, but about satisfying a psychological craving for the comfort of the soul? Hunger is a void, a negative, a lack of something awaiting fulfillment. There are far, far deeper hungers than the kind that can be satisfied by snack foods. I think it likely that everyone has a moment that comes when an inchoate yearning takes hold of the psyche, a hunger for something that you often cannot name, but that takes the form of the near-universal human question: *Is this all there is?*

I STILL BELIEVE I can claim that I reached my dreaded fortieth birthday without feeling any sense of crisis. To the contrary, I felt my life was full if not overflowing with a soul-satisfying job, house, husband, child, dog, and a roster of fabulous friends—all of which kept my calendar so busy I had no time to wallow in middle-aged self-pity. Why is it, then, that the racetrack driving bug hit me like a long-lost answer to a question I'd never even considered posing? Was I hungry for something I didn't even know I lacked? There are things that come to you in life, unexpected pleasures, that fill voids you don't even know dwell within you. I think physical hunger and psychic hunger are interrelated, and it's curious the effects that the high-performance driving has had on my appetite on many different levels. As I think back on it, hunger has taken any number of different forms in my life.

Take garlic—please, take *lots* of garlic. I endured a garlic-deprived if otherwise perfectly happy childhood, raised as I was by a north-German mother in central Pennsylvania where garlic never crossed our threshold or our taste buds. The local vampires were perfectly at ease in our house. It's possible that in other houses I was occasionally served, on warm squishy white bread with lots of margarine, some of that powdered yellow substance that passes for garlic in the spice aisles of the grocery store—and, okay, I have to admit here that, topped with dried supermarket oregano and plenty of salt, this is a flavor combination that still has the capacity to make me weak in the knees—but real garlic, cloves peeled from their papery heads, sharp and pungent and downright stinky? I'd truly never had the malodorous pleasure. It wasn't until I went to grad school and bought my first cookbook—the first cookbook I'd ever seen that wasn't *Joy* or *Farmer's Fanny* (as it was called in my house)—that I came across recipes calling for garlic. Here was a hunger I'd never known I'd had, but once I discovered garlic, I couldn't get enough of it. I imagine I went through grad school in a garlic-infused fug, and for this I take a moment to apologize to my professors and fellow students. But when you've never had garlic before, and suddenly you become aware of it, there is a sleeping giant that awakens inside and clamors for that powerful allium punch.

And pesto, orgasmic pesto: A fellow grad student introduced me to pesto, which elevated my garlic-lust to new heights. The heady combination of fresh basil, unctuous olive oil, poignant garlic; the slightly resinous pine nuts and rich salty cheese: nothing beats it to this day, and if I got nothing else from grad school, that alone would have been worth it. As I was learning about the rich history of art and architecture in my studies, these racy flavors were teaching me about new areas of exploration in the field of life.

When I'd finished with my grad school coursework and Mr. B had settled in New York, even more new exciting flavors opened up to me. For a girl raised in central Pennsylvania, none was more challenging than the first sublimely terrifying sushi encounter. It would be hard to imagine anything more foreign and revolting than raw fish to the girl I used to be. I still can't quite believe I found the courage to take that first bite of *tekkamaki*, the red, quivering, slightly obscene raw tuna at its center. And then, what exactly was that little bright green pyramid that, when compared to every edible object this girl had ever known, looked more like minty toothpaste than anything else she could think of? One sinus-clearing, brain-tickling bite later, and I was hooked on one of the most dangerous items I'd ever seen classified as food before. Wasabi: Cowabunga!

Mr. B and I have had many fun and exciting food discoveries since then, including the joys of the grape, and it's thanks to him that our life adventures have included other mind-expanding experiences, from tandem bicycle-riding to jazz music to international travel, and now I can thank him for introducing me to high-performance driving—as if life itself weren't dangerous enough already. Besides the obvious source of excitement that such a hobby might be expected to present, the excursions to the racetrack have had some unexpected effects on hunger and my appetite, both physical and psychic.

Given the not-in-my-backyard appeal of the racetrack ambience, motorsports parks tend not to be located in high-rent districts. You don't go for the food, which is usually supplied by local diners or national chains—fine for sustenance, but nothing to write home about. Far worse is the food available within the chain-link compound of the track, which tends to be prepared in as many ways as the Model T was painted: You can have anything you want, so long as it is fried. The standard repertoire consists of hamburgers, hot dogs, chicken nuggets, French fries, and tortilla chips covered in that orangey sludge optimistically, and I suspect fraudulently, called nacho cheese: No cheese was harmed in the making of this sauce. A quiche could saunter right through the paddock and exit completely unmolested, not to mention a head of lettuce with a whole posse of vegetables in crime.

It appears to me as if this kind of food causes a regression in men who, when at home, would not stoop to such depths of culinary depravity, but when surrounded by powerful engines and the company of other men, wantonly abandon all standards of taste for the nitrate-tainted glory of the concession-stand hot dog. At a garage banquet (halt: Did you ever in your life think you could see those two words compounded?—like: painless electrolysis) held by a hospitable club, I have watched in horror as my urbane Mr. B, perfectly at home at a Michelin 3-star in Paris, wolfed down one pig-in-a-blanket after another. I have to confess that from the isolated sanctuary of my porcini-mushroom-dusted, Himalayan-pink-salt world, I was blissfully ignorant of the ongoing manufacture and consumption of pigs-in-blankets. I had until then labored under the misapprehension that they had died the same ignominious death as the meatballs bathed in sauce made of equal parts ketchup and grape jelly. At the track I sometimes feel like a cultural anthropologist, doing fieldwork on archaeological foods from the TV-tray era that have somehow survived into the present day.

Yet neither am I immune to the effects of the racetrack on the appetite. Confession time: I am the kind of person who buys whole nutmeg and then grates it on an itty-bitty little grater when a recipe calls for ground nutmeg, because the flavor is just that much superior to the kind you buy pre-ground in a jar. Which is not to say that I don't from time to time enjoy sinking my teeth into that irresistibly aerated, orange-colored piece of paradise known as a Cheez Doodle. But my standards are high. When at home, I am a yoga-loving, organic-buying, lapsed vegetarian. I cook a lot of pasta, bake a lot of bread, stir a lot of fries. Our home diet is largely centered on vegetables and grains and dairy products. Still, I love a blanket of salty, chewy prosciutto draped over a melon, or a crumbling of bacon on my salad, or a bit of sausage studding my pizza. My philosophy about meat is to deploy it as a condiment rather than a centerpiece. I believe this benefits my health, my family's health, even the health of the planet—but the simple selfish fact is that this is my personal preference anyway. Love them carbs.

MY INITIAL EXPERIENCES at the racetrack were so terrifying that I had no appetite whatsoever. I wouldn't eat at all, so knotted up were my bowels. I was running on fumes, and I swear I lost several pounds with each outing to the track—that is, until I returned home and ate like a horse to make up for it. But once I began to settle into the racetrack routine, I found I had a most peculiar gut-level reaction to the atmosphere. The first time Mr. B and I enjoyed the luxury of a sit-down lunch at a driving event, I opened up the menu and began to peruse the familiar columns that are home to me in a restaurant: Appetizers, Salads, Soups: the waist-watcher's food columns. *Hmm, that's odd,* I thought: Nothing looked good. I skipped over to Sandwiches and Hamburgers. Suddenly a Neanderthal voice growled out from the depths of my gullet: Want meat. Need MEAT. Feed meat NOW. I obeyed and ordered a ham sandwich. The ridiculously overstuffed sandwich that emerged looked to me like a whole pig had sacrificed itself for my delectation. I'm not used to such big piles of meat. But I bared my canines, uttered a little snarl, and attacked the great wad of meat with a gusto that took me completely by surprise.

I had never denied myself meat in some holier-than-thou, self-sacrificing attempt to keep my girlish figure. I just never liked big amounts of it, finding it boring to be confronted with a big steak or pork chop or chicken breast. After a few bites, I simply grew tired of it. Now suddenly the meat looked as good to me as it seems to look to my little dog, who scrabbles unabashedly at the garbage can when the odd chicken scraps get tossed inside. *I want it I want it I want it* he whines with a pure animal hunger. Something about the visceral ferocity of the high-speed chase around the track had ignited a similar hunger in me, and all of a sudden, I realized: *Hey, puppy, I get it. Meat GOOD.*

My carnivorous alter ego awakens every so often like a werewolf when I am at the track, but my racetrack-inspired, newfound love of bourbon has followed me home like a docile new pet. For just as you can't eat petit fours and cucumber finger sandwiches at the racetrack, you really have to adjust to the drinking culture as well. When Mr. B graduated from college and moved to the city and began working at a big money-center bank, he decided he needed to learn about wine. Chiefly this was in order to stave off embarrassment when confronted with a wine list at a business luncheon or dinner.

"Ummm," he imagined randomly jabbing his finger at the wine list, "I'll take a bottle of *that*."

"Very good sir," the sommelier would reply, "a bottle of Sauternes with your steak."

Like me, he mostly came to terms with alcohol in college, after some admittedly illicit experimentation in high school. Booze in college, as we all know to our cost, is a rancid affair involving sour-tasting cheap beer from kegs and vile concoctions whose high-proof contents are masked by super-sweet, artificially flavored mixers. Raise your hand if you ever suffered the nauseating aftereffects of too many Jell-O shots at a celebratory post-football-game party.

Looking back on it, moving from frat-house hooch to high-class connoisseurship was a pretty major leap into adulthood for both of us. I happily followed along as my own personal sommelier started buying and tasting wines from all over the world, as exotic to us both as commuting by camel would have been. What we knew about wine could fit in a half-bottle of Blue Nun. I grew up in a basically teetotaling house, and he in a whisky-and-soda-with-Walter-Cronkite sort of environment, at a time when no one more than twenty miles inland from either coast was particularly interested in wine. This was especially true in Pennsylvania, where *alcohol* meant either beer or the hard stuff, and where the purchase of alcohol is still strictly regulated in state stores. Having left the safe confines of our home state, we tipsily rode the wave of wine's popularity into an agreeable acquaintance with cabernet and merlot, Old World and New World, Bordeaux and Barolo.

You simply can't drink wine at the racetrack, though. Not long ago, a minor furor was caused by a professional football player's supermodel girlfriend when she quaffed a glass of wine from the skybox while her beau played on the gridiron below. Wine, scoffed the press and the bloggers, is a poseur's drink not to be tolerated in the all-American environs of the Monstrodome. Football is the bastion of beer. So is the racetrack.

Meditatively sipping a Montepulciano while turbocharged engines belch out their noisome fumes is simply inconceivable. Actually, no alcohol is permitted at all while the track is "hot," or active. Very sensible. But afterward? Let the pull-tabs pop. So what do you order when you belly up to the legendary bar at the Seneca Lodge in Watkins Glen—a bar festooned with decades of racing paraphernalia and surreally bristling with arrows shot into place by local archery champions? A beer, of course, is always acceptable, and there are times when an ice-cold brew is supremely delicious.

Pondering this important question and not in the mood for a beer, I eyed the offerings behind the bar one night and asked myself what a self-respecting racecar driver could drink. A pretty pink Cosmo or a Pineapple Flirtini was definitely out of the question. The bartender would probably spit in such an order anyway. And then I spied the plain-labeled bottle with the dripping red wax on its cap and read: *Maker's Mark*. Perfect. Bourbon is a serious, home-distilled, hairy-chested potion that fairly shouts: I am hardcore. I don't mess around. No namby-pamby thingum-*ini* drinks for me. So what if it tastes a little like race fuel? Small price to pay for drinking the right drink. I take it with a couple of cubes of ice, and sip at it very slowly, for the stuff will knock you on your ass if you're a lightweight like me. It's become something of a habit for the post-driving debriefing at the bar, and I feel in my bones when I order my bourbon that it is the right drink for the occasion. I've kind of gotten used to it. Sometimes at home I'll pour one just to transport me back to a good day at the track.

Not all alcoholic experiences that come with the track are worth repeating, but the whole environment has certainly broadened my horizons, and I find myself trying all sorts of things I might never have tried before. One of the most memorable dinners we ever attended took place at the sort of local watering hole that you'd never find in any guidebook but that is worth a pilgrimage in its own right. Nestled in an inlet on the Delaware Bay in Newport, New Jersey, the Bull on the Barn Bayshore Crab House is the kind of place that makes out-of-towners feel like they've

post-racing beer at the Bull on the Barn Crab Shack

discovered some well-guarded secret, and it will prompt them to go back home and proselytize about it to their friends who wish they'd shut up about this place at the godforsaken end of nowhere. The Bull on the Barn isn't just located on some back road: Nope, its address actually *is*—honest to God—100 Back Road. Which is accurate. It's the kind of place that has a marooned crab boat with a jury-rigged TV in its cockpit as décor for the outdoor dance floor, and inside the barn you sit at long picnic tables while you gaze at buoys and traps and chum buckets.

The owner was a friend of one of the track club members and arranged to stay open for one more night before shutting down for the season. We feasted on oysters and shrimp and of course plenty of crab, and it was all delicious and very jolly. We were told to BYOB, and so Mr. B and I brought a six-pack of beer and my companion bottle of bourbon, prepared to share in the name of hospitality and good will. It was not long into the festivities when the guy who had organized the evening pulled out a mason jar filled with a clear liquid and announced that he'd brought a sample of local corn moonshine, and who would be the first to try? In all my sheltered life, I had never encountered moonshine before. I'd thought it was the stuff of Prohibition-Era lore and *The Beverly Hillbillies* TV-land fantasy. Who knew that enterprising twenty-first-century bootleggers in southern Jersey were operating illegal distilleries? *Hell, why not,* I thought, *let it be me,* as I reached for the jar to take the first communal swig. The encouraging gentlemen circling the picnic table cheered me on.

"Hoo, *doggie*," I gasped, as the fiery liquid burned its way down my throat, bringing tears to my eyes. I wiped my mouth in the time-honored style on the back of my sleeve, hoping to recapture my composure. I passed on the jar, observing that no one need fear any communicable diseases— this stuff could wipe out the bubonic plague. A far cry from merlot, corn moonshine is not one of those experiments that I will take home with me to try out at my next dinner party. Yet despite the fact that it is not on a level with the mystical experience of my recent first encounter with Chateau d'Yquem, I nevertheless feel in some indefinable way richer for having sampled the moonshine.

In the end I suppose that the driving adventure has stoked my hunger for all kinds of new experiences. I'd like to think that I was always pretty open-minded about trying new foods and doing new things, but I've since become even more adventuresome. I'll take on baby octopus, or roast a whole piglet, or make my own *fleur-de-sel* caramel ice cream (awesome, by the way—come to my house and I'll make it for you). If there's anything chili-infused on the menu, be it cocktails or chocolate, I'll be the one who's ordering it. From flaming waffles to Angry Lobsters, if it looks like a dare, count me in.

I went to visit a friend in San Antonio not long ago, and as we passed by the Alamo, there out in front was a Mexican lady selling shaved ice by the cone. It wasn't that hot, and we'd just had a snack, so I was about to cruise on by when I spotted the pump-bottle flavor marked *Pickle*

Juice. A pickle-juice snow cone! I came to a halt. *When, I reflected, will I ever again have the opportunity to sample a pickle-juice snow cone?* It seemed like a dare, so I couldn't refuse, and I ponied up my $2.75 for the privilege of trying it out. I'll tell you right now, to reduce the suspense, that it tastes just exactly like sucking on a frozen pickle. The salt fiend enjoyed it, at least at the start, but the peculiar combination of ice, which is thirst-quenching, and salt, which is not, got old after a while. I will confess to running out of enthusiasm for the novelty about one-third of the way through, and consigning it to the rubbish bin of my culinary history not long thereafter.

Despite all the adventure I've recently embarked on, the Hunger Slam still strikes on a disturbingly regular basis. I have been unable to replace my beloved Wheat Thins with either carrot sticks or motor oil. There are all sorts of hunger, and fortunately the nosh monster can be pacified with a little salty cracker. But if the hunger of the soul is a void not of physical nourishment but of rich and varied experience, then I suppose I've awakened a new kind of hunger. I never thought for a moment, before it all began: *Yep, what's missing from my life is piloting a sports car around a racetrack at face-flattening speeds.*

Like the garlic I never missed in my childhood—how could I be hungry for something I'd never tasted?—now that I've sampled the burnt rubber and sucked in the high-octane fumes, I keep coming back for more. And it's way more than simply the driving itself—I want *more* of everything. You can fill that gaping hole with food and drink, but you can also fill it with the new experiences that following life's invitation to adventure can bring. If you feed that hunger, then the answer to *is this all there is?* is a resounding *no*: There's always more, and no matter how old you get, or how far you travel, there's always the next pickle-juice snow cone waiting around the corner. It's the unexpected surprise that reminds you: Keep on going, make the next turn, and always say yes, because there's always something new up ahead.

Just as I couldn't know how much I would love garlic or wasabi until they unexpectedly entered my life, neither could I have had any inkling that learning how to control my car at the outer edge of physics and finding my own capacity for bravery would teach me more about myself than anything my life had thrown at me so far. From behind the wheel of a car speeding down the track at 135 miles per hour, suddenly the life of the wife, mommy, and college professor looked to me as dull as it sounds on paper. Just as I can now no longer contemplate life without garlic or jalapeños or chocolate laced with sea salt (divine), I can now no longer tolerate a life without the spice—the heady elixir—of nailing a high-speed turn, wheels screaming in protest and all neurons firing on high alert: Feed the hunger and, man, look out, 'cuz here I come.

CHAPTER NINE

Always Wear Your Lacy Panties and Other Fashion Advice for the Racetrack

Gearing up for the next weekend at the racetrack takes enormous amounts of preparation: more friggin' *maintenance*. After the cars have been cleaned and prepped and outfitted and safety-inspected comes the human preparation: arranging for childcare and sleepovers (I owe so many favors, all over town. Lord help me if they are ever called in. I would not be surprised one day to find a half-dozen teenage girls sitting on my doorstep, demanding college tuition as payback); dog-sitting; packing of food and drinks—lots and lots of water and the all-important post-racing bourbon; and finally, there's the not-to-be-forgotten packing of your own bag of toiletries and, of course, clothes.

Nowhere have I seen it written that you can't love fashion and still be a rockin' good feminist at the same time. Furthermore, I have solid proof of this. One of my best friends is a gorgeous Haitian-born accountant whose accent and fashion sense are both stylishly tinged with French. She is always—enviably—effortlessly chic. By all rights I should hate her, but instead I adore her and occasionally try to copy her shoes. This girl-friend works in publishing and not long ago had the opportunity to meet Gloria Steinem at an industry reception. Approaching Our Lady of Seventies Feminism, she nervously wracked her brain: What on earth do you *say* to the woman who founded *Ms.* magazine and changed the dialogue for women everywhere? Increasingly desperate as the gap between them closed, she blurted out the first thing that came into her head, which was: "You look fabulous!"

And she did look amazing, my friend later confided to me, fit and fashionable and totally chic. Apparently delighted by my lovely friend's compliment, Ms. Steinem returned it, telling her she looked beautiful, too. Which just goes to show that: (a) even icons of feminism like to be told they look fabulous; and (b) my own love of clothes doesn't necessarily make me a Real Housewife of New Jersey, even if I am a Real Wife, living in New Jersey.

Thus it is with a totally straight face, and no shame whatsoever, that I come to one of the most important questions a fashion-forward gal who loves to look stylish must grapple with if she engages in high-performance driving as a sport: What on earth are you going to *wear*?

As with so many things in life, I think it's important to begin with fundamentals, and so I will begin with that most fundamental of fundamentals: underwear.

From personal observations and perusal of the shopping malls, I think I may safely say that men just don't think about underwear very much. Boxers or briefs, most guys have taken their stand sometime between Bar Mitzvah and BA and have stocked their underwear drawer with a week or a fortnight's worth (depending on household laundry cycles) of one type or the other—and that's pretty much that. They don't generally give it much more thought until holes start to appear or the elastic starts to give out and then they just restock with more of the same. Which is why there's no national chain called "Albert's Secret."

Women's undergarments, on the contrary, represent not only a whole market segment but also a complex taxonomy of sign, symbol, and function. The average woman's underwear drawer is a vast arsenal of panties and brassieres for different purposes, different moods, different audiences. Venture into my own—if you dare—and you'll find:

- COTTON BIKINI BRIEFS: With firm elastic at the leg openings, these generally don't ride up and so are the most comfortable for athletic activities, sleeping, and wearing around the house when no one will actually see me, because their downside is a highly visible pantyline, which renders them unsuitable for public display;

- COTTON BOYSHORTS: Without the firm elastic and somewhat resembling a man's briefs, these can be worn casually with jeans and don't leave a strong pantyline but are not as comfortable as bikinis for, say, working out because the lack of elastic means that during vigorous activity on the elliptical trainer, they will almost always ride up and make an uncomfortable wedgie; plus they are too visible for really form-fitting pants or skirts;

- LACY BOYSHORT PANTIES: Pretty with the lace but designed to ride about halfway up the butt, these are suitable for most form-fitting outfits and are somewhat cheeky but remain slightly more comfortable to wear than a thong; and then there are their evil sisters, the

- THONGS: The go-to choice for being absolutely, positively sure that you will get no pantyline whatsoever, the drawback of these bad girls is the perma-wedgie that never quite lets you forget you have them on. Why, why, why do we do this to ourselves? Would any man in his right mind ever consent to spend an entire day with a piece of fabric wedged in his buttocks? We all know the answer to this.

[Note: This list excludes the special-occasion underwear from Agent Provocateur and similar slightly-naughty-yet-still-tasteful lingerie lines which is none of your damn business.]

WOMEN HAVE STORED in their internal hard drives a complicated mental spreadsheet of outfits and occasions for each type of panty: light-colored work trousers = thong; low-riding skinny jeans = hipster boyshorts; couch-potato sweatpants = bikini briefs; denim pencil skirt = lacy boyshorts. Date night, big interview, shopping in the city, all = thong. Going to the gym, having a sick day, eating ice cream while watching *Mad Men*, all = definitively bikini briefs. A single day may also embrace multiple panty changes. There are few things that take a higher priority in my world than changing out of the thong as soon as I have gotten home from a long day at work. Lord, what a relief it is to take that piece of string out of my ass. Gentlemen, you have no idea.

If you are a woman with the usual complicated assortment of lingerie, and you then take up the hobby of driving racecars, the moment will inexorably arrive when you are packing to go to the racetrack and you open up your underwear drawer with all its subtle choices and then you have to ask yourself: Which panties do I take to the racetrack?

Now, you might think that the fallback panty position, given the somewhat grungy and frequently sweaty atmosphere of the track, would be the panties of choice for your athletic activities—the sensible, stay-put cotton bikini briefs. And truly, there'd be nothing wrong with that selection. You could go with that. You'd have the usual pantyline issue, but maybe you are willing to trade that for comfort in the car. The cotton boyshorts might be a better choice, making you feel more serene about your rear view while providing you with a certain sense of camaraderie with the guys, since they are the closest thing in appearance to men's briefs. But thongs? You'd have to be either insane or dangerously masochistic.

Me? I go with the lacy panties.

There's that scene in *Bull Durham* in which Kevin Costner's character convinces the cocky young hotshot played by Tim Robbins to wear a lacy black garter belt under his baseball uniform for one game. The idea is that the unaccustomed women's undergarment will serve to distract his frontal lobes enough that instead of thinking too hard about the mechanics of his pitching, he will be pitching from some deeper, more instinctual place. He ends up pitching his best game ever, and we as the audience get to eavesdrop on his inner conversation and discover that he kinda likes the feeling of the garter belt's dangly little doodads brushing against his thighs. Wearing lacy panties to the racetrack is a little bit like that. (For me. For the guys? Dunno. You'll have to ask them.) Under my nondescript track-ready clothes—the jeans or cargo pants, the long-sleeved T-shirts, the helmet, and the driving shoes—I get to remember the girl underneath. At the racetrack, if you sit to pee, you are mightily outnumbered by those who urinate from the vertical. Throughout a long day of driving and the rehashing of the sessions and discussions of horsepower and tire pressure and brake pads, every time I go for a pee, I catch sight of my lacy panties and I remember that I am a girl. I can be discussing Turn Seven or carbon-fiber front splitters with the guys in the paddock, but a little piece of my brain will remember that I have my lacy panties on. It's both comforting and a little bit funky. I highly recommend it.

Plus, there's the deep, secret satisfaction of knowing, when I pass a guy who's really made me work for it, that I could say, if I *really* wanted to crush his male ego into little tiny quivering bits: "Dude, I just passed you, and I'm wearing lacy panties."

Girl power!

HOW ABOUT THE rest of the driving wardrobe? It's mostly a big disappointment for a Jersey girl who loves her clothes as much as I do. If you caught me on a normal day, and you gave the possibility any thought at all, you'd probably peg me as Least Likely to Be a Sports Car Enthusiast—at least from a fashion perspective. I adore my overpriced designer jeans. I'm addicted to chunky heels and boots. I love silky tops and flowy scarves and eclectic prints and dangly earrings and layered necklaces. I am absolutely unapologetic about thinking that dressing up is one of the best things about being a girl—including the lingerie. So it's rather hard on me to leave all that behind when I pack for the racetrack.

Out go the heels: Driving shoes are essentially thin-soled sneakers. They must be flexible and sensitive so that you can feel every nuance of the accelerator pedal underneath your toes. My biggest consolation, shoe-wise, is that I found brightly colored driving shoes that match my adorable car. I definitely had to ditch the designer jeans: You don't want to put rips into your artfully distressed Sevens in the wrong places. You actually want to buy cheap jeans and distress them, for real, yourself. What a novel concept. As for shirts: At many tracks you're required, no matter how hot it is, to wear a long-sleeved shirt made out of natural fibers (sometimes short-sleeved tees are okayed, but long sleeves are still recommended). A good combination, I found, is to wear a short-sleeved T-shirt or athletic tank with built-in support and then layer the long-sleeved one over the top when you go out on the track. I figure this is my chance to show my cheeky side, so I like to wear cute pink T-shirts with cartoon skulls, or tight tees with tattoo prints, or racerback tanks accessorized with a leather-thong choker. It's my way of getting a little bit of fashion in and reminding the guys who and what I am. I suspect they think it's cute, and I like that it probably disarms them. It can be good to be underestimated. Someday, when I am very, very fast, and very, very good, the sight of me in my hot-pink skull T-shirt may inspire shock and awe as I pass by. Hey, a girl can dream.

The rest of the ensemble is a real fashion disaster. The helmet looks silly when you're wearing it, and it leaves you with the worst hair ever when you take it off: sweaty, and plastered to your skull. The neck brace, the gloves—none of it does much for the fashionista, but it's part of the gear and since there are excellent reasons for wearing it all, you simply

what the fashion forward driver wears

have to shrug and go with the cranium-protecting equipment. The biggest fashion conundrum on this score is represented by the flame-retardant jumpsuit. Shopping at the racetrack is an extremely limited endeavor. There are indeed shops at the racetrack, but naturally, they deal exclusively in driving paraphernalia for the petrolhead. Without a doubt the single most expensive item of clothing you can buy there is the racing jumpsuit. A standard one will set you back about as much as a modestly-sized, entry-level Chanel bag—around $1500. And like the Chanel bag, you have to possess a certain amount of street cred to be able to pull it off. You can't just tote around a Chanel bag with an ensemble courtesy of Kmart. The Chanel bag must be honored with a commensurately high-fashion outfit. (Or so I believe. I have never actually owned a Chanel bag, so I'm theorizing here.) Similarly, the racing suit is only for the deadly serious—the ones who have made the leap from wishful weekend track outings to competitive against-the-clock racing. If you wear one, you have declared your allegiance with the registered racers, and then your driving skills had damn well better live up to the suit, or you will be a pathetic object of ridicule and scorn.

Secretly I've been eyeing the jumpsuits with envy. Although they are not especially kind to the female figure—do not ask if your butt looks big in a jumpsuit, because the answer is, sadly, *yes*—the guys and gals who wear them belong to a club I don't have entry to. There's nothing like exclusivity to make something desirable (see Chanel bag, above). And there's a certain sartorial rightness to them—they look like what you should be wearing to the track, and their techy, sporty panache works with the industrial styling of the track-dedicated racecar. Also they get to wear jaunty red or blue booties. How cool is that?

But while the jumpsuit is a creature perfectly at home at the racetrack, the recent resurgence of the jumpsuit as street-appropriate gear is something that needs to be addressed—and sternly. I would like to take a moment to plead with the fashion industry for some mercy and common sense.

An Open Letter to *Elle* Magazine Concerning Jumpsuits:

Dear *Elle*,

In a recent issue you asked me to trust you regarding that one-piece sartorial concoction known as the jumpsuit. *Trust us*, you said. Look, I want to trust you. I really, really do. The jumpsuit is a fantastically appealing idea—one item of clothing, and you're dressed. Like a dress. Only with pants. Brilliant! Like Emma Peel's sexy number in *The Avengers*: The jumpsuit is, theoretically, a secret double-agent garment for every occasion. But, dear *Elle*, aside from the very obvious whaddya-do-when-you-gotta-pee concern, I have reservations.

One issue I have with your genius recommendation is that I've already been a brave, card-carrying jumpsuit-wearer. It was brilliant then, too. It was 1989, and the jumpsuit I owned was a little bit Ralph-Lauren-going-on-safari, a little bit Ingrid-Bergman-in-*Casablanca*. It was khaki-colored, and the top half was double-breasted and resembled a trench coat, with wide lapels, a strong shoulder (read "shoulder pads"—it was, just barely, still the eighties), and bronzy buttons. Paired with a brass collar-style necklace and cuff, I believed it was the most glamorous and urbane thing I owned. When my then-boyfriend, newly employed in New York, invited me for drinks in the Rainbow Room, that's what I wore as I sipped the most expensive drink I'd ever quaffed in my life ($20 for a cocktail!) and watched the sun set over lower Manhattan, the Twin Towers still innocently gleaming in the distance. Absolute magic. It was also what I was wearing when I experienced my first and only lesbian come-on, when a fellow intern at the Guggenheim, where I worked for that summer, whispered in my ear, "Hey, sexy lady." I was *hot* in that jumpsuit. So one reason I can't get another jumpsuit is that it could potentially spoil my precious memories of the jumpsuit from two decades ago.

Here's the other problem with your jumpsuit recommendation: Let's face it, jumpsuits are for superheroes. Big screen, small screen, or real life, only superheroes can really pull them off. Uma Thurman in *Kill Bill*. Elastigirl in *The Incredibles*. Supergirl. Catwoman. Elvis: The Fat Years. What do they have in common? Uncommon physiques, for starters: Jumpsuits are designed for the cartoonishly svelte (or, in the case of Elvis, the drugged and self-deluded). Superheroes never have to go to the grocery store or pump their own gas. Plus, you never actually see them go to the toilet, which is absolutely fine for a superhero, who is unencumbered by such mundane consider-ations. The rest of us who dare to don a jumpsuit need either to disrobe completely or install a trapdoor. In real life, only astronauts and racecar drivers look good in jumpsuits. Sally Ride and Danica Patrick may be able to rock the jumpsuit, but the rest of us mere mortals should simply worship from afar.

So although I really do want to trust you on this issue, I for one will have to sit out this round in the jumpsuit revivals. Maybe when I am sixty and it comes around again, I will try one more time. On the other hand, maybe I do want to encour-age other girls to try it, because precious sartorial memories don't just happen, and there will come a day when you'll need to unpack some of those memories for a good, hearty laugh. And the next Danica Patrick has to come from somewhere. But, listen, dear *Elle*, no matter what: Dhoti pants are *right out*.

Yours sincerely, Track Girl

MAYBE SOMEDAY I will make the leap from untimed events to official racing, and at that point I'll be required to don a jumpsuit, for safety rea-sons. Until then, though, I can really only fantasize about both the jump-suit and the Chanel bag. Perhaps when I win my first race, I will make the circle complete and spring for the bag with the interlocking "C" logo. Until then, I leave you with some fashion thoughts for the girl at the racetrack:

Track Girl's List of Fashion Dos and Don'ts for the Racetrack

DON'T WEAR STILETTOS:
They can make heel-toe downshifting difficult.

DO MAKE FRIENDS WITH THE BASEBALL CAP:
There's a whole new meaning to "helmet hair" here.

DON'T OVER-ACCESSORIZE:
Chandelier earrings won't fit under your helmet.

DO COORDINATE YOUR NAIL POLISH WITH YOUR CAR:
All the guys will underestimate you.

DON'T WEAR LEGGINGS:
Spandex is not flame-retardant.

DO WEAR A MOISTURIZING LIP GLOSS:
Going at a 130 miles per hour with the windows down
can be very drying.

And always keep your lacy panties on.

CHAPTER TEN

Yoga, the Zen of the Racetrack, and the Mommy Mind

I f the clothes are so awful, and the packing and the maintenance and the preparation are all such chores, why, one might sensibly ask, do I go to so much trouble to get to the racetrack? What about it is so compelling that I willingly expend massive amounts of my precious time, limited energy, and nonrenewable financial resources to keep going back? What, in short, is so great about it? While a childfree weekend away from home is near nirvana in its own right, why do I not instead take a spa weekend or a yoga retreat? Wouldn't something relaxing and restorative be better for both my physical and my mental health?

The very first time I climbed into my car in order to drive around the racetrack, I was so petrified that I was nearly hyperventilating. My poor instructor, sensing imminent doom, or maybe vomit, first tried to get me to calm down by getting me to do some deep breathing. The guy had only known me for about five minutes when he asked, "You do yoga, right?"

Sheesh, I thought, *am I that much of a stereotype?*

If I am a suburban New Jersey mom of a certain age, I must do yoga, right? Well, okay, right. I *do* do yoga. Once a week, I submit to my beloved

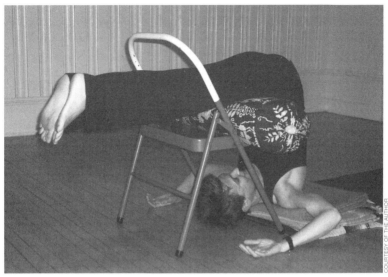

COURTESY OF THE AUTHOR

Supported Halasana, a.k.a. Contemplating the Underside of a Yoga Chair

yoga instructor, who looks like what Janice Joplin would look like now if she had chosen yoga over hallucinogens, and who harbors a slightly sadistic streak beneath her benign Earth Mother façade. I go to curl myself into complicated pretzels and humiliate myself when I can't for the life of me cantilever into a handstand. I go because I know how important flexibility is for my overall health—it's like the flossing of the exercise world. And I go because I love feeling like warm, gooey, tired taffy after all that stretching and pulling is over.

What I do not go for is the meditative state of mind yoga is supposed to induce in its dedicated practitioners. After an hour and a quarter of Downward-Facing Dogs and Cow-Faces and the whole menagerie (another pose I cannot manage is the Peacock Pose, properly called Pincha Mayurasana, which when pronounced sounds exactly like a naughty suggestion on a crowded subway car), Yoga Janice will put us into something restful like Supported Halasana. So, there I'll be, ass over teakettle, my body an inverted C with my legs resting (theoretically comfortably) on a chair. You could perch a serving tray on the backs of my thighs; my petard is hoisted high up in the air; and my head is scrunched under all this on the ground. Now we're supposed to breathe (uh-huh) and rest.

Sri Joplin turns down the lights to assist with the meditative mood. Immediately my eyes fly open, and I stare at the underside of the chair. I scan the pattern on the fabric of the bolster cover. I examine the tops of my thighs. I worry that they are getting squishier. I wonder how much longer we're going to be like this. I think about how much there is left to read in my monthly book club selection and whether I can finish the book in time for the next meeting. Did I prep the fruit for Miss M's morning repast? I worry about whether her complaints of a tummy ache were just the result of eating too many Doritos at a friend's house or whether she'll be up in the middle of the night. I think about the lecture I am going to give tomorrow, the re-set button on the daily to-do list, whether I need to refill the dog's prescription medication. I'm not even sure what's supposed to happen in my brain when my body is contorted like this, but I imagine it's ideally supposed to be some blissed-out goddessy state in which my consciousness floats in a sweet celestial Jell-O (definitely the blue kind). Mine resembles something more like the opening of a sample sale of Jimmy Choos at a *Sex and the City* convention.

I think of it as the Mommy Mind. I see the Mommy Mind as the by-product of emulsifying the oil and vinegar of personal and professional lives. You maintain a home, which always needs new stuff brought in while old stuff is breaking down. You make appointments, run errands, over-see projects. You raise a child or two or four. You make appointments, chauffeur these offspring all over town, oversee homework. You have a pet or two. You make appointments, walk these pets, administer affection and discipline. You have your family and friends. You make appoint-ments, send greeting cards, go on date nights or girls' nights out. Oh, and you have a job—full-time, part-time, volunteer. You make appointments, dress the part, commute, work, mentor. And you do this all day, every day. The Mommy Mind embraces all these facets and more by being able to think simultaneously about annual budgets, department meetings, a child's band concert, a husband's birthday, buying holiday gifts, feeding the cat, getting your nails done, taking the steak out of the freezer to thaw, and whether to do cardio or strength training today. If you could cut off the tops of our heads and look inside, it would look like a stampede at the circus, with elephants running one way and the bearded lady the other.

I don't pretend that my days look any different from those of millions of other working moms. And by my definition, *all* moms are working moms. All the women I know juggle responsibilities associated with jobs, children, school, pets, friends, family, spouses, and home maintenance. One has four boys, ages five to thirteen, has trained to be an EMT, and rides with the ambulance one night a week. One quit her journalist's job to tend to her son with leukemia (now in remission); she's turned to fiction writing and is working on a novel. One, recently divorced, raises three children by herself while running a custom cabinetry business. And I know all of them have trouble getting to sleep at night because their brains are buzzing and popping with the minutiae of the day gone by, and the demands of the day to come. The Mommy Mind. It's part of being a busy woman with a full life, and what's so wrong with that anyway?

Nothing, really, if you ask me. We have so much to do because our lives have so much good stuff in them. We could have chosen not to get the dogs, have fewer or no children, live in a low-maintenance condo. Nobody put a gun to our heads and said: You must live the suburban idyll, woman, or die. None of us would really want to give up the jobs we have, all sixty-three of them. But what it does mean—for me at least—is that when I am supposed to be relaxing, like when I am meditating at the end of yoga class or getting that rare massage or trying to commune with my pillow at night, I simply can't empty my head. There's too much in it, and it's clanging around too noisily for any Zen-like peace to descend on the Grand Central Station that is my consciousness.

Enter the racetrack. It's not exactly yoga, my friends, and it's not a day at the spa. It's very, very loud. It's stinky. The gear is uncomfortable. The helmet is heavy and restrictive and looks stupid. The seat belts are uncomfortably tight. The gloves are hot. If I'm not sweating like a pig while marinating on the hot tarmac then I'm freezing my ass off. And above all else, screaming down a straight at 135 miles per hour is *not* relaxing. Adrenaline is having a house party in my nervous system. My heart is thudding. My brain is calculating wildly as my sensory input approaches maximum overload. My palms are sweating. Every nerve in my body is thrumming with the effort of keeping up, and the lizard part of my brain is just repeating and repeating: *You're gonna die, you're gonna die, you're gonna die.* And yet I find this mental activity to be so therapeutic, so beneficial, so seductively desirable that I go back again and again for the brain fix. Why?

Simple: High-performance driving is the only activity I've encountered in my life that is powerful enough to counteract the Mommy Mind. Well, that, and a really unhealthy amount of tequila. When I am hurtling around a corner that is embraced by a concrete wall, it is a matter of life and death that I concentrate on doing one thing, and one thing only: coming out the other end of the turn in one piece. To paraphrase Samuel Johnson, nothing concentrates the mind like the prospect of total vehicular carnage. For the twenty or so intense minutes that the average driving session lasts, I cannot think about my stalled career, my child's math grade, the fight with my spouse over which family we bless with our Thanksgiving presence, or the five pounds I'd optimally like to lose. There is simply no room for anything else but the need to get the car safely around the next corner.

I'm really not a scatterbrain. The Mommy condition requires me to think about many different things, often at once, but that doesn't mean I'm an idiot or an incompetent boob. I do many things rather well. I am, after all, a college professor, so I can achieve a fair amount of focus when called upon by the task at hand. But the laser-like intensity that driving at the limits of physics and biology requires is something unparalleled in my experience. The entire world, with all its complexities, all its demands and frustrations, shrinks down to a plutonium-dense pinpoint of the space-time continuum. There is only the next few hundred yards of track; there is only the next five seconds. The last turn I just executed is ancient history, and at this speed, even the corner I'm currently in is already a thing of the past.

I had understood conceptually the Zen notion of living in the present moment, but I had never truly experienced it until I took to driving on the racetrack. There, it is absolutely essential to forget everything that has just happened. You can have no regrets. You must be 100 percent in the present moment, and every power you have must be focused on the continuous flow of the moment that is about to arrive—and those moments come at you so swiftly that that single moment stretches out seemingly to eternity, as if it were the only thing that ever has existed or will exist. Until, that is, the checkered flag is waved and the session is over.

(Drivers can get so absorbed in this flow that it is not uncommon for them to fail to see the checkered flag and continue blithely on. It slowly dawns on them that they are the only one on the racetrack, and they have to suffer the exquisitely embarrassing agony of a complete solo lap—there is only one exit in the circuit—around the track with everybody watching. Ask me how I know.)

Whole books have been written on the mental aspect of racecar driving. Just about anybody who immerses him- or herself in the discipline will assert that it is almost entirely a head game. Yes, the elite professional Formula One drivers need to be in top-notch physical condition, and driving an endurance race takes tremendous stamina—but good physical condition is merely a framework for them, a better support system for the supercomputer that is running the show: the machine under the helmet. The intense mental focus called for came as a huge surprise to an intellectual like me. I suppose I'd always thought (if I'd given it any thought at all) that racecar driving was simply about macho aggression, and that all it took to go fast was more horsepower than the other guy and a heavier right foot. And while it certainly is true that you have to be aggressive to win races, and plenty of horsepower helps, it's really the brain that gets the job done.

The mental journey goes something like this: First, shed all the noise, all the extraneous garbage. Breathe out the to-do lists, breathe in the burnt-rubber-tinged air. Breathe out the Mommy Mind, breathe in the race fuel. Next, you have to accomplish two things simultaneously: Narrow down your focus so that you are paying attention only to the world that matters—the fine network created between your car, your body, and the track. Then, open up all your senses to tune into that network. Your eyes—accustomed to flitting from computer screen to barking dog to matching socks—zero in on the surface of the road, the topography it winds over, the markers that tell you a turn is coming up. Your ears are overwhelmed and preoccupied by the roar of the engine, but this, too, is something you must be as attuned to as the differing cries of a baby. A baby has a repertoire of cries that correspond to hunger, neglect, or dirty diapers. Your car does, too. If it's revving too high or too low, it will behave differently, it won't feel settled, or it won't give you the power you want. Even your nose needs to be tuned into the smells of things—but as with babies or cooking, this is mostly important when things go disastrously wrong: the automotive equivalent of diarrhea or burnt lasagna. Finally, and perhaps most significantly, you need to turn your whole body into a sensory receptor for the car's connection to the road surface. As your entire body melds with the seat, you have to envision something like those kooky braid-connectors from *Avatar* that allow the indigenous blue Na'vi people to plug into their six-legged horses or pterodactyls. Hands, feet, and derriere all need to become one with the car, and it helps to think of the four wheels of the car as extensions of your own body. It's amazing how much of the road, and your car's connection to it, you can feel if you focus.

It is, in fact, my theory that middle-aged mommies may be better equipped to be racecar drivers than any other demographic. Who is better at putting aside the self-centered ego and concentrating their energies into watching and listening and feeling? Who is better at brain compartmentalization and sensory analysis? Who has faster reflexes when a glass of Kool-Aid is about to spill or a baby is teetering at the edge of the stairs? And who has practiced more yoga? All these things allow you to understand the Zen of the racetrack and open yourself up to the sensory input and heightened awareness that high-performance driving demands. More than that, though—who needs it more? For a few hours, once a month or so during the driving season, *I'm not home.* No part of me is at home—the Mommy Mind disappears and Track Girl takes over. Without child, dog, house, email, and to-do lists, my brain gets to go on holiday, and the resulting mental enema is so cleansing that I crave it again and again.

When this process goes well—when brain and hands and feet and car all work together, I become so immersed in the present moment that I believe I experience what one writer has famously referred to as "Flow." This is a theory of optimal experience in a book of the same name by psychologist Mihaly Csikszentmihalyi, who I suspect must be enjoying a bout of orthographic Flow himself in order to get his own name spelled right. He posits that Flow is experienced when you are completely immersed in whatever activity you are doing. The activity must be one that stretches the body and the mind to their furthest capacities. This activity is usually very difficult and not necessarily fun at the time, but the result of this total engagement is a profound sense of presentness, and it is so rewarding that you'll do pretty much anything to get to that state again.

I've experienced this sense of Flow before. There are times when I've given lectures about one of my favorite subjects, and all my points ease naturally one to the next, and I come up with references and colorfully illustrative metaphors effortlessly—stuff I didn't prepare but can dispense on tap like hot and cold running water—and the allotted hour and a quarter goes by, and I've hardly noticed the passage of time. I'm wrapped up in my topic, my brain is drawing deep into the well of knowledge I possess on my specialized subject, and I feel like a DJ at a big rave, spinning from one song to the next and knowing just exactly what to put on the turntable after that. When I'm in that Flow, I know I'm good, and my students share that absorption—I can sense that I've got them, and I feel like I could wrap them around me like a colorful feather boa. It's the biggest reason I keep returning to the classroom despite the lack of conventional academic career success. I suspect it's a nerdy version of what a stand-up comedian feels when she's got the audience in the palm of her hand and she just knows that her next joke about plumber butt or faked orgasms is going to slay them in their seats.

Now, not every session on the racetrack produces Flow, just as not every lecture I give is going to shoot me to the top of the rankings on ratemyprofessors.com. Certainly there are bad sessions and so-so sessions just as there are good ones. Sometimes things don't click, and I'm not as fast or as smooth or as accurate as I know I can be. Being on the racetrack does not inherently guarantee Flow in and of itself. But because the demands of the racetrack are so powerful and the penalties for getting it wrong are very tangible, even a bad session demands total mind and body engagement, and a good session is enough to make me feel in control of the entire universe: to infinity and (redundantly) beyond.

It is a powerfully transcendent joy, and it is mad addictive.

It is also unbelievably tiring. You might think that sitting behind the wheel and driving isn't much of a physical challenge. In part, this is true. There are plenty of guys packing big fuel reservoirs in their midsections who can drive very well regardless. And—good to know—plenty of drivers at club events, both men and women, are well beyond traditional retirement age. There are even some handicapped drivers who use paddle shifters or automatic transmissions. So, no, the driving itself won't do much for getting you into your skinny jeans. Nevertheless, the intense mental effort it takes to create the proper focus, to open your senses to every nuance of the track and the car, and simply to deal with the adrenaline pouring into your system, is wonderfully exhausting. You know that total exhaustion that comes after a full exploration of the post-holiday sale racks at Bloomingdale's, or a marathon bout of vacation sex? It's like that, only better. Or better than the shopping, anyway. I come off a day of driving so worn out that the insidious Mommy Mind has no way to worm itself back in again—or at least, not until I walk back in the door at home to find the stack of bills and piles of laundry that have accumulated in my absence.

So, thanks for all the yoga. I'll still come every Monday night to try and Pincha Mayurasana. But I'm pretty certain the best place for me to look for my Zen is at the racetrack. Gimme my *om* and I'll make it *vroom*.

CHAPTER ELEVEN

High-Speed Chases and the Pursuit

The attractions of high-performance driving may in part be the Zen-like flow and the mental spic-and-span-ing that it forces onto the messy Mommy Mind, but I'd totally be bullshitting if I didn't also 'fess up that just plain going fast is capital F-ing Fun. Here is the first question I am always, always asked about my adventures at the racetrack: "How fast do you go?"

I'll answer that first with the simple answer. I have, on my very best and fastest session in a more powerful car than my beloved Mini, on the back straight at Watkins Glen, come pretty near to 140 miles per hour. Which, I can tell you, is blazingly, breathtakingly, snot-fuckingly *fast* ('scuse my French, but sometimes the extremes really do call for it). Indy-type cars regularly go around 230 miles per hour, so Danica Patrick is lots faster than I am when she's behind the wheels of one of those 650-horsepower babies, but still, it's over twice as fast as the highest legal speed limit in New Jersey.

So, yes, going that fast is really, *really* fun. But the real question is: Why? The sensation of speed all by itself is exciting, sure. It's more than that, though, because it's also about breaking the bonds of convention and my usual obedient relationship with society and The Law. Release from those shackles of conformity is enormously exhilarating.

Here's a tale that will help explain why:

> Accelerating to over a hundred miles per hour coming out of the curve, I glanced in my rearview mirror again and saw that the big black Crown Vic was gaining on me: Yep, the fuzz was on my tail. My little Mini and I could outmaneuver the heavy-duty cop car in the curves, no problem, but as soon as we got to a straight stretch, there he was, gunning for me and pulling ever closer, looming large in my rear view. A very sharp couple of curves came up, and I lost him. The road straightened out, and he almost caught up with me again. This game of cat-and-mouse continued for a good fifteen minutes, but I couldn't shake him. It was the crazy cinematic car chase come surreally to life, and my palms were sweating and my heart was racing. I held out for as long as my frayed nerves could stand it. Finally, I couldn't take the pressure any longer, so I found a gentler stretch, eased up a little, stuck my hand out the window, and gave him the signal to pass me by. Go, buddy. Go chase some other poor schmuck down.

THIS SCENARIO UNFOLDED during one of my early track events, when I was still struggling with basics like learning The Line and dealing with the utter ridiculousness of the predicament I had put myself into. Just as I was beginning to feel like I might eventually get the hang of this new venture, I found myself being chased by a cop car. Most of my fellow students were in typical track cars—Porsches, BMWs, some Subarus—but this guy appeared to have come to hone his skills in his unmarked, state-issued Crown Victoria. So there I was, mild-mannered, middle-aged me

high-speed chases

in my tiny but stylish little car, being chased down by a cop as if I had just hot-wired and stolen my ride. And I felt every bit as guilty as if it had been the truth.

Driving Americans have a funny relationship with the law. Like most Americans, I am an honest, upstanding, law-abiding citizen. I pay my bills, file my taxes, and would no sooner shoplift or park in a handicapped spot than I would drown kittens or set fire to my neighbor's house. Once, when I was still dating Mr. B and he was living in New York, I went jogging in Central Park, and I spotted a twenty-dollar bill on the ground. I picked it up, ran up to the next person I saw ahead, and demanded, "Did you drop this?"

That equally honest and equally stupid person replied, astonishingly, "No."

I'm glad I'm not alone in this. I am an orderly member of an orderly society, and I like it that way. I believe that our laws—proposed, enacted, and enforced by democratically elected officials and paid for by those honestly-filed taxes—are there to protect our way of life. They are what prove we have evolved from pillaging Vikings and raiding Huns to more or less civilized human beings, although when I watch *Survivor,* I'm not entirely sure about this. Like most Americans, though, when I am behind the wheel, I break the law on pretty much a daily basis, and multiple times a day at that. By the strictest of legal standards, I may be above Bonnie and Clyde, but I am not above reproach. I am a scofflaw, and, technically, I suppose I am a criminal, though of a pretty milquetoast sort. Of course I am talking about speed limits.

Ask almost any member of the Upright Citizens Brigade, and the vast majority of them would agree that speed limits are a good idea. We can't have people racing at top speeds around neighborhoods where small, innocent children are walking their cute, big-eyed puppies. We don't want people picking Chihuahuas out of SUV grilles, and social Darwinism aside, it's a pretty good idea to protect ourselves from driving off cliffs when an unexpectedly sharp turn looms ahead. Even on the highways, speed limits are a good thing, so that most people are driving around the same speed and there isn't too much of a discrepancy between the slowest and fastest drivers.

Yet by some tacit and nearly universal agreement, as unspoken and as irresistible as the movement of geese south for the winter, we Americans instinctively ignore the speed limits we have ourselves—if by proxy—enacted. If one were to enter, say, the Garden State Parkway and actually obey the posted fifty-five-mile-per-hour speed limit, utter havoc would ensue, and the perpetrator would as surely be the cause of an accident as the drunken teenager careening around at ninety. Like the geese that fly tip-to-tip yet never touch, our smooth lines of travel may flex and bend, but we mostly stay in congruence with one another. There are outliers, to be sure—the elderly or the terminally timid on the one hand, the Richard Petty wannabes and the overly entitled on the other—but for the most part there's a pretty democratic agreement about what the "real" speed limit is, and it's around seventy or seventy-five, give or take. To be fair, this is also what is generally enforced, too. Still, it means that mostly we are on the wrong side of the law when we drive, we deserve tickets we aren't getting, and we have to look over our shoulders constantly in a kind of uneasy moralistic dance with our consciences finger-wagging at us while we justify ourselves with the everybody-does-it excuse. For heaven's sake, my seventy-something-year-old *mother* does it as she's on her way to her knitting group.

So, yes, I drive faster than the speed limit. All the time, every day. I don't feel great about it, because I don't like breaking the law. But I don't obey the limits, either, because they just feel *wrong*. I drive what feels safe, and we all know the studies that have shown that most people instinctively do drive a safe speed, whether that's higher or lower than the posted speed limit. Usually, of course, it's higher than the posted limit. In New Jersey, that's often *way* higher than the posted speed limit. Here, speeding is the unofficial state pastime, right up there with outlet shopping and bad dye jobs. There's a spot on I-78 where our men in blue actually set up a duck blind—a burlap screen behind which two of them hang out on lawn chairs, picking off speeders with their laser guns while three or four chase cars reel in the poor unsuspecting motorists like it's open season. This seems hardly sporting: like shooting fish in a barrel. But maybe New Jersey has the highest insurance rates in the nation for good reason. I recently took a trip to Colorado and was shocked by how law-abiding the state's citizens were as regards to speed limits. Just amazing. At the same time, I saw very little evidence of law enforcement by the side of the roads. Coincidence? I think not. Then again, I also saw a herd of elk cross a four-lane highway against the traffic signal, so I suppose in Colorado, all bets are off.

Because I'm such an honest person, though, I always feel guilty when I see a police officer on the roads. I know you are just like me, too, because you brake just as sharply as I do when you spot that speed trap on the side of the road, even if you are going somewhere reasonably near the speed limit. I've seen you—and we all slow down to something below the actual speed limit, and when we've driven safely by, we think, *Phew, today's not my day to get nailed.* And then we press down our accelerators again, to get back to the speed God meant for us to cruise at.

All of this constitutes one of the reasons why I feel extraordinarily liberated during my driving sessions at the track. I don't have to look over my shoulder because I'm not breaking the law. For a brief, shining moment, the Jiminy Cricket on my shoulder can stuff his constant chirping, and I feel serene in the knowledge that whatever else might transpire here—wrecked cars, ruined bodies, explosive crashes—it is all legal. Dangerous, perhaps, but still *legal.*

I suspect that for nearly all the participants at the kind of track driving events I go to, there is a similar feeling of release. The men and women who populate these events are pretty much all hardworking professionals—and occasionally retirees who were formerly hardworking professionals. They come from many walks of life, but given that high-performance driving is not an inexpensive hobby, they collectively hold an array of high-profile careers. They are doctors, computer programmers, bankers like Mr. B, businessmen and businesswomen of every stripe. These are people who spend all of their time working within the systems of societal expectation and the bonds of convention. They do what they're supposed to do—they pay their mortgages, they make sure that the inspection stickers are up to date, they get permits for renovating their bathrooms. When they come to the racetrack, though, they get to shake loose at least one of those strictures: They can drive as fast as they want to, and doing so will only get them congratulated. It feels very outlaw to drive at these speeds. I have a feeling that the joy of breaking the law—if only vicariously—partially accounts for the suspicious number of lawyers I have encountered at the track. We've met a minister, too, so it looks like even God needs to unbutton His collar and cut loose once in a while.

Perhaps the appeal of occasionally letting loose is undeniable even at the other end of the radar gun. One day, when Mr. B was moving his fabulous but, let's face it, somewhat ostentatious track car in town between the mechanic and the garage, he was waiting to turn at the light of the main intersection of our really very nice, not to say tony, downtown. Typically on weekends, there at the Starbucks, a police officer is often stationed to shepherd latte-toting pedestrians safely across the zebra stripes. It was a fine day, and Mr. B's window was rolled down. As he idled at the light, the officer on frappuccino duty approached him, complimented him on his car, and asked him if he lived in town.

"Yes, sir," Mr. B answered, wondering guiltily what he could possibly have done wrong.

"How would you like to let 'er rip?" the nice officer wanted to know, on a local highway he named that is not an interstate but is limited-access, four-lane, and divided.

Mr. B, utterly flummoxed, said, "Um, that's okay, I take it to the track."

"'Cuz," continued the undaunted gentleman in blue, "I'll let you take it out to the highway and go as fast as you want to go, and you won't get into any trouble. No tickets, no problem, no nothing." And then came the kicker: "You just have to let *me* drive it back."

Stupefying. It just goes to show that no one is immune from the seductive allure of all that gorgeous horsepower—and that even the Law has its devil-may-care moments. It is uncanny, though, how pervasively the prospect of violating the law penetrates our consciousness when we are driving on the highway in the normal course of daily life. It's like a nasty little beast sitting there, reminding us that we must restrain ourselves, quash the impulse to go faster, because the Law, like Santa Claus, knows when you've been bad or good. Can they see even into the depths of our souls to know how badly we *want* to speed? Some officers seem to know what you are thinking, as we once discovered driving on the highway outside of Binghamton, New York.

There's no question that when you are driving the nation's highways in a candy-colored buzz-bomb like mine, or a mighty-winged Porsche like Mr. B's, you have to be, like Caesar's wife, above reproach. We both make a point, whether driving singly or together, of not being the fastest cars on the road. And though we do not maintain strict observance of the speed limits, we do drive quite conservatively, given the rip-roaring equipment.

Mr. B and I—each in our own racy car—formed a minor convoy of two as we were returning home from the track at Watkins Glen in upstate New York one beautiful fall afternoon. We were approaching Binghamton on Route 17. Now, it is well known among the track rats who need to travel this stretch to get to and from The Glen (as those in the know call it) that it is pretty routinely policed for speed. So we were more than usually conservative in our stately march down the highway, and though we were in the left-hand lane, we were in line with a number of other cars doing a pretty modest five to seven miles per hour above the posted speed limit. Even the most rabid of law enforcement officers wouldn't get their shorts in a twist over that.

It caused us neither surprise nor concern, then, when we spotted a police van parked and facing our direction in the center median. As I neared him, I reflexively eased up a bit on the gas pedal and eyed him warily as the rabbit does the cougar. Nevertheless, my conscience was perfectly clear, so I couldn't help but be startled when I looked at the officer and saw him raise his arm, and point—nope, not the dreaded radar gun—his *finger* at us, and start shaking it. *Tsk, tsk, tsk,* the finger chided as we both drove on by. *Shame on you. You were clearly THINKING about going fast.*

Which was true, but it was hard to see how we could be condemned for the high-speed lust in our hearts. There is, thankfully, no way to ticket you for having wistful *thoughts* about breaking the speed limit. Yet.

BUT WHAT IS it that we're always speeding towards, anyway? We spend most of our adult lives engaged in pursuit. We're constantly chasing our goals, our ambitions, our dreams. Our whole lives are set up as the pursuit of one thing or another, loosely defined as success. As Americans we are theoretically guaranteed life, liberty, and the pursuit of happiness, but how much time do we really spend pursuing happiness? Mostly the pursuit consists of achieving mileposts, which, once reached, are quickly replaced by new ones. You pursue a college degree. You reach your goal, you wave that degree in the air, but then you decide to pursue an advanced degree, or a career. You embark on your career, and that, too, provides goals that, once reached, are always succeeded by new goals: the next promotion, the next bonus, the next level of responsibility. You pursue love, and though perhaps the hierarchy isn't as clearly defined, there are mileposts there as well: you have a girlfriend or boyfriend, then a fiancé (or fiancée), then a spouse, a house, a baby, maybe two, maybe more.

When you're younger, you tend to think naively that there will come a time or situation you'll reach when the pursuit will stop. Once I buy a house, you think, I will have reached the end. But the house needs an addition, or it becomes too small to hold your family or your dreams. Or it needs a new hot-water heater, or roof, or French drain, or updated appliances. Once you reach a certain level at your job, if you're fortunate enough to have a job, you tell yourself, I will become financially secure. But there is always a higher position, a better job, more money, or a company car (or are those golden days over?). The highway of life for the gainfully employed is one that stretches to the horizon, and the thing about horizons is that they are infinitely moving targets. Possibly this thought could be depressing, but it really shouldn't be, because we need new challenges to keep life interesting. It is stasis that is terrifyingly close to death.

Still, that unending highway can be daunting, and there is something enormously liberating about getting off it once in a while. The highway of life unfurls infinitely and irreversibly in one direction only—you never get a chance to go back and see the same scenery again. By contrast, at the racetrack you go, really fast, in circles. To the uninitiated this may look as

© FENG YU/123RF

silly as a dog chasing its own tail. But here's the beauty of the thing: When you are going in circles, clearly you are not in pursuit of any particular object or larger goal. Instead, you are engaged in pure pursuit itself—pursuit for the sake of pursuit alone—and it is extraordinarily liberating. Going places without needing to get anywhere, speed without repercussion, sheer, exultant velocity without looking over your shoulder—for the responsible taxpayer and otherwise law-abiding citizen, this experience can be as heady as a drug. Engage in it at your own peril, for you may never be able to go back to the slow lane again.

Moreover, where the only end to the highway of life is the assisted-living community (and, shudder, beyond), at the racetrack there is temporary closure. When I go, I pull out all the stops, I go like blazes, and then the checkered flag is waved, and I gratefully step off the merry-go-round. So far, Mr. B and I only participate in club-based Driver's Ed events, which means we aren't even racing against other people. So when the checkered flag comes out, we win every time—and every time, it feels like a celebration, and a little bit like we are getting away with something.

SO HERE'S TO high-speed chases with no bad guys and no cops—to a place where bankers and college professors and people who always tip at least 15 percent can go and feel a little bit badass without running afoul of the laws we usually support. Here's to pursuit in its purest form—the chasing down of rainbows with no pot of gold in sight.

I once spied a Corvette with a custom license plate that read HI OFICR, and I thought he was probably tempting fate, or perhaps relying a bit too heavily on a state trooper with a sense of humor. Me, you'll find in my racy little car going not too far over the speed limit, heading to the track, and only *thinking* about going fast. Ticket *this*.

CHAPTER TWELVE

The Question of My Internal Apparatus

E nough with the touchy-feely stuff already. It's time to get down to brass tacks—or balls, as the case may be. This chapter is not for the anatomically squeamish. Feel free to skip ahead to the next one if you don't want to read about testicles. And by that I mean: read *a lot* about testicles. Because here is what your faithful correspondent can report back from her time on the front lines and in the hairy, sweaty, squalid trenches of the masculine battlefield: your husbands, your boyfriends, your coworkers and neighbors, your doctor and your lawyer and your insurance agent and the guy behind the cash register—when they are out together with a whole lot of other men, and they are engaged in a physically competitive activity, they talk about balls *all the time.*

If you are a woman at the racetrack, you will inevitably have to come to terms with your lack of testicles. Oh, sure, I was already acquainted with the whole biology of it—I've had a baby, after all, and as early as 1970 I noticed the salient anatomical difference between my little brother and me when we were given baths together—but I had never before realized how important testicles are for your ability to drive a car. I was confronted by the issue of my lack of balls the very first time I drove at the racetrack, and I should have realized right then and there how central a theme balls would be in my new hobby.

As is customary at many of these events, the instructors who ride with you in your car will have multiple students—often, one in a novice group, then another more advanced driver in an intermediate group. The instructor assigned to me for my maiden voyage at the track was a guy who lived for speed and drank high-octane for breakfast. He was a dedicated amateur club racer and loved the whole atmosphere so much that he was an instructor of instructors for the club Driver's Ed events. Thus, I was not his only student. Consider: Student A was middle-aged and terrified me, in a completely unmodified, civilian Mini Cooper, and Student B was a guy with a track-ready Ferrari. Wondering whether it was utterly frustrating for a race junkie like him to be stuck in a little Mini with a tentative Nervous Nellie like me, I asked him how it was going with his other student in the Ferrari. What was that like? I asked him. He proceeded to give me all the stats on the car—which sounded to me something like what dogs hear in *The Far Side* cartoons: "blah blah

© KLAUS SCHNITZER

a minnow among the sharks

blah *Ferrari* blah blah blah blah *fast.*" I nodded politely and thought miserably how glacially slow I must seem to him.

"The Ferrari has ceramic brakes," he added, "but the guy just doesn't have the balls to use them."

I gave a dutiful chuckle and let the conversational ball (as it were) drop, since we were waved on to the track to begin the session, and everything I had—testicular and otherwise—needed to focus on my driving. But later, I chewed worriedly on what my instructor had said. Should I have asked him, "Are testicles required for braking?" If so, what will happen when I need to stop my car? Here I have been braking all my adult life with just a pair of ovaries to go on, and now this guy was telling me that I cannot brake without completely different equipment down yonder. And what about accelerating? Or steering? Can you do either of those things competently without testicles? If not, then I supposed I'd better hang up the helmet immediately and go back home, because not only have I never owned a pair of testicles, I've never really coveted a set for myself, either. The silly things clang around down there and are so fragile and prone to injury, too. Don't get me wrong, I'm all for them in principle, and if we didn't have them, the human race would be in sorry shape indeed—extinct, even. I'm an especially big fan of the one particular set that provided me with the raw materials to build my very own Divine Miss M. It's just that they inspire no envy in me. I much prefer the tidiness of my own internally stored apparatus.

Or was my scornful instructor speaking in metaphors, forsooth? There, too, I guessed I'd still be in trouble. Metaphorical balls would be the ones you use to go bungee jumping or skydiving or disarming muggers in dark alleyways. I don't have that type of balls, either. I've just never thought of myself as a particularly brave person. Until now, I had never signed up for daring sports or activities. I'm a professor of architectural history. The thrill of my week is the arrival of the Sunday *New York Times* crossword puzzle. (Which I do in pen, thank you very much. How's that for ballsy?) Running, fine; bicycling, okay; cross-country skiing, I can manage. But I tried rollerblading when it was popular, and found it too scary, too uncontrollable. Downhill skiing always looked even more menacing. Rock climbing was right out. Keep your feet in contact with the ground, don't go too fast, be in control at all times—these are my mottos. So far this philosophy has kept all my bones unbroken and my skin intact. It's a *modus operandi* with an excellent success rate.

PSYCHOLOGICALLY SPEAKING, I'VE never been very brave, either. I've usually shied away from conflict. I don't like aggression in others, and have always had trouble accessing it in myself. Whenever I encountered it, I went into retreat; I shut down. I got stony-faced and nonresponsive, and I let other people's aggression, when completely unavoidable, roll over me as much as possible. Even in daily life, I'm usually kind of a wimp. I find it impossible to be rude to telemarketers. True, I have often fantasized about being rude to them, but I just can't seem to bring myself to do it. I actually find myself apologizing to them as I tell them I'm not interested in their chimney cleaning services or taking a survey about cable companies. I also don't like to haggle over prices, even at antique shops or flea markets where it's expected. I'd be a disaster in a Turkish bazaar. I understand you insult the vendors if you pay the asking price.

On a recent nature show, I watched the delicate-legged, white-spotted calf of an elk engage its only defense against the roving wolves looking to enjoy a little elk snack. It found itself a hidey-hole in the tall grasses, under a fallen tree trunk or behind a rock, and it hunkered down and tried to make itself invisible. Sure, I get it that the wolves have just as much of a right to a full stomach as the elk calf has to live, but I was rooting for the elk calf just the same. *You go, little guy,* I thought, much relieved when the wolves gave up and trotted away. I'm all for the nonconfrontational elk calf approach.

I'm like that on the highway, too. Aggressive drivers give me the heebie-jeebies, and I would much rather just move over and let them pass than get into any pissing matches on the Garden State. It happens a lot in New Jersey. So when some wolf in a Corvette starts breathing down my neck, I happily pull an elk calf and just hunker down and let him by. My theory is: I'd rather have the assholes in front of me where I can see them—and where they can usefully serve as cop bait—than behind me.

So what does the elk calf do at the racetrack where it's nothing but wolves as far as the eye can see? That was one of the aspects I had the hardest time dealing with at first. The racetrack is a super aggressive atmosphere. The noise of those souped-up engines, with their big, bad sports exhausts, is deafening. Put twenty or more of them on the track and let them run wild in their wolfish packs, and you'd think the Four Horsemen of the Apocalypse were on their way. Even the smells are aggressive—hot rubber, cooking motor oil, high-octane gasoline fumes. It's enough to singe your nose hairs. And aside from the pungently real smells, there's the practically palpable musk of testosterone hanging in the air. The guys who bring their speedy cars to the racetrack may look like professional sheep when they're in their streetclothes—all those seemingly domesticated doctors and lawyers, computer geeks and corporate tools—but they shed their sheep's clothing at the track and let their inner Big Bads out to play. The aura of testosterone there is so strong, I'm always afraid that if I breathe in too much of it, I will start growing facial hair.

What's a certified double-X chromosome carrier to do? I discovered recently that one possible solution would be for me simply to go out and buy a pair. When you drive the nation's highways as much as I do, with a regular long-distance commute and frequent weekend trips away from home, you inevitably end up seeing some strange sights out there on the roads. Sometimes they are just bumper stickers or personalized license plates whose statements I ponder briefly before the highway lulls my consciousness away again. If they are good enough, I try to remember them to tell my family when I get home. (My current favorite: a truck belonging to James Brown's Lawn and Garden Service: *The Godfather of*

Soil.) Sometimes you see an interesting or exotic or antique car—a Lamborghini or a Bentley—sometimes, a license plate that you don't expect to see in the northeastern United States—Alaska, Hawaii, or even, once, Guam. If you're out there long enough, you, too, will eventually spot a set of truck testicles. When I first glimpsed them on the New Jersey Turnpike, I couldn't quite believe my eyes. It was the gentle swaying motion that first caught my wandering attention as I gained on the pickup truck that was sporting its special apparatus. What was that, I idly wondered, swinging back and forth under the truck's tow hitch? It looks like—no, it can't be—yes, it really is: Your brain processes what it just can't quite believe is there. But there, indeed, they were: larger than life and anatomically accurate masculine genitalia appended to the vehicle. I gaped, briefly, alternately repelled and fascinated with this novel automotive accessory.

As soon as I returned home, I felt compelled to learn more about how to gender your vehicle. I briefly mulled over just how to look up automotive genitalia, then I tentatively typed in *truck testicles* on my Internet search engine and instantly came up with the startling revelation that there are at least four different companies that specialize in this product: thatsnutz. com, trucknutzandbikerballz.com, bumpernuts.com, and bullsballs.com all sell the devices. What an amazing country I live in, I thought. Surely there is no place else on earth where four different companies can exist, and, presumably, make a profit, selling testicles to hang from a truck. You just can't envision the Japanese or the French festooning their trucks with replica testicles. The Russians maybe. But I digress. As if to affirm our capitalistic superiority, there is a gloriously wide selection to choose from. There is the understated set of black testicles, which unobtrusively harmonizes with your truck's undercarriage and tow hitch. The more realistic flesh-toned pair is a little creepy by any standard. There are the considerably more expensive cast metal ones, which are available in classic Detroit chrome—and, of course, brass (get it?). Then, as surely as there had to be brass balls, there just had to be blue ones (it is at this point that you start to think about all the metaphors in the English language that reference that particular part of the male anatomy). Somewhat bewildering are the shocking hot pink testicles—for the sensitive guy?—as well as the internally lit ones that can be wired into the vehicle's electrical system. Glow-in-the dark testicles! Who knew?

Astonishing, I thought, as I reviewed the magnificent array of ersatz masculinity. Consider the possibilities—oh, the possibilities! The first thing I wondered was whether I would ever consider hanging a pair of breasts off my car. Breasticles? Was there a new business concept to be exploited in this? A fortune to be made? The first stumbling block to this idea would have to be a technical one. Where would you display a pair of breasts on a car? Testicles clearly belong down low on the vehicle. It makes instinctive sense that you'd put them on a tow hitch, between the two rear wheels. If cars really had reproductive systems, you feel sure that this is where they'd be. Mating would be awkward—but then, when isn't it? Surely this is how Smart cars are made. By contrast, vehicular breasts would either have to be located on the undercarriage, where they couldn't possibly be seen anyway, or on the front of the car, attached to the grill. *Wait,* I thought, *we already have car bras.* Why not breasts to fill them? But all cars already sport a set of headlamps, don't they? Breasts, I concluded, would be extraneous. Besides, nobody would look me in the windshield anymore.

I thought of my offspring-blessed brother, whose fully operational manhood is unquestionably evidenced by his three small children. Everything south of the border is clearly in excellent working order. Yet when baby number three swelled the ranks of backseat passengers requiring safety seats to a point that mandated a new family vehicle, he experienced a crisis of confidence that hit him just below the belt. For if powerful pickup trucks are the swaggering *machos* of the road, what are the bloated, slow, and ungainly minivans but the eunuchs? You may as well just hand over the testicles in exchange for the car keys. It was clear that he felt his masculinity was being threatened by the purchase of the dreaded minivan. Oh, how he hated to give in! The only way he could soothe his injured sense of masculinity was by pointing out that the bed of the minivan, when folded flat, could fit an entire sheet of plywood, one of those other measures of masculinity. At least if you have a saw and a hammer and some nails, you must still be a bona fide guy, even if you're loading the raw materials into a (say it with pride) *minivan.*

Maybe the testicles are being sold to the *wrong guys.* Aren't testicles on a pickup truck at the very least redundant? If you've got the big, powerful truck with the heavy-duty axles and double sets of wheels, maybe even the erect, chromed exhaust pipe, aren't your testicles already on display for the whole world to see? I've never seen a pair on an eighteen-wheeler. The operator of a Mack truck knows he's got 'em and apparently doesn't feel the need to double up. The guys who really *need* them are the ones driving the minivans. The companies that sell these specialized accessories could benefit from a whole new marketing push: Instead of preaching to the choir and selling their testicles to the owners of pickup trucks, they should aim to provide replacement testicles to the drivers of the minivans. I see a whole new world for the disgruntled daddies who could reclaim their rightful patrimony with a click of the mouse and the simple expedient of a set of injection-molded testicles appended to the rear of their minivans. The suburban streets, soccer-field parking lots, and elementary school pickup lines would be filled with anatomically correct carpoolers, and a vehicular gender injustice would be righted. Now *that* would be nuts.

And what about me? Should I just buy a pair, and hang them on my car, and consider myself fully equipped? Would that give me the balls I seem to need to be a success at the racetrack? Or could I somehow learn to run with the wolves on my own estrogen-based terms? Where I needed them the most was in the whole culture of The Pass. The act of passing that we take for granted on our nation's highways is, at the track, a highly nuanced and psychologically fraught system that lies at the heart of why most of the participants are there in the first place. One of the biggest differences between club-based DE events and official, winner-takes-all racing is the system put into place for passing. At a real race, passing is, of course, how races are won. There are no rules for passing—you do it whenever you can, however you can, and that's where much of the excitement lies. It's also, not too surprisingly, when accidents are most likely to occur. Thus, in the (theoretically) friendlier arena of club-based high-performance driving events, there are strict commandments regarding passing.

The First Commandment of Passing is:

THOU SHALT NOT PASS WITHOUT A POINT-BY.

In other words, no one may be a Passer without the explicit consent of the Passee. The ritual goes like this: The overtaking car politely requests a pass by nosing right up to the slower car's hind end. The Passer remains glued to the Passee's tail until the Passee notices and admits that he is slower than the driver on his ass. This, as you may imagine, is a moment of great sadness for the Passee. Sometimes he will deliberately ignore the request of the Passer, hoping that perhaps he may in the next corner prove to be faster after all.

Which brings us to the Second Commandment of Passing, to wit:

THOU SHALT GIVE THE POINT-BY IF THOU BE SLOWER
THAN THY BROTHER. OR SISTER, AS THE CASE MAY BE.

The Passee is enjoined to stick his left arm out the window and indicate where he would like to be passed—a point to the left means *pass me on the left*, and a finger pointing over the roof of the car means *pass me on the right* (not, as you might think, *go take a flying leap*).

The Third Commandment of Passing, then, is:

THOU SHALT LIFT THY FOOT OFF THE
ACCELERATOR IF THOU ART BEING PASSED. JUST A TITCH.

This is especially difficult for the Passee if the Passer is in a lower-horsepower car, because it constitutes the Passee's tacit admission that the Passer is a better driver through the corners. The Passer then swings out to the indicated side, floors it, and blows by the Passee. An extremely polite Passer may give a friendly *thank-you* wave, but this is strictly optional. It is, on the other hand, considered poor form to yell "sucker!" as you pass by, and in any case, you won't be heard.

A corollary to polite passing lies in the Fourth Commandment:

THOU SHALT NOT CUT OFF THE PASSEE.

As tempting as it may be to teach the slower driver a lesson, and as irresistible as the allure of getting back to your line may be, plenty of room and a courtly step around indicate respect for one's dance partner. In my anxiety to get back to my place on The Line and because of my lack of feel for where the guy I was passing stood, I once veered too close on the return from the pass and got thoroughly reamed out by my instructor. I felt so bad I had to find the guy afterward and apologize to him. *Mea culpa.*

In deference to the sacredness of The Line, the Fifth Commandment of Passing is:

THOU SHALT NOT PASS IN CORNERS.
(UNLESS THOU ART AN INSTRUCTOR, IN WHICH CASE THOU ART
CLOSER TO GOD AND CAN MAKE UP THINE OWN RULES ON THAT.)

This is a simple matter of safety and means that fewer cars end up meeting their (Auto) Maker before their time.

Further safety requirements lead to the Sixth Commandment
of Passing, namely:

THOU SHALT NOT PASS UNDER A YELLOW FLAG.

Since a cautionary yellow flag means, à la *Madeline*'s Miss Clavel, *something is not right*, all passing is out in this situation. Fair enough.

AND WHO ENFORCES these commandments? The prophets are the flaggers, who can cast you into outer darkness if you break one of the Passing Commandments. If a corner worker spies a driver who passes without being given a point-by (Commandment Number One, and the most important), he will be called off the track and given a lecture, followed by penance in the form of Time Out from the track before being permitted back into play. Repeat offenders may be stoned, castrated, or, worst of all, sent home. Thus endeth the lesson.

So it is with the intricate politics of passing where the oft-mentioned and not entirely accurate talk of "testicles" is heard. There is no question that this is what it all comes down to at the track. Do you have the chutzpah to drive more aggressively, go faster, and thus pass someone else? The notches in the fan belt are the cars you have passed. The Pass is far more gratifying if the car you passed was your equal in terms of horsepower— or, even better, someone who had more horsepower than you but, clearly, less in the way of intestinal fortitude.

So where does this all leave me, the one without balls, purchased or otherwise, the one who prefers to let people pass on the highway? It should come as no surprise that I am someone very generous with the point-by. If there's someone filling my rearview mirror, I prefer to let him go. And I just don't go all out when I drive. I figure there's time for me to develop the skills that eventually will allow me to use the car's remaining potential that I have kept in reserve. Perhaps this is easier for me to do because I have no testicles at stake? Or perhaps it is my internally stored apparatus that gives me a calm in the face of aggression and a knowledge that I will get my turn?

BUT RECENTLY I seem to have begun to access my own Inner Apparatus. I'm driving a little harder, daring to push the accelerator right down to the floor (you can really do that!), braking later, keeping more speed through corners. I had a particularly good session not long ago in which I was feeling very on, very powerful, very grab-your-crotch-and-hock-a-loogie good. When you are on like this, everything seems to go right, and suddenly, I was not merely playing with the big boys—I was passing them. I jumped one or two of them and bestowed a nice little Queen Elizabeth wave upon them after they gave me the point-by and I sped past. No need to be rude about it.

But then came the moment I think I've been waiting for my whole damn life. Slowly but surely, I was gaining on a wicked-looking Darth Vader of a Porsche Turbo, all dressed in black. This in itself would have been cause for celebration, but the motor oil on the cake was the fact that this was a *flame-spitting* Porsche Turbo. I rather doubt that there is anything more enchanting to the male of the population than the idea of a car that spits flames when you drive it. I know it is something Mr. B fantasizes about. This slightly older model of Porsche does it, for real. When the driver downshifts, the car dumps a little bit of fuel into the exhaust, which ignites in the tailpipe and comes out as flames. Friggin' *awesome*. And I was catching up to him. Oh, he made me work for it all right, but I reeled him in, stayed on his ass—but not too close, so I didn't char my headlights—and he was forced to give me the point-by.

Heh heh heh, I chuckled evilly, in my head. I am Track Girl; hear me roar.

SO IF I'VE located my Inner Apparatus, have I become a braver person? Well, maybe. I still won't be rude to telemarketers. Those poor reviled people are just trying to earn a living, even if they are interrupting the family mealtime. I'm still happy to step aside on the highway to let the other driver pass. It's just not very important. But I have to admit that, having found the psychic wherewithal to hold my own on a racetrack filled with men who like to pull it out and waggle it around, my attitude to life has undergone something of a testosterone-tinted makeover. I think it is inevitable that if you enter a venue like that and come out not only intact but also victorious, you will be changed in some important respects. In the passing lanes of life, men have a tendency to put themselves first. They put themselves out there, they engage in the contest, they put the foot to the floor, and when they see an opportunity to pass someone else by, they take it, and they don't apologize for it. By engaging in a little actual passing my-self, I've been forced to put myself—quite literally—ahead of the other guy. And it's brought me to realize that maybe I can do that for myself out here in the real world, too: put myself first, the way many men would. Certainly there have been times recently when I've found myself thinking, dammit, if I can pass a flame-spitting Porsche Turbo, then maybe I can, after all, eat a snail. Or go downhill skiing. Or try on a miniskirt. Or change careers and write a book.

CHAPTER THIRTEEN

How to Make Physics Your Bitch

For all that metaphorical testicles are extremely useful for in the highly charged, competitive, masculine environment of the racetrack, it turns out that high-powered brains are actually an even bigger asset if you are going to be any good at this lunatic thing. Experiencing the Zen-like flow of the racetrack was in itself an eye-opener for a sports car novice like me, but I think I was even less prepared for the revelation that the interactive relationship between car and driver would be such a profoundly intellectual experience, and that it would please the bespectacled professorial persona to no end. Being introduced to the math and physics of the racetrack re-awakened the eternal nerd in me—someone who, you will recall, loved school so much she chose never to leave its navel-gazing confines. It's been tremendous fun to be a student again and to rediscover my long-lost appreciation for the unyielding, leather-clad, whip-cracking dominatrix that is physics—once upon a time my favorite academic subject.

Despite my perfectly normal humanoid ears and complete absence of a tail, I persist in my belief that I am genetically part basset hound. This is because like a dog I often construct my mental topography of the world around me through my sense of smell. I regularly astound my husband

and daughter with seemingly Sherlock-Holmesian deductions about what they have been up to derived very simply from the way they smell. Mr. B will never be able to cheat on me without my smelling the damning evidence on his shirt, and the Divine Miss M can never pretend to be sick. I would only have to lean in and give her a whiff to know whether she was faking it or not. Her body chemistry when she is ill gives off a very distinct odor I recognize immediately as *Eau de l'Enfant Malade*. Had I been raised in France I might well have trained to be a professional "nose." Nearer to the refineries of New Jersey than the lavender fields of Provence, I am the one who sniffs suspiciously at spoiled foods ("Here, honey," says Mr. B, "smell this and tell me if it's off") and tracks down possum carcasses after they've crawled under the deck to die. Ew.

On a more positive note, I revel in the bouquet of smells all around me, like the juicy-crisp fragrance of a grapefruit when I cut it open, or the luxurious tannic scent of leather and polish in a shoe-repair shop. There are some slightly weirder smells I really like, too: the musky animal smell of my tiny dog that develops weeks after his last grooming; a very faint residual remnant of skunk; Elmer's glue; packing tape; Band-Aids. For me, the most erotic scent in the world—with the possible exception of a snuffle at Mr. B's clavicle after he's freshly showered and has applied a dab of his Italian cologne that smells like burnished saddle leather and oak trees and rosemary and . . . ummm, where was I? The sexiest non-male aroma I know of—is jet fuel. God, I love that stuff. There's a stretch of the New Jersey Turnpike sandwiched between the IKEA and the runways of Newark Airport, and every time I motor past it, I go nearly faint with the pleasure of breathing in the fumes that billow out from the tarmac. I have loved that smell since childhood, and partly it's the smell itself—sharp, pungent, oily yet clean—and partly it's the association. The smell of jet fuel means I am going somewhere. It fills me with anticipation and excitement—the promises of a new destination and new sights to see. If it weren't for the fact of its probable carcinogenic properties, I would dab it on my pulse points.

Even today, shuffling ignominiously barefoot through the dreary purgatory of the security lines at the airport cannot squelch my adoration for jet fuel and airplanes. I love the smell of airports; I love the smell of jet fuel; I love the smell of the air that whiffles out of those little overhead jets above your seat. Airplane bathrooms: not so much. But every paradise must have its cesspool. Still, nothing thrills me quite so deeply as the moment when the big bird gathers its mighty weight as it speeds down the runway, and, counter to all reasonable expectation, lifts off the ground as your stomach gives a last little lurch earthward. Almost as good as sex, if considerably more expensive and requiring a great deal more foreplay.

The physics of liftoff, and how those massive machines stay improbably airborne, has always fascinated me. That is why, when given the option of choosing a subject for a high school physics makeup exam, I elected to work out the physics of the jet airplane. I had missed a big exam because of a trip my parents had taken me on, and my teacher gave me the opportunity to make up what I'd missed by doing an oral examination. I had one of the most memorable and enjoyable educational moments of my life as he and I used basic mechanical physics to work out the lift necessary to hoist a 747 into the air. Perhaps you can already tell by this that my high school physics teacher was something special. His name was Steve Jacobsen, and he had a PhD in physics, which made him embarrassingly overqualified to be teaching in our rural Pennsylvania high school. Our school was too small and there were too few students who advanced far enough in science to merit a full-time physics teacher. Dr. Jacobsen taught part-time at the local university and part-time at the high school. From galloping bridges, to returning the previous year in a rocket ship traveling faster than the speed of light, to the seemingly impossible liftoff of a hulking 747 into the wild blue yonder, "Shaky Jake," as we called him, explained why the world behaved the way it did. He did it with such clarity and wit that we all loved both him and the class.

Many years later, I spent a good ten minutes collapsing in laughter as I attempted to split a lunch check with another art historian. We sat over the remnants of a civilized meal, two highly intelligent women, both possessing fairly prestigious doctorates, and all we wanted to do was divide a simple bill in two and provide our waiter with a reasonable tip. The complications arose as we were trying to work out how to do it in cash with the denominations we held in our respective wallets. As we traded tens and twenties and singles back and forth, we began to lose count and feel increasingly silly.

"This is yours," I said, handing her a ten, and she replied: "No, wait, I think it's *yours.*"

"Are you sure? Because I think that means you paid too much." And so on.

As we swapped the bills, we were soon helpless with hilarity as we realized that despite a collective total of at least fifteen years of advanced education, we could not manage a brainlessly simple arithmetic problem. Brilliance at maths, as my lovely British friend is wont to call it, is clearly not the art historian's forte. So why did I love my high school physics class so much?

Part of it actually was the subject matter, but most of it was the teacher. I truly did enjoy learning the mechanics of how the world around me operates. Lunch checks aside, I was actually pretty good at math back then, but what I enjoyed most about physics wasn't so much the mathematical nuts and bolts, but the ah-ha revelations of how and why a sailboat angles its sails a certain way against the wind, or how resonance frequencies could make a bridge dance, or why it is that in movies the horse-drawn carriage wheels always seem to be revolving frantically backward. All of this would have been much, much more dull if it weren't for the inimitable Shaky Jake. It was thanks to his lively teaching style, particularly the translation of arcane formulae into real-life examples, that made physics come alive for me and the rest of my classmates. When I graduated from high school, he encouraged me to sign up for college Physics for Poets classes aimed at liberal-arts types like me, but I have to confess somewhat sheepishly that I never did. I've had a fortunate number of brilliant teachers over the years, but my favorite one of all time remains my guru of high school physics. Here's to you, Steve Jacobsen: May all your vectors line up and may all your reactions be equal and opposite.

I'VE THOUGHT A lot about both Shaky Jake and my early fascination with physics during my recent adventures at the racetrack as I've tried to convince my car to go where I want it to go around each corner. Whether your car makes the turn or ends up plowing the surrounding fields is purely a matter of simple Newtonian physics. At the same time, whether you understand both the physics and the driving techniques has a lot to do with the highly varied and sometimes random quality of the racetrack pedagogy. When you start out doing high-performance driving events, you are always assigned an instructor. Instructors are first and foremost skilled drivers who have been doing this sort of thing for years. They have made a decision to undergo instructor training, and they've committed themselves to climbing in the passenger seat of the vehicles of strangers who are often complete novices to the sport. Their only payment is free or reduced-cost track time for themselves, and the satisfaction of helping somebody else improve. All of them may be brilliant at driving, but—as with any group of instructors in any field of endeavor—not all are gifted at communicating how to do it.

I've been pontificating in classrooms all over the New York metropolitan area for over a decade and a half now, and I've been a mommy, too, for much of that time. I'm used to telling other people what to think ("the Sistine Chapel is the greatest single contribution to human civilization") and what to do ("I don't care if you don't feel like it; go to the potty before we leave the house because we're not stopping on the way"). I was even pretty sure I knew how to drive. Suddenly, poised on the racecourse, I was a rank beginner, a student all over again, something I had not experienced since graduate school. When you are used to being the teacher, it's not that easy to turn off the authoritative persona and submit to someone else's instruction. It's humbling, and I'm sure that like all things that taste slightly bitter, it's got to be good for you.

If a student ignores my summary of Frank Lloyd Wright's contribution to modern architecture, the worst thing she will suffer is a bad grade and the guilt of flagrantly squandering her parents' tuition check. At the track, though, it can be quite literally a matter of life and death to listen to what your instructor is telling you. I've had wonderful instructors who were simply instinctively good at teaching. Luckily for me, my very first instructor was one of the good ones. He seemed to understand how much I could absorb during that initial experience, and once I reached a level of basic competence, he talked less and less, ultimately reducing our communication to waves of the hand, almost like a conductor with an orchestra. In just two short days, although I had a glimmering of just how much I still had to learn, he left me with a deeply compelling urge to pursue mastery of the skill. I can only dream of inspiring my own students to the same extent.

Since then I've had quite a number of different instructors whose styles varied as greatly as they did. I've had some who talked too much and some who talked too little. I've had some who have dictated, and some who have taken the time to explain. I've had old-school dashboard-thumpers and low-key analytical types. Once I took that important step back and acknowledged that I had a great deal to learn, it was fun to be on the receiving end once more. For a former honors student and an eternal nerd, discovering a whole new use for physics was more fun than I would have thought possible. Prior to this discovery, I never gave any serious thought to the mechanics of what a car does on the road. Instead, I was prone—as so many of us are—to anthropomorphize my automobile.

braking, turning, accelerating:
it's all about the grip

MAYBE BECAUSE MANY of us spend more time with our vehicles than with our dearest friends, we often provide them with names and personalities. I have read of a study that concluded that over 80 percent of car owners consider their car to be a member of the family. One of my friends named her Mazda Bertha, and besides my first car, the Putterbug, I have had cars named Thor, Gertrude, and Bubba Trump, as well as a GPS named Helga. Rationally I know it's silly, but I talk to my car, praising it when it does well, encouraging it, especially at the track, when I need a little extra oomph to make it around a corner.

As it turns out, though, everything a car does on the road is governed by simple mechanical physics, not talking nice to it as I'd previously thought. Whereas The Line is geometry (my most favorite math subject way back when), adhesion and grip—braking, turning, accelerating—is all just Newtonian physics. I've even bought books on the subject and read up on how I could maximize my vehicle's performance through the delicate manipulation of brake, gas, and steering wheel. Shaky Jake would be proud.

What I learned was this: Your car, just like a cat, balances on four, black, grippy paws. Everything it can and can't do is dictated by the four small squares where the rubber of your tire meets the asphalt—called in the lingo the "Contact Patch." Whether your car will do what you want it to do all depends on whether you have the grip to do it. Think of the cat as it gathers up speed for a run at a mouse. Fluffy's power all comes from her muscular rear haunches, and as she catapults forward, her weight, and thus the grip in her paw pads, shifts towards her rear. Thus: Acceleration shifts weight, hence grip, towards the back. Suddenly the mouse has disappeared in its hole, and she needs to come to a halt. Out shoot her front paws as she tries to stop herself, and her weight shifts to the front as the carpet gathers in little ripples ahead of her. It's the grip she has in the front that will allow her to save herself from conking her head against the wall. So: Braking shifts weight to the front.

If the cat spies the mouse darting around a corner, the principles of weight shift start going side-to-side. As she tries to turn right, say, the forces acting on her body (especially if she's gone overboard on the cat chow) pull her out to the left, and she has to counteract that by leaning in and shifting her weight towards the inside (the right). Most of her grip is in her left side, as that is where the weight has been thrown. Likewise, in a car, if you maintain too much speed as you enter a turn, the car will generate too much sideways force to keep its grip on your intended arc. It will lose its grip and swing in a larger arc instead. If this larger arc is also larger than the arc of the road, then off you will slide into the gravel pit if you are lucky, or the tire wall if you are not. Simple. If, on the other hand, you ease up on the accelerator—which shifts the weight towards the front of the car—your front or steering wheels will get more of their bite back, and they will allow you to turn better.

It is chiefly through pushing your car nearer to the limits of its ability to adhere to the road surface that you can begin to understand and therefore manipulate the physics of your car. My most favorite eureka moment on this score came when I first understood and was able to employ what is called throttle steering. An instructor was helping me to negotiate a tight but fairly high-speed turn and told me to watch the nose of the car while I was making the turn and then to ease up ever so gently on the accelerator pedal (called *feathering*). I obeyed, and as I feathered off the gas, I could see—without my having turned the steering wheel in the slightest—the nose dive down just slightly and turn the car into the corner more tightly. It seemed like magic, and I felt like an absolute genius. As it turns out, this is just a basic tool in the racecar driver's bag of tricks, but it made me feel like a master of space, time, and dimension to understand and use it. Like someone looking at a wall full of nails who has just been taught how to use a hammer, I now take any opportunity I can to throttle steer, just because I love the feeling of total domination that it gives me. Wham-wham-wham-*wham!*

Ultimately the physics of the track come down to a subtle and interconnected ballet of weight shift and adhesion. Going fast in a straight line, whether on a highway or a track, requires little skill. All that takes is a brick on the gas pedal. Making a car dance around turns, however, requires the interplay of hand, foot, and eye coordination, coupled with a feel for the distribution of balance and the immutable and lovely laws of the physics that govern the behavior of inanimate objects on this earth. It is one of the things that keeps drawing me back to the inconvenient, expensive, rather ridiculous pieces of asphalt paradise that are the race-tracks of the mid-Atlantic region. For when so much else in life seems unpredictable and uncontrollable, from the wildly vacillating economy to the unpredictable weather that floods your (carpeted, of course) basement to the hormonal mood swings of a preadolescent daughter, there is something profoundly comforting in being able to control one unexpected thing. When even inanimate objects seem to have it in for you—the television, the plumbing, the coffee maker, the hard drive on your computer— how magnificent, how authoritative it feels to experience dominion over the ordinarily docile machine that makes its rounds to work or the grocery store or the kids' [fill in overscheduled offsprings' activity here]. Although contemplating relativity or the Big Bang can sometimes make me feel both insignificant and unintelligent, understanding and manipulating the physics of my car can, for a brief, shining moment, make me feel like a superhero. Is it any wonder that the dusky, pungent, nose-hair-singeing aromas of burning rubber and overheated brake pads have joined the list of my top favorite smells? They may not quite replace jet fuel as the most erotic smell I can name, but when I inhale that heady, petroleum-based mixture, my heart takes a leap, my pulse begins to race, and I know that I'm about to take possession of a powerful machine and turn physics into my bitch. Take that, you toasters and programmable DVRs of the world, and bow to your mistress.

CHAPTER FOURTEEN

Tracking the Grey Wolf

K illing some time at the track between sessions one day, I chatted with the chief instructor who was running that particular driving event. I'd never met him before, but he seemed like a nice man, and I was a little bored. After covering a few of the expected topics—cars, driving, cars, and then some more about cars—I decided to ask this unassuming, silver-haired man with the T-shirt and ball cap what he did in real life. Did he, I wondered, run a garage, or maybe a car dealership? Was he an engineer, perhaps, or a computer programmer who loves to tinker? Nope, nope, and nope again. Turns out, he's a professor of neuroscience. Whoa.

So, while piloting a sports car around a racetrack may not be brain surgery, I have proof that it is something some neuroscientists do for fun. It felt a little bit like finding out your plumber is a big fan of Kierkegaard or Gilbert and Sullivan—delightful, if unexpected. Since the conversation with the neuroscientist, I've felt the need to know more about these people who spend so much free time driving fast cars at the racetrack. Who are they? What do they do? What do they find so appealing about this bizarre and addictive hobby? I enjoy asking questions to get to know people at the track a little, and I love hearing their backstories. I am often surprised by who emerges from under the helmet. The instructor in one classroom is a dentist. My instructor behind the wheel is an insurance salesman. The chief instructor is a retired chemical engineer who shares my alma mater. The guy I sat next to at lunch is the smoking anesthesiologist (with apologies to Mr. B: He was smoking in more ways than one). There's the eye surgeon recovering from thyroid cancer. The veterinarian. The philosophy professor (I speed therefore I am). And probably everybody's favorite, the Bimmer-driving minister. Go, God, Go.

Belonging as I do to a relatively rare minority at the track, I pay particular attention to my sisters in acceleration. Who are they, and what brings them here? We tend to gravitate toward one another anyway, so it's easy to strike up conversations. I've casually befriended a very stylish blond architect who happened to be dating the philosophy professor. The second time I saw her at the track, I noticed she'd traded in her lovely white Porsche for an outrageous track car called a Diasio that looks like a slightly shrunken Formula One racer. She's a poster girl for grown-up babedom, in my book, and I am just slightly in love with her. I wish I could pull off those D&G sunglasses she sports. Not to mention the Diasio.

Fabulous women in fabulous cars: You just never know what combination might show up to the track. At a non-marque-specific event where drivers arrived in everything from a souped-up, track-ready pickup truck to the family station wagon, I was unpacking my things onto the asphalt when the unmistakable sternum-rattling vibrato of an Italian sports car distinguished itself from the general thrumming of the paddock soundtrack. I glanced up to come face-to-headlamps with a wicked-looking, screaming orange Lamborghini Superleggera.

Wow, majorly outclassed, I thought, feeling a little like I'd brought a butter knife to a grenade-launching party. I waited to see who would emerge from this exotic supercar. I was picturing hairy chests and thick gold chains. What I got instead was a sturdily built woman, around sixty, with a beautiful crown of snow-white hair feathered in the front and tied into a teeny-weeny ponytail in the back. As she unpacked her car, out popped a fat teddy bear, dressed to match its mistress with a polka-dotted kerchief tied around its furry little neck. "He goes everywhere I go," she later informed me of her stuffed mascot. Lady Lamborghini, it turned out, was a professor of engineering and a Russian who spoke her English with a beautiful vodka-infused accent. I did not dare ask where the car came from.

Some women are more dramatic, some less so, but it's always a pleasure to meet one of my own kind and find out how she got there. I love to collect their stories and in the process uncover an entire subset of women who love this outrageous thing as much as I do. It makes me feel like we are members of a super-secret sisterhood, a slightly dangerous cabal of rule-breakers, out to subvert the normal order of things, ready to take on whatever the men and the asphalt may throw in our paths. Join us, and I will teach you the secret handshake.

There was a woman who used to compete in club races and now just likes to drive these noncompetitive events in between managing her horse farm. There's a very nice, gray-haired motherly woman I regularly see who shares her Porsche with her husband. There's the pony-tailed instructor who goes by the name of Speedy, and who is the only person I've met in real life with David Bowie eyes: one green, one brown. Mesmerizing. And there's plenty of terrific support staff in the form of wives who come to the track but do not drive, like the lovely Hawaiian lady I met who happily sits in the shade of the trailer and works cross-stitch samplers for her grandchildren while her husband flies around the track. The women of the racetrack are the members of my own, self-declared secret society, and so it is a constant source of interest to me to meet them and find out what I can about them in the very short amount of time we are thrown together by these events.

OF ALL THE women I have so far encountered, none of them has awed me as deeply as Miriam the Grey Wolf, who has completely transformed the way I picture myself in the upcoming quarter century of my life.

Quick, what's your favorite scene from *Top Gun*? Well, okay, *besides* the shirtless beach volleyball game (possibly the finest slice of beefcake ever to be served up on the silver screen). But no—mine comes earlier in the film, shortly after the scene in the bar where Tom Cruise attempts to pick up Kelly McGillis. Sexy Tom is here at the height of his cinematic scrumptiousness, and he pours on all of his considerable charm, including the famous rendition of "You've Lost That Lovin' Feelin'," but his target is bulletproof and roundly rejects him. Crash and burn, baby, crash and burn. The next morning, Tom Skerritt welcomes the cocky new Top Gun recruits to the program, and the boys visibly preen as he informs them of what they already know deep in their loins: that they are the best of the best. And then comes one of my favorite moments in film history: Skerritt introduces the hotshots to their instructor, and in strides the gorgeous, confident McGillis, curly blond bob bouncing in slow-motion splendor— and Cruise sinks into his chair as he realizes that this is the woman who spurned him in the bar the night before. I've always loved that scene for the way it upended all expectations about who would be in possession of the knowledge and the power over those big birds in the sky. And for the way Kelly McGillis rocks her Ray-Bans.

I never expected to see this scene played out in real life, but some-times truth is even more wondrous than fiction. The *de rigueur* classroom instruction sessions at high performance Driver's Ed events are provided to supplement the on-track driving experience with an understanding of the physics and mechanics of your car's behavior on the track. When you first start driving at the track, you tend to hang onto every word that drops from the instructor's sage mouth in the hopes that some kind of magic will transfer from him to you, and there's no doubt that there is much use-ful information to be gleaned from these highly experienced drivers and the theory they have to impart. Still, after you have gone to eight or ten such events, the information starts to get a little repetitive, and the class-room experience becomes somewhat routine. I always attend the sessions because I'm such a Goody Two-shoes anyway, and because you never know what new and useful things might emerge. Not everybody goes in with such a good attitude, though, and such was the case when I attended an event at Summit Point, West Virginia. I was in a group of intermediate drivers, and it was a glorious spring day, so no one was especially thrilled to have to go to class inside the cement block building when all the excitement was happening outside. Nevertheless, when the time came, in we trundled, not anticipating anything different from the usual rundown of driving theory.

I seated myself in the classroom, waiting for my dose of apexes and trackouts, correct braking techniques and maximum acceleration points, when up to the whiteboard stalked a tiny little gray-haired woman. She looked to be all of five-foot-one, and she sported a brindled gray but sharply cut bob, with super-stylish eyebrow-grazing bangs. When she turned around and pulled off her jacket, I realized with astonishment that she was wearing a T-shirt with an allover pattern of grimacing skulls. I estimated, from her compact build and smooth face, that she was probably in her late fifties. She began by unpacking a funny green box which soon sported multicolored blinking lights and the word EGOS mounted on the top.

"We begin, gentlemen," she addressed the room, "with you putting your egos in this box—you can pick them up again when you leave."

Oh, hang on a sec, I thought, perking up, *this is gonna be fun.* The macho guys who make up the usual assortment of track rats think they already know everything there is to know about how to go fast, and being told how to do things by a diminutive gray-haired granny has *got* to get their undershorts in a twist.

I was not wrong about the fun factor. Our instructor, who introduced herself as Miriam, proceeded to unpack a container of sparkly green *Go Faster Pills* and another of pinkish goo labeled *Apex Crème.* A bloody stump of an amputated arm flopped onto the table along with the familiar set of flags. She then took us through our usual paces—safety, flagging signals, optimal lines, the traction circle, and so forth. It soon became apparent that not only did she know her stuff, but she was gifted at communicating it. She had an artistic talent for drawing, and used this skill for visualizing complex theoretical information and making it simple to understand. Along with some of the standard material that gets covered repeatedly in these classrooms, she came up with innumerable head-scratchers that soon earned her a grudging admiration from the big bluff know-it-alls in the classroom.

At the end of the first day, she took the class on a "track walk." This sounds exactly like what it is: You walk the two-plus miles of the track on foot, assessing from the ground what your optimal driving line is, observing the elevation changes that are not apparent when you are at driving speed, feeling the imperfections and surfaces of the asphalt. Miriam took us through it yard by yard. It took an hour and a half, and it was clear by the end that what Miriam didn't know about the track wasn't worth knowing. All of us were just about numb from exhaustion and sensory overload by this point, but Miriam seemed completely unperturbed.

We took one shortcut. It eliminated a single turn of the track, and as we crossed through it, she pointed out the broken automotive safety glass that glittered in piles along either side of the pass.

"This," Miriam announced, nonchalantly gesturing at the glass, "is where the ramming exercises are done. For seventeen years I used to teach this, but now I've stopped."

I think I may have kept my mouth closed, but mentally my jaw dropped. This little woman conducted *ramming exercises?* As in, smashing cars into each other *on purpose?* I had to know more, and I made it my business to get to know Miriam a little better.

AFTER WE WERE finished with the track walk, I chatted with Miriam as she walked to her car in preparation for leaving for dinner. Her car? A beautiful charcoal silver Porsche 911, circa early 1980s. It bore a personalized license plate: GRY WLF. It dawned on me that this was her signature—the gray hair, the gray jeans, the gray skull-patterned shirt, the gray car. She was the Grey Wolf (I discovered she prefers the more elegant spelling of grey with an "e"). I managed to weasel in on the dinner plans so that I could talk some more with this remarkable woman. My first revelation: This woman with her stylish hair, fabulous car, energetic body, and cheeky attitude was not, as I had guessed, in her fifties or even her sixties, but was seventy-four!

"I work out every day," she proudly proclaimed over dinner. "That's why they threw me out of the hospital two days after my hip replacement this winter."

Hip replacement? The woman had just exhausted a group of younger men by trotting them around a racetrack with four hundred feet of elevation changes, and she was doing it on a hip that was less than six months old. I was utterly smitten.

It got even better. The track where all this took place is in a corner of West Virginia about seventy miles west of Washington, DC. Next to the track is an entire campus dedicated to training federal agents, diplomats, and security professionals in all kinds of driving techniques. The track contracts with government and private agencies to provide counter-terrorist driving exercises in ramming techniques, high-speed chases, and criminal attack evasion. They also go off-track to do route analysis and surveillance detection, and they include instruction in a mysteriously-named Personal Protection Module. Whatever they do, it involves gunfire, because during down times at the track you will often hear the *pop-pop-pop* of the firing range in the distance. It's real straight-from-the-movies stuff. If you drive around the grounds, you will come across a whole lot filled with white Chevy Impalas with protective ramming cages wrapped around their bumpers. It kind of makes you want to try some ramming exercises yourself.

It turned out that this is just what the Grey Wolf did for seventeen years, retiring from it only when she was in her mid-sixties.

"Was it lots of fun to teach all of this cloak-and-dagger stuff?" I wanted to know.

"It was a living," she said, a bit dismissively. "But I sat in the car with three other students, and they each took turns driving. I didn't get to drive very much myself, and that's what I love to do most, so it wasn't quite as much fun as it sounds."

I conjured up a mental image of the Grey Wolf in her skull-patterned T-shirt sitting in a car with three identical Men in Black, all sporting black neckties and earpieces, dutifully ramming targets as this sexagenarian rattled off instructions.

"Once I hit sixty-five, I decided I'd had enough of it," she added.

Fair enough. When you've hit the age when many women are enjoying grandmotherhood and bridge club, then it's probably okay to stop with the ramming exercises. Today, the Grey Wolf is the chief instructor for the DC-area Corvette Club, but they loan her out for other driving events like the one I attended with the Porsche Club.

NOW, I'VE LOOKED to many different women to provide me with role models for how to live my life. I've always wanted to be the smartest person in any room, so my role models have mostly been other professors who have made it to where I always dreamed of being: published, popular, and tenured. I guess I did okay. Having other professors as role models was not a bad way to shape my career, but that story line has essentially played itself out. Understanding that circumstances have conspired to prevent me from a secure spot in the traditional academic hierarchy, I'd come to accept that I was in a mighty fine place, teaching great students at a wonderful college where I could research and publish what I wanted and never have to attend any committee meetings. All this was well and good, but it was also kind of complete: I knew how to do it, had done it, and I put the little gold bow on it, too. It also gradually dawned on me that I myself—wife, mother, smarty-pants with a kickass fashion sense—had become a role model for the young women I was teaching. They could do worse.

So where does the role model look next for a role model? *The New York Times* doesn't have my obituary on file yet. I've accomplished some pretty awesome things: earned a PhD, written several books, established a good career and a great marriage, raised a well-adjusted kid (in itself a minor miracle), and became part of a circle of fabulous friends. But if I'm not done living and learning and growing—well, what do I do for an encore? It's not so much about growing old as it is about simply *growing*.

As I found out more about Miriam, I learned a wonderful story about her and her Porsche. For starters, it is her first and—she adamantly asserts this is the case—her last. She was working as an illustrator and graphic designer when one day, out on the streets of DC, she spotted a now-classic 911 sporting the style of spoiler that is descriptively known as a "whale-tail."

Her artist's eye caught by the distinctive sweep of the aerodynamic accessory, she turned to the man walking next to her and demanded:

"What kind of car is that? It's beautiful. I'm going to get one of those."

Her companion laughed and informed her, "That's a Porsche 911. But it's a car for men. You don't want one of those."

This was, of course, all Miriam needed to hear. She went in search of a 911 like the one she had seen on the street. She found one in a barn in Maryland and persuaded a friend of hers—a pilot—to go out with her to fetch it. He, too, attempting to dissuade her, condescended to say, "I'll go with you, but I won't teach you to drive it."

For here's the kicker: Miriam didn't even know how to drive stick. And no self-respecting Porsche of the era came as an automatic. Even now, Germans view automatic transmissions as a peculiarly American automotive abomination. True to his word, the pilot brought her to the Porsche, but once there, he left her to her own devices.

"To this day," she told me, "I don't know how I managed to get it back home. But I did, and then I decided I needed to learn how to control this amazing machine. So every single weekend I went out to the track. I left Friday afternoon, I stayed until Sunday, and I drove and drove until I understood everything I possibly could about the car, the track, and how to go fast. From there I became an instructor, and eventually I was hired by the track to do the government training courses."

This was already enough for me to fall head over heels for this woman. Damn, did I want to be like her! Sure, I still like to be the smartest person in any room. But how much better to be the smartest *and* the fastest?

But wait, as they say in the Veg-O-Matic infomercials, there's *more*. My admiration for the Grey Wolf is not only about having the guts to follow one's instincts and passions. It's also about embracing who you are, at any stage in life. I have decades to go until I'm seventy-four. And I only have to look as far as my own mother to find a role model for how to be a grandmother and still Skype and Facebook with the grandkids. My mom is magnificent. At age seventy, she organized a quilt show in a small local museum. She plays badminton every week and has just picked up canasta and mah-jongg. She and Dad keep jetting off to places like Turkey and Egypt and New Zealand. They still bring me T-shirts, which gives me the not altogether unpleasant feeling that I am twelve again. So, yeah, I could do *way* worse than to be like my mom when I am seventy.

But her chief hobby is knitting, and (sorry, Mom!) the shameful fact is that I hate to knit. Oh, I'm capable of it. My fingers are clever enough to manage this retro-feminine skill, and I have a scarf and even a modest little mohair sweater to prove it. But whereas my mom derives great pleasure from knitting her woolen masterpieces, I do not. To her, a ball of yarn looks like a great steaming plate of spaghetti Alfredo, waiting to be savored, guilt-free and with no saturated fats. To me, it looks like a hairy and cantankerous octopus needing to be beaten into submission. There I'd be, tensely hunched over the needles and clickety-clacking away, furiously churning out another row, just waiting for that pile of yarn to concede that it was going to be a sweater, come hell or high water. This is to say: not therapeutic.

So it seems unlikely that I will be knitting when I am seventy-four and, I hope, a grandmother. My mom remains a role model for the next three or four decades of my life, but the Grey Wolf has given me yet another way to think about how to tackle becoming the person who's still in development.

WHEN MIRIAM FIRST encountered her beloved 911, it was painted a fashionable, deep chocolate brown (remember, it was the early '80s; they liked brown cars then). This was fine with her, for it matched her own dark auburn tresses. Over time, however, two things happened: The paint job on the Porsche started showing its age, and to put it bluntly, so did her hair. Miriam decided to embrace her gray, and though she maintained a sharp cut, she let the color be what it would. When her hair went completely gray, so did her Porsche: She had it repainted in that elegant metallic charcoal which, really, suits it so much better. Even her wardrobe went gray, and thus completed the transformation to the Grey Wolf. All that remained was to get the personalized license plate and proclaim it to the world. Of all the famous silver manes out there, no one, but no one, owns it like Miriam the Grey Wolf.

So, I still want to be like my mom, learning new things and still going places for the next three or four decades. I just don't want to have to knit. It's a little—well—*slow* for me. The Grey Wolf has given me some other things to think about. First, I can grow and change at any stage in my life. She went from artist and illustrator to counter-terrorist driving instructor. If she can do that, maybe even I can dare to go from professor to (drumroll, please) writer.

She's also solid proof that there's plenty of time for me to continue to build my skills and rock the racetrack just like her, and for decades to come. If I keep practicing, keep learning, and take the skills acquisition process seriously enough, then I could progress from student, to confident solo driver, to track instructor, and even to classroom or chief instructor.

I probably will never instruct federal agents in counter-terrorist driving techniques, but maybe I could carry off the skull-patterned T-shirt? I still have time to decide what my T-shirt will look like. It's my new goal in life to be terrorizing young men in my Porsche when I am seventy-four, and teaching them a thing or two not just about how to carry more speed through a corner, but also about readjusting expectations and never, ever underestimating what a feisty and determined woman can accomplish, at any age.

Of course, I'll need my own moniker. Feel free to write in with suggestions.

CHAPTER FIFTEEN

Never Try to Teach
a Pig to Drive

In my year of learning to drive fast, certainly the most important personal interactions I had at the racetrack were the ones I had with my instructors. Miriam, my new idol, was a classroom instructor, so her role was more removed from the direct, one-on-one experiences I had with my in-car instructors. These relationships are in some ways really strange because they are highly artificial. Two total strangers are suddenly thrown together in the intimate confines of a very small car. Both of us are wearing helmets, which means we could theoretically spend an entire weekend together yet not be able to pick each other out of a police lineup. Despite this helmeted anonymity, we must have total trust in one another: My instructor, who is putting his (occasionally her) life in my driving hands, has to trust that I will listen and obey, and in return, I have to trust him enough to do as he says. We hold each other's lives in our driving gloves— and yet, when the weekend is over, we will amicably part ways and we might not ever see each other again.

Talk about speed dating.

The oddity of this relationship is that it is at once clinical and formal as well as very intimate. My passenger is my instructor, and I have voluntarily agreed to this really stunning thing, when you think about it, which is:

I have given him total license *to tell me how to drive.*

And this is a world-class head-thumper because normally nobody, NOBODY, gets to tell me how to drive.

I am a woman who is used to being in charge. I am a competent driver, an independent person, and since I'm also an educator, I am *really* comfortable with telling other people what to do. Behind the wheel, then, few things annoy me more than when my passenger feels motivated to comment on my driving. The level of the annoyance has a tendency, I have noticed, to rise faster when the relationship is more intimate. If a friend has the effrontery to comment on my driving, I can swallow my annoyance without too much trouble. If my mother comments on my driving, it is harder to squelch the urge to snap back at her. But the good Lord above (or whoever it is who looks out for the wretched objects of acid tongues) help my poor Mr. B should he have the audacity to make some sort of suggestion about how I should handle my car.

What is it about intimate relationships that makes it so hard to learn from someone you love? Learning about driving from a series of strangers has given me some interesting insights into the power relationship behind the wheel and in a marriage—especially when I invited the intrepid Mr. B to sit beside me at the track. I was reminded of the incident that occurred when Mr. B and I were adorably naive new parents and we decided that it was time that our own small fry should learn how to swim.

No two ways about it: Mr. B is a suit. When he's on duty, he's a serious-looking guy with great taste in ties who wears his tailored Italian wool ensembles to work every day. His biggest fashion dilemma each morning is choosing between a gray suit or a blue one. I never see him in the morning because he gets up too early for me, but I love to see him when he gets home in the evenings because he looks so handsome and authoritative. He's a serious guy in a serious business, so I've always been sorry that I never saw him in action at one of his first paying jobs when in summers off from college he taught swimming lessons to preschoolers. It cheers me to envision my suit-wearing Banker Boy in swim trunks, hair plastered to his head like an otter's, with a bevy of small, non-swimming children clinging to him for dear life. I imagine him prying their little vise-grip fingers out of his chest hair and coaxing them to trust the Styrofoam bubbles he strapped to them to keep their heads out of the water. He did this for several summers, and not only did he teach a fair number of fearful tadpoles how to swim, but to my knowledge, he never lost a single one to drowning.

All of which was why, when it came time for the angsty Miss M to learn how to swim, we thought: Great, her daddy is a certified pro so he can teach her during summertime outings to the community pool. Simple, efficient, obvious, right? So it seemed—until he took her to the waist-high water where it was too deep for her to stand, and he tried to get her to relax into floating on her back while he supported her from underneath.

"No Daddy," came the childish, high-pitched, instantaneous response.

He asked her to put her face in the water and blow bubbles. "No Daddy," again.

He politely requested that she hold on to the edge of the pool and kick her legs.

"No Daddy."

It came out as a flat statement, not so much a rejection to the specific request, but as a definitive assessment of the entire situation, and it became such an integral part of her repertoire that summer that it merged into a single word: *Nodaddy.* It was not long before I began to think that *Nodaddy* was our offspring's new name for her sire. You can also imagine that poor Nodaddy quickly tired of this exercise in frustration and feared that his excellent record of swimming-lesson drownings might be compromised if he continued. The charming familial fantasy was abandoned, consigning yours truly to the steamy chlorinated hell that is the poolside stand of bleachers at our local Y. The mutinous Miss M, of course, learned to swim from a series of young men and women exactly like her daddy of fifteen years earlier. They gave her the same set of instructions Nodaddy had tried to give her, and she followed them without argument and, lo and behold, learned to swim.

Far, far worse than fathers and daughters in the swimming pool are husbands and wives who occupy the two front seats of the same automobile. I have a German cousin who is a police commissioner. She has gone on international undercover sting operations. She has worked murder cases. I'm rather in awe of her, frankly. Who wouldn't be? She's a perfectly competent driver but lets her civilian husband take the wheel whenever they are in the car together. He drives, and she delivers instructions to him. If I am along for the ride, sitting in the back, I work avidly on focusing my attention elsewhere, *anywhere* but on the interaction of the Commish and her hubby as they turn into squabbling children over whether he is going too fast, whether the windshield wipers should be on or off, whether they should take this exit or the next one, or how close to the restaurant to park the car. How is it, I wonder, that the Commish hasn't become a homicide victim herself? Yet husband and wife emerge from the vehicle unscathed every time and continue on with life as usual, and when dinner is over, they return to their seats in the same configuration and resume the Punch and Judy routine where they left off.

I DON'T KNOW of any couples that can coexist peaceably behind the wheel. My mother-in-law simply won't let her husband drive anymore when they're both in the car because she thinks he is a mortal hazard (though she has apparently no compunction about letting him go out alone). At the same time, he lives in fear that she will someday take out the entire passenger side of the vehicle because he thinks she drives too far to the right. My mother refuses to pay attention to what my dad does anymore, and she studiously ignores his actions on the road by maintaining all attention on her knitting. It's the only way, she says, to keep her sanity while he waffles about whether to pass someone until he finally does at the last possible moment and swings out directly in front of someone else who is approaching fast from behind. Take just about any two people who have sworn to honor and cherish each other in sickness and in health for as long as they both shall live, and put them in the front two seats of an automobile, and dignity and respect just seem to fly out the window.

Mr. B and I are by no means a model couple in this regard, despite our good record on Valentine's Day cards and remembering anniversaries and, well, just staying married to each other for closing in on two decades now. We do fine around town, usually, but there have been some jaw-clenching moments when we've been on vacation. The source of our discord lies in the fact that at birth, Mr. B underwent experimental carrier-pigeon brain implantation surgery, whereas I am woefully stuck with my mortal and highly fallible sense of direction. Endowed with underwhelmingly average map-reading skills, I can generally figure out where it is that I want to go. My chief difficulty lies in the challenge of ascertaining where I currently am. Where, oh where, is the *You Are Here* spot when you need it? *That* is never on the map. Blessed with his homing-pigeon sense of direction but cursed with the patience of a flea, Mr. B's tolerance with my map struggles in a decision-making pinch is somewhat south of saintly. You can probably imagine the difficulties that transpired when, without a GPS and faced with the labyrinthine tangle of streets that is your average quaint historic European city, yours truly desperately twisted the map this way and that in an attempt to locate our current whereabouts while figuring out how to get to a *centre-ville* hotel on the other side of a pedestrian zone at the wrong end of a one-way street. It took only a couple of these teeth-gnashing episodes to determine that the better arrangement was for me to drive and the compass-headed Mr. B to navigate.

Having arrived at a solution in which Mr. B read the maps, programmed the GPS, and issued commands while I obediently directed the car where he determined it should go, the two of us arrogantly thought we had solved our marital-navigational challenges to such an extent that not long ago we decided to attempt our first road rally. Such an event is not a test of speed or even driving skill. Instead, a group of drivers is given a set of highly cryptic instructions and then turned loose on public roads to find their way along a predetermined route. All directions are calculated so that drivers never need to go over the posted speed limits, and the winner is the car that comes closest to the ideal time—neither under nor over. Here is a sample of the sort of instructions you might see:

mileage 5: BL after "Quick Chek"

pause 2 minutes at "State Law"

mileage 5.6: CAS 40 at "United States Post Office"

mileage 6.9: R after "620" CAS 26

Mr. B and I said to one another: We have driven in and out of the canal-lined maze of Amsterdam; we have entered and exited the Place de l'Etoile in Paris without incident; we possess five advanced degrees between the two of us. We are invincible cartographical masters and a superior example of marital communication and collaboration. We will kick ass at this rally thing.

How devastatingly wrong we were. We entered the fray feeling pretty damn cocky. We left the rally, *forty-two* humiliating minutes over time and much the worse for wear, utterly crushed and dispirited. It was, of course, a great deal harder than we thought, and our misunderstanding of the logic of the instructions led to much confusion and some reality-TV-worthy moments in the cockpit. So disgusted with ourselves were we that we handed in our time sheet and stalked off without joining the post-rally party. We were simply grateful that we had told no one about our delusions of competency beforehand.

It was, then, with a pang of remembered defeat that we perused the write-up of the rally in the club newsletter several months later as it arrived in our mailbox in the dead of winter. Mr. B flipped it to me, saying, "Look, here's that rally we attempted last fall—maybe you want to read about it?"

Clearly he hadn't read it through to the end, for when I did, I stumbled with horrified recognition upon our own names. The team that had won the novice category was lauded first, and then, much to my consternation, there were we. We had pulled off, according to the newsletter, an "impressive second-place finish" in the novice category.

"Impressive!" I shrieked to my beloved copilot, "Look here! We were im*press*ive!!"

Mr. B bent over my shoulder to locate the offending sentence and ascertain the mortifying truth of it. "Why, *yes*, my dear," he intoned, assuming his best Charlton Heston impression, "we *are* impressive."

It has since become a secret code between us, a watchword for hubris, and whenever we need to remind ourselves not to become too big for our britches, we congratulate ourselves on just how *impressive* we are.

Undaunted, we plan to try another rally at the next possible opportunity. It may sound like we are marital masochists cruising for an appearance on *Divorce Court*, but it has more to do with licking our wounded pride. Dammit, we *will* get the better of this thing and show that we are smarter and stronger than a set of diabolical instructions and the emotional pressure cooker of the inside of a very small car. It's a case of us against the world, so whatever tensions might have existed behind the dashboard, we are determined to present a united front against all those other couples who by virtue of beating us at the rally might think their union beats ours. We'll show them.

But if the rally rite of passage emboldened us to think that love is a mighty speedy thing, what evil do you suppose may befall the state of the marital union when you separate us out at the racetrack? What happens to the us-against-them mentality when it becomes him-against-her? For if the normal state of affairs on the highways and byways of America presents a challenge for any romantically linked couple in a car, how much worse is it when you add insanely high speeds, turbocharged competitiveness, and a *soupçon* of real, physical danger to the mix? The opportunity to join my own better half at the track presented all sorts of interesting challenges to our relationship, not the least of which was the reappearance of the decades-old thorn in my side of a latent but utterly hopeless competitive streak with my husband as its object.

For here's my romantic albatross: Mr. B is one of those excruciatingly annoying people who excels at everything he tries. Okay, so he can't spell worth a damn. And he has never attempted counted cross-stitch, as far as I know. But everything else he tries, he is disgustingly good at. A skinny but wiry little kid, he played soccer and joined swim team and peewee football, but eventually he gravitated to running when it became clear he had a natural talent for it. In high school he grew to six feet tall and a rail-thin 135 pounds, won a state championship, and was actively recruited for college track and cross-country teams. After college he took up bicycling, and all along the way I puttered along behind, mostly content to admire his long-limbed grace and resigned to follow in his wake and catch up to him while he waited for me. Ice skating. Rollerblading. Tennis. *Clue.* There is nothing he cannot do. If he says it's Colonel Mustard in the library with the candlestick, never doubt it: It is so.

The winter after my first complete season at the racetrack, I had the opportunity to try downhill skiing for the first time in my life. My newly increased sense of bravery and adventure compelled me to grab my inner testicles and carpe diem. The Divine Miss M and I spent a week in Colorado with family, taking ski lessons and thrilling to the outdoorsy excursions in the spectacular Rocky Mountains. By the end of the week

COURTESY OF THE AUTHOR

my Mr. B and his fearsome machine

we were enjoying ourselves so much, schussing down the long slopes and feeling fairly confident in our skills, that we thought we'd want to do some more family outings with Mr. B over what remained of the winter. Nearly a quarter of a century earlier, Mr. B had once gone skiing for two days with some family friends. Characteristically—when we next hit the slopes as a family—he took one shot down the bunny slope, and by the end of the day he and the mogulous Miss M were skiing short black diamond sections while I, once again, watched admiringly—if just a touch jealously—from the base of the lifts.

Mr. B, in return, thought he'd try the yoga I'd been enthusing over for the previous eight years, so in the interests of his increased flexibility and serenity of mind, I heartily welcomed him to join me. When in short order he mastered both the headstand it had taken me years to achieve and the handstand that to this day I still cannot manage, it finally did strike me as a bit thick. I admire his mastery of many skills. I love that I am hitched to so competent a star. But, really, couldn't I outdo him at *something?*

So here's the thing about driving: There is absolutely no inherent advantage in being male once you are positioned behind the wheel. There's no getting around biology, and why would we want to anyway? They can keep male pattern baldness. And somebody has to open the pickle jars and kill the spiders (Yes: I may possess a PhD and drive racecars as a hobby, but still I say, killing spiders is for single girls. Go report me to Gloria Steinem. I don't care). Men may be physically faster and stronger, and that is ostensibly why there are different leagues for them in individual sports like skiing or swimming or tennis or Ping-Pong. But put them behind the wheel of a car, and their physical advantages disappear. In fact, ask any of the driving instructors at the type of events I attend, and they will unanimously assert that women make better students.

Racecar driving may be the only professional sport in which women can compete on an entirely genderless and level platform with men (is poker a sport?). Danica Patrick and her slightly less high-profile compatriots—Milka Duno, Sarah Fisher, 2010 Rookie of the Year Simona de Silvestro—have triumphantly quashed the accepted notion that driving fast and well is an exclusively male talent. I was thrilled to my very feminine core when I realized that high-performance driving is in fact a largely cerebral sport that is based on a series of competencies that have little to do with brute strength and everything to do with calculated brain power, deftness of hand and foot, and precision finesse. Mental toughness and endurance are non-negotiable requisites: But I ask you, doesn't the nine-month incubation and ultimately thorny production of an entire human being out of one's own body necessitate at least as much of those qualities as any man may possess?

In any case, my own personal goal is nothing so lofty as joining the IndyCar sisterhood. My no-longer-secret ambition is much more modest, although it would be a heretofore unimaginable triumph for permanently sidelined me. I want, I yearn, I crave with all my heart and soul and every fiber of my little being, after nearly three decades of being bested in every imaginable sport and every type of physical activity by my beloved, to kick his cute, muscular butt at something. ANYTHING. Unfortunately for me, he has many years of experience over me and there is the pesky problem of his innate talent at all things physical which makes him a superlative driver on top of all his other accomplishments—but still, I am cautiously optimistic that if I concentrate all of my considerable mental acuity, and exercise my feminine doggedness, I may, just possibly, have a shot at equaling or—dare I say it—surpassing my skilled and speedy mate.

What does any of this have to do with romantic togetherness behind the wheel? Mr. B, having advanced so far in the driving club ranks that he qualified as an instructor himself, sagely removed himself far from the role of teacher when it came time for me to take my first lessons on the track. Conventional wisdom both on and off the racetrack holds that husbands should never try to teach their wives *anything*. Or vice versa. I believe this is very wise.

When I was in high school, our choir director had this piece of advice posted on the rehearsal room wall:

Never try to teach a pig to sing.
It wastes your time and it annoys the pig.

It is an ageless piece of wisdom that really should be taken to heart by daddies in swimming pools as well as men and women in cars, on golf courses, tennis courts, everywhere—both the relationship, and the talent, must be in concert for the undertaking to be successful. On the racetrack there is the additional peril of the one quite literally killing the other if the mechanical or pedagogical failure is disastrous enough to cause a crash—not to mention the risk of manual strangulation if the attempt at instruction sours irretrievably for either student or teacher. Anyone at the track, if asked, would tell you to stay away from giving or receiving instruction from a spouse in the strongest of terms. As in: Are you effin' *insane?*

Halfway through my first complete season, however, I found that the quality of instruction was somewhat variable. Some instructors were excellent, some more perfunctory. Sometimes the advice coming from the current instructor would be in contradiction to the advice received from a previous instructor. Most frustrating was the fact that, since I had a different instructor every time, there could be no continuity in the assessment of my progress or the building of my skills. There was no good way for me to get a sense of overarching improvement. What inevitably transpired was that after each event, the connubial pillow talk would turn to what I had just done or learned or wished I had done or learned, but Mr. B could only offer generalized, objective advice because he had never actually been in the car with me during the events in question. Thus it was that, one night over the post-racing beer and chips, Mr. B somewhat hesitatingly, and with understandable trepidation, offered:

"Would you like *me* to be your instructor sometime?"

Time-out for a multiple-choice question:

My Mr. B is:

(a) very, very brave

(b) very, very stupid

(c) suicidal

(d) secretly seeking divorce

(e) a hopeless romantic

Answer: Ask him yourself.

I am not yet divorced nor serving time behind bars for homicide, so I believe that leaves some combination of bravery, stupidity, and/or romanticism. I actually do not know what evil imp prompted him to come up with this lunatic suggestion, but my hope is that it was based on a possibly misplaced faith in his wife's calm good nature and propensity for rational behavior.

MY RESPONSE? DID I do the sensible thing and run screaming from the room? I did not. I mused over the suggestion for some time, and decided that if our relationship, which has lasted our entire adult lives, could not withstand one twenty-minute session behind the wheel on the racetrack, then it was not as strong as I had always presumed. Ultimately we agreed that we would try it out just once at our next event, while the instructor of record would continue on as my principle teacher the rest of the time. When the time came and my own private automotive Mr. Chips climbed into the car with me, I was, more than anything, almost paralyzingly nervous. The anticipation of going out on the racetrack always gives me the flutters. But having my husband sitting there beside me made me nearly sick with the desire to climb back out of the car again. True, I did not want to kill the both of us and leave the Divine Miss M an orphan. But I was not nervous because of my responsibility for my husband's continued earthly existence. What I was really afraid of was that this man I adore and whom I consider my fully equal partner in life would be sitting in judgment of me—and would I continue to measure up?

And that, I suppose, is the crux of the matter when any couple sits together in the two front seats of any car. By definition, the person who controls the car has assumed an implicit position of power over the one sitting in the inherently passive seat to the right. The supposed parity between a husband and a wife has to shift as the one who drives is more literally in control in a car than in almost any other situation in daily life. Conversely, the passenger has simultaneously relinquished any real participation in the physical path the two are embarking upon together. If it is nearly irresistible to the passenger to try to insert him- or herself into the equation, it is because the desire to remind one's mate that the relationship is one of equals is desperately important in order to correct the temporary imbalance of power. Absolute trust and the exceedingly difficult maintenance of a clamp on one's trap are necessary to turn over all control to the driver. No wonder so few of us are able to do it. Allowing Mr. B to instruct me while behind the wheel was one of the most difficult things I think I've ever done in the context of our lengthy relationship. It required me to relinquish my absolute power as the driver and open myself not merely to technical instruction from him but also to the possibility of hurtful critique. It took far more trust for me to allow him to be my driving instructor than it had ever taken to have him drive me somewhere while I was a passenger.

So how did this experiment in marital self-destruction work out? To Mr. B's eternal credit, he was a wonderful instructor—the best I've ever had. Since he kept his commentary strictly technical, his instructions calm, and his praise generous, I never once felt threatened or inferior. Since the areas of possible improvement he pointed out to me were ones I could recognize as both legitimate and valuable, and since he displayed a genuine interest in making me faster, I could feel like he was treating me as a real fellow enthusiast, and not as an inferior in an unequal power structure. When, after adopting some of his suggestions, I caught up to another car, he said sotto voce as if to the other driver, "She's all over you like a bad rash, buddy—c'mon, scratch it, scraaaaatch it, you know you want to."

I laughed and laughed at both the triumph and the absurdity of it when the other driver finally signaled me to pass. It was not just because he'd helped me refine my technique, as he might have with any other student. It was not just because we'd both enjoyed the pass, which is after all one of the principle joys of the track experience. It was, I think, because we had just proved to ourselves how—well—*impressive* we both were. It was impossible, at that instant, to think of a more romantic moment in our union. Unfortunately you can't smooch with your helmets on, and anyway at that point I was humming along at over ninety-five miles per hour.

I liked having him as my instructor so much that from time to time I request it. Neither of us thinks it is a good idea for him to be my instructor all the time. Probably no marriage is up for that. And there are always different and valuable things to be learned from other instructors. But it's confidence-inspiring to think that he respects me enough to want to climb in there beside me and help me to go faster—because that's what he is always encouraging me to do. How many wives can claim *that*? The last time he sat in that passenger seat, he urged me to be more aggressive with the accelerator pedal coming out of the turns.

"Hard on, hard on, hard ON!" he'd shouted.

"You *wish*," I replied.

The thought of his confidence in my skills and his desire to help me improve upon them just about gave me the female equivalent.

Plus, I figure if I go out with him often enough, I will plumb all his secrets, and when I have learned all he knows, maybe someday I will whup his darling ass.

CHAPTER SIXTEEN

Bug Guts on the Windshield

Both through the formal instruction I've received at the racetrack, and just through the repetitive process of the driving itself, I feel I have learned a great deal about my life and myself during my adventures in high-performance driving. Most instructors, like the inimitable Mr. B, are practical-minded. They have taught me about The Line, about how to deal with rain, about braking and turning, and about such technical tricks as throttle steering, trail braking, and heel-toe downshifting. As a by-product I have learned all sorts of lessons about being tough, open, aggressive, and adventurous. But if there is one lesson more valuable than any other I have learned at the racetrack, it is this: Positive visualization is a technique of incredible power.

I am not naturally one of those people with a cheery disposition. I have to work at it. My ingrained tendency towards negativity is one I have legitimately inherited and must do constant battle against. My dad—someone who always likes to see the glass half post-apocalyptic—likes to say that while the optimist is frequently disappointed, the pessimist rarely is. His take seems to be that we are all, and always, on the brink of total annihilation, and if society hasn't yet degenerated into complete anarchy and steaming heaps of garbage—well, just you wait. It's a stance that seems to work for him, though sometimes listening to him could depress a hyena. Perhaps it's the Danish heritage that dogs his darker moments. That he brought his children into this hopeless state of affairs seems to be an unfathomable leap into the sunny side, but perhaps it was a momentary lapse of judgment brought on by the heat of the moment and the come-hither attractions of my petite German mother. Pessimism is a way of life for him, and it is this congenital negativity that causes him to clutch his umbrellas on even the most cloudless of days. The world could come to an end today, and it is best to be dressed for it. He represents the dark side of the psychological coin.

And then there's the sunnier flip side. Recently Mr. B and I attended the musical Miss M's middle-school band concert. First off, this warning: You never, *ever*, believe you are going to be old enough and square enough to be one of those tired-looking, middle-aged parents sitting in the middle-school auditorium—and then suddenly there you jolly well are. Life is funny that way. So—on the stage sat all the lovely children, gussied up in black and white, looking like little professionals, waiting for their band director, when in he bounced like Tigger with a baton, just radiating positive energy and gladness all over the place. From his exuberant entrance and his smashing tuxedo with tails, you would have thought he had just made it to Carnegie Hall. It struck me that an unquenchable—and really, completely unjustifiable—optimism must be a prerequisite for being a middle-school band teacher. He raises his baton, up go the children's instruments, and his expectation clearly is that beautiful harmonies will emerge from the 120 eleven- and twelve-year-olds arrayed before him. At that moment, I am filled with love for this man who is exchanging many years of musical training for the less-than-lovely sounds we are about to hear. If this is not the very definition of optimism, then I don't know what is.

I suspect that somewhere between the doom and gloom of my father's worldview and the unsinkable buoyancy of the middle-school band teacher hovers the average psyche. Sometimes we may veer from one extreme to the other, wrestling with the dark demons of negativity when confronted by a series of setbacks; other times we may revel in unbridled optimism when for a time everything seems to be going our way. Given my psychological inheritance, it should come as no surprise that I have had to wrestle the dark bastard demon off my back. I envision him as an ugly, snot-nosed little gargoyle, and he had his sharp little talons sunk into me when I was in my late twenties. I had completed my doctorate and had done so with prizes and flying colors, so I expected a rewarding if not exactly glamorous career would duly follow. I didn't aspire to an endowed chair at Harvard, either, just a nice steady job at a small, second-tier liberal arts college. But as I bounced from secretarial temping to SAT prep to adjunct teaching to community college and back again to adjuncting, I became increasingly frustrated and defeated. Where was the cozy office in a little brick colonial building on a leafy campus that I'd envisioned? I'd even entertained the modest fantasy of a fireplace, or a rocking chair, in that office. I'd have students in for tea, and we'd discuss the bleak sense of isolation in Winslow Homer's seascapes, or the not-so-understated eroticism of Georgia O'Keeffe's flower paintings. Where, oh where, were my adoring acolytes?

As I grappled with the increasingly obvious fact that I was never going to land the tenure-track professorship of my dreams, there were times when I felt really, really black. What had I spent all that time and energy on writing a dissertation for? If nobody hired me, then wasn't that an indication that I wasn't nearly as smart and talented as I hoped I was? Even though I could legitimately rationalize the depressed academic job market as the spanner in the works, it all felt very personal, and very damning. I know I was difficult to live with at this point, and I know I complained a lot. It is a tribute to Mr. B's constancy that he stuck with me during this definitely less-than-attractive period in my life. Was I even clinical? It's possible; there's some of it in the family. I am as mulishly obstinate and stupidly proud as my own dad, though, and never dreamed of doing any-thing but digging myself out of it on my own. Do not try this at home.

It is hard to pinpoint what brought me out of it. There was no blind-ing flash of light or profound revelation. I suppose I just gradually realized that, no matter how hard I tried, nothing could change the external cir-cumstances that seemed to stand in judgment of my efforts. I could either continue to pound myself with recriminations and negativity, or I could ease up, accept it, and start to appreciate and enjoy what I did have. I'm no Pollyanna, but I simply made the choice to be happier. And that's all I do. I remind myself, on a daily basis, that I have a great deal of good in my life, and that I have a choice to be happy, or not.

A former colleague of mine had a one-frame cartoon pinned to her bulletin board. It depicted a psychotherapist delivering a roundhouse slap to his patient's face while he yelled, "Snap out of it!!" It bore the title: Single-Session Therapy. When I start a negative thought spiral and I catch my-self at it, I try to give myself a mental slap and remind myself not to be a solipsistic, spoiled ingrate. It works most of the time, and when it doesn't, I'm fortunate enough that a bracing dry martini with a jalapeño-stuffed olive often does.

I believe I've learned a little bit through my own experiences about the insidious power of negativity and the genuinely difficult exercise of thinking positively. It is easy to be negative. It is the weaselly way out. If you think you can't, then you almost certainly can't. And when you fail, you triumphantly and self-fulfillingly think, *Hey, I was right, I knew it would never work out.* You get to feel smug about things turning out badly, which makes you feel like you remain in control. Thinking positively is much, much harder, partly because of the riskiness of exposing hope. It's like letting people see your underwear.

DOES POSITIVE MENTAL imagery bring good things to your life? If I keep repeatedly visualizing the Hermès Birkin bag, will one magically appear in my closet? Is the reason I don't have a Birkin bag in my closet because I have never put great energy into thinking that there ought to be one in there, somewhere? Should I now start meditating, say, ten or fifteen minutes every day, on buttery leather and fine French craftsmanship, and await the Birkin's manifestation? I suppose it's possible, though I suspect that in addition to intense visualization, an American Express black card with an inflated credit limit would also be really helpful.

No: I don't believe in any New-Aged power-of-positive-thinking, if-you-build-it-they-will-come stuff. What I do believe in—now more than ever—is the power of positivity and the incredible capacity of the mind to visualize. Coming to reluctant terms with the lack of conventional success in my academic career taught me the uselessness of persistent negativity. But it was, surprisingly, the racetrack that has taught me a great deal more about the incredible potential of the brain when harnessed constructively.

One might argue that climbing into the car—any car—in the first place is a pretty big leap of faith, and by that argument you are an optimist if you are planning on coming home alive. I often reflect on this as I try to cross a busy intersection near my house, a homicidal cocktail combining a steep hill with a blind curve and New Jersey drivers celebrating a rare long run between traffic lights. I marvel every single time I make it across this intersection and I don't die. Certainly you have to be even more of an optimist if you climb into a sports car at a racetrack and expect to complete twenty laps at top speed without incident. This rock-bottom optimism helps—at the very least, you need to have it to get in the car at all—but this is also not really the essence of positive thinking that the experience taught me, either.

WHAT REALLY CAME as an epiphany was the discovery of the brain-power I am able to harness and the way I can use it to make my car go where I want it to go. It was only at the racetrack that I began to understand what positive visualization really meant. Not only is it a magnificent tool, but its power is curiously addictive. Getting it right made me feel like the superhero Brainiac 5, able to exert mind control over all I could see. Harnessing this has made me feel more powerful, and, oddly, smarter than I've been in any other subject. Perhaps it is the immediacy of the result, since teaching a class or writing an academic treatise is a much more plodding, long-term cultivating of mental effort. At the racetrack, if you make the car go exactly where you want it to go, you feel as if you have triumphed over matter and the perverse powers of the universe. Track Girl powers, activate!

We hominids are hardwired to love puzzles. Think of those marvelous sequences on nature programs in which mama chimpanzees teach their babies how to choose a slim, leafy twig, strip it of its greenery, dunk it into a termite mound, and then remove it to slurp off the tasty fat termites that cling to it. What a brilliant solution to the puzzle of how to get at those yummy little buggers who stubbornly hide inside the impenetrable cement-hard mound! How empowering, how deeply satisfying it must be to conquer that challenge. The gratification is two-part: The emotional reward of feeling superior to the situation at hand, and the more immediate and visceral reward of the chimpanzee equivalent of a free bag of Fritos. Is it any wonder, then, that we, as the distant relatives of chimpanzees, have made Sudoku and KenKen puzzles an international phenomenon? When we solve such a puzzle, we get a rush of those addictive beta-endorphins that tickle the pleasure centers of the brain and make us want to try again. The mathematical Miss M's teacher was at one point running a KenKen competition for her students, and it was all I could do to keep my mitts off the puzzles she brought home. Once, after we'd been stumped while working on a particularly gnarly one, I hunted for the puzzle's weak spot to see where it would fall, and unwisely filled in three or four squares in my darling daughter's absence. I caught absolute hell when she found out and was forced to erase the whole thing so that she, and only she, would be the puzzle's conquistador.

Without question, a great deal of the racetrack's appeal for me is the mental challenge of conquering the three-dimensional puzzle of it. My personal favorite is a newer track at the Summit Point Motorsports Park in West Virginia that from above resembles a plate of linguine. Because of its many twists and turns, it is not an especially fast track, but among track geeks, it is widely considered to be one of the most technical road tracks of the newer generation. The official count declares that it comprises twenty-two different turns in a devilishly complicated configuration that also involves a great deal of elevation changes and a carousel that is banked at twenty degrees. Mentally mastering this track feels akin to solving an expert-level KenKen, since each turn is connected to the next, and getting it right involves a cascading series of solutions in which each one must be right for the next one to fall in line.

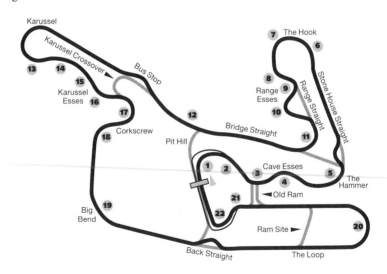

the circuit at Shenandoah

The first time I tackled it, I felt utterly at sea. There seemed to be no way to predict what would come next. My initial bewilderment soon gave way to the determination that I always feel when presented with a fresh

Sunday *Times* crossword puzzle: Dammit, I'm going to get the better of this thing. I could practically feel the neurons firing at quantum speed as I tried to wrap my head around the complexities of the track. Then I recalled watching an Olympic downhill slalom skier running the course in his head before the final heat. Eyes closed, his body gently swayed and his hands swooped in elegant arcs before him as he visualized the path he must take to win his gold medal.

Huh, I thought. *Let me give that a try.*

I took a map of the track with me and climbed to the top level of the timing tower, and I followed one and then another car visually around the course, as much as I could actually see, connecting the dots in my head where I could not. Gradually a picture of the track began to emerge in my head, and when I got behind the wheel, I started to get that endorphin rush when I could picture the contours of the track ahead of me before I arrived at them. The startling expansion of my field of vision from the immediate foreground to the unseen horizon reminded me of the philosophy embraced by one of the members of my extended family. She is the daughter of my father-in-law's second wife, making her, I suppose, my stepsister-in-law. Stepsister-in-law is a converted Texan whom I admire for her unfailing optimism in the face of the many challenges life has thrown her way as well as for her adoption of the Texan habit of delivering pithy aphorisms for all occasions.

My favorite such aphorism encapsulates her attitude toward the difficulties life presents when you are a single parent to two pre-teen daughters, work two jobs, and manage your own horse farm. When I asked for the secret to her equanimity, she offered: "Don't fixate on the bug guts on the windshield."

The implications of this wondrous piece of advice are both obvious and yet somehow subtly brilliant: If you focus on the small messes that dot the mental landscape like the goose-turd land mines in a public park, then you will never see the lake and the landscape and the sunset beyond.

All our lives are filled with bug guts: the red sock in the white laundry, the squirrel in the attic, the water in the basement, the sudden, panicky discovery that you're out of toilet paper. If you dedicate all your energies to the bug guts, then you have neither the energy nor the interest in the larger vision of the road ahead. It can also affect your psychic outlook, because if you are solely mired in the small stuff, then it's difficult to maintain a positive attitude toward the larger goals of job satisfaction or finding (and keeping) love. Those who accomplish the really big things rarely think about the bug guts. This is a huge luxury that simply isn't possible for most of us—we have to mix in a certain amount of attention to the bug guts. First, if you don't clean enough of them off the windshield, then you can't see the panoramic view before you. And, if you only ever look at the stars, you may end up walking around sockless in the winter snow like Albert Einstein. Clearly the trick is to strike a middle balance in order to keep from getting frostbitten ankles, but most of us tend the other way by letting the toilet paper shortages run our lives.

What I also naturally like about the axiom is that it speaks directly to the experience of being behind the wheel of a fast-traveling racecar. Novice drivers—and I was no shining exception—have a tendency to concentrate their vision on the small piece of real estate that is directly in front of them. This is only natural as you are desperately trying to calculate exactly how to remain on that particular piece of asphalt and not drive right off it. All people, when subjected to stress, have a tendency to narrow their focus to what needs to be accomplished in the very next instant—in other words, the bug guts. In high-speed driving, this tendency must be fought against as much as possible, for the high speed dictates that the patch of road in front of you is already a done deal, and any decision you make behind the wheel will be enacted in a path that is far ahead of you. It turns out that the high school Driver's Ed platitude, Aim High in Steering, is one of the most important lessons you can absorb not only for the car but also for life.

ANOTHER OF THE most common admonitions you will hear at the race-track is: "Your car goes where your eyes go." It's sometimes also referred to as the Pothole Effect. Have you ever wondered how it is that if you are on the lookout for potholes in a particularly poorly maintained stretch of road, you seem inevitably to hit every one of them? The reason is simple: Cars are so well designed as an extension to the human frame that a driver will instinctively put the car wherever his eyes are focused. By the same token, it is often difficult for drivers to avoid an accident because in order to avoid it, you have to envision the path around or to the side of it, whereas invariably our attention is focused on the obstacle itself. Often this means that the witness to an accident drives right in and becomes a part of it himself. The faster you are going, the more important it becomes to look further and further ahead—above and beyond the bug guts, until often you must mentally envision a path in your head that is not physically visible at all.

It was at the super-tricky track in West Virginia that I felt as if I had discovered the incredible power of visualization. Because it is so twisty, much of the time I could not actually see the turn that was up next. So intensely did I work on trying to see the track in my head that eventually I found sections in which I could picture the path of the car, its compass and sweep, around blind turns or straight through low impeding hillocks. Like solving a KenKen, every piece seemed to lock into place, and I felt like a master of the universe, able to move mountains with the power of my brain. That triumphant moment is so heady, so powerful, it acted like a drug: This is your brain on race fuel.

And then there's breathing. I'd always thought the emphasis placed on breathing was more New-Agey stuff—not for me. *Of course I am going to breathe, you moron,* I scoffed (silently), as various people in positions of authority used to exhort me to breathe—the teachers of gym, aerobics, music, yoga, prenatal classes. Breathe through your eyes, a singing teacher once told me. Huh? As I lay on the hospital bed, trying to give birth to the rhinoceros that was lodged in my belly, the nurses and doctor told me to breathe. How, I wanted to scream, is breathing going to improve this situation? I pretty much ignored them, breathed according to my need for oxygen, pushed when I was told I had to, and eventually, with much sweating and grunting and eye-popping effort, the rhino morphed into my daughter. To this day it is beyond me why anyone has a second baby and the human race hasn't yet fizzled into extinction. Breathe indeed.

In all my failed attempts at breathing in sync with a physical effort, I never really saw what all the hoo-ha was about—until I started to visualize the racetrack and relax enough to allow my body to respond to the rhythms of what I was directing the car to do. It was at the same track where I had successfully managed to visualize the course and see through solid landmasses that I also began to tap into the power of breathing for the first time in my life. This particular course begins with a series of short, rhythmic esses—right, then left, then right again—gently uphill as you attempt to build up some speed after the initial turn out of pit lane. Such turns are called esses when they don't really require braking or hard turning, but instead allow you to sweep along in more or less continuous motion. I would straighten out of the first sharp turn and then begin the run through the esses, balancing the car first on one side and then the other, gently moving the wheel and applying delicate modulating pressure to the accelerator, when I began to realize that I was breathing in synchronization with the shifts in the balance of the car. It felt effortless and harmonious, as if the car were itself an extension of my brain and my body, and—oddly—it was very, very beautiful.

THE HARNESSING OF mental energy that the sport of high-performance driving encourages came as a major revelation to me. It is a far more cerebral exercise than I would ever have given it credit for. Breathing, focusing, and positive visualization were exercises that not only enhanced my driving skills but naturally enough enhanced the rest of my life as well.

I found that if I could drive the track in my head, then my physical self would generally agree to participate, and my body would put the car where my eyes and brain told it to go. On those occasions when I found my Flow, and I managed to get brain, body, and car working harmoniously together, the resultant sense of mastery over the physical world was so hugely empowering—thank you, beta-endorphins—that I found I desperately wanted to carry that sense of mastery over into the rest of my life.

The touchy-feely metaphorical lesson about positive visualization goes something like this: Sometimes you see best with your eyes shut. If you visualize the future—what you really want, where you really want to go—with a positive mental outlook, and if you aim your vision beyond the bug guts to the larger panorama of the life you have, and if you keep your focus on that larger goal, then you can see right through the windshield and the little hillocks and steer your life where you want it to go.

I am someone who is deeply suspicious of anything that sounds too cheery and too easy. What I get from my pessimistic father—and from my own life experiences generally—is an ingrained skepticism that tells me that if it sounds too good to be true, it pretty much always is. Positive visualization, however, isn't good because it's easy. It's damn hard. In fact it's exhausting. Attempting to master the complicated track in West Virginia was completely exhilarating, it's true, but it was also one of the most mentally depleting exercises I've ever undertaken. Afterward I was almost stupefied with the effort it had required. How very much harder it is to take that approach with life. I won't try to declare that I'm entirely successful at it, but the mental exercises I've undertaken on the racetrack have helped me think about reprogramming the path of my professional life.

All this made me realize that the path I had earlier envisioned—the comfy, tweedy professorship in an ivy-covered enclave—wasn't the only path that it was possible to envision. For too long I guess I'd allowed the bits and pieces of a scattered career splatter on the windshield of my life and prevent me from seeing around other potential corners. The track made me think: Hey, if I can see through mountains and make a car dance through an impossible-seeming set of curves, then I can envision other corners and see around them, too. I can wipe off the bug guts and stop letting them dictate my current path. I haven't cut off all my academic ties just yet—I'm not quite ready to go into professional freefall—but the mental exercises have allowed me to see that there are other things I can do, other roads I can drive, and it has also given me the courage to turn on the blinker and explore them. If you are reading this right now, then you know I have succeeded.

Drive your own road. Ignore the bug guts. And give the snot-nosed gargoyle a tequila on the rocks.

CHAPTER SEVENTEEN

The Best Booty Ever

B efore my first year of racecar driving was over, it was clear that things had gotten pretty serious pretty quickly. My beloved Mr. B watched, indulgently, as I fell, and fell hard, for this addictive activity. (A guy I chatted with once at the track said: "It makes a heroin addiction seem like a vague yen for something salty." Also, I think a heroin addiction might be cheaper.) Mr. B listened tolerantly to me gabble about turn-ins and track-outs, who I'd passed, what I'd done, and when could I go next, please? Inevitably, my car came up for discussion, as well. How could I make it go faster, brake harder, be grippier, turn flatter? Should I upgrade brake pads? Buy new wheels and racier tires? Install a race harness? Tighten up the shocks and suspension?

And that's when, suddenly, I found myself behind the wheel of the new love of my life.

It was the most hilarious thing I had ever driven. By the first screaming quarter of a mile, I wanted it with all my heart. The teeny-tiny Lotus Elise, weighing in at slightly under one ton (your average SUV is over double that), is like a foul-tempered Chihuahua on amphetamines—tiny, fast, noisy as heck, and you can just imagine wanting to swat it

COURTESY OF THE AUTHOR

without a doubt, the best booty ever

with a rolled-up newspaper. The five-year-old gently used one we were test-driving was a Tonka-Toy yellow, and the upward-curving lines of the front of the car—its grille, its lights—made it the friendliest-looking thing you'd ever see bearing down on you in your rearview mirror. How could a gal resist a car with such a high cuteness factor? It seems made for a girl, too—one with as much yoga practice as I've had, since you need to be small, lithe, and highly flexible just to get in and out of the thing. It gives a whole new meaning to the Lotus Position. And with an accelerator pedal the size of a pack of Juicy Fruit, daintier women's feet seem like a prerequisite to driving it.

The adorableness ends, though, once you manage to wedge yourself in and take it for a ride. With a four-cylinder Toyota engine whining in your ear (it sits right behind your head), and your rear end maybe half a foot off the ground, the Lotus revs high, jumps fast, and plays hard, sticking to the road like a bad toupee. Its tiny size and extreme light weight lend it demonic acceleration and extraordinarily quick handling around corners. I probably shouldn't reveal just how fast I wound it up on the forty-mile-per-hour picturesque back roads around Princeton, but I'm sorry to say a third digit enters in.

"Sorry, sir," I imagined myself explaining to the frowning man in blue, "the car made me do it."

Mr. B and I, hooting at the top of our lungs, both felt like children who'd entered a real-world Hot Wheels set. Suddenly I could see myself unleashing some major whup-ass at the racetrack, and I wanted this addictive machine for my very own.

Mr. B is a serious romantic; he always has been. We'd only known each other for two months when he gave me a box of chocolates for Valentine's Day. This was no cheapie Whitman's Sampler purchased at the local drugstore, either, but locally handmade ones, with a charming note whose contents I refuse to indulge on account of some things should just remain private. I was sixteen and this was small-town Pennsylvania, and all this made Mr. B a pretty classy guy. Throughout the course of our long romance, both prenuptial and post-, he's gifted me with better swag than any girl having grown up in central Pennsylvania (if you're from there, you say *pee-aye*) could ever have dreamed of—sparkly jewelry, status watches, yummy handbags—the usual suspects that make most any woman's covetous little heart go pitter-pat.

As good as all that booty is, his best and most romantic gestures in my eyes have been the gifts that promise a future shared activity. *We are in this together*, those things say. The mountain bike he surprised me with was maybe not the most traditionally romantic gift a girl ever got, but it said to me, *Join me in this thing I like to do*. And surely a tandem is all about togetherness—you can't ride it by yourself, and no matter how hard you pedal, you can't get away from your partner. The second-best gift he ever gave me was a flashy, tasseled, patent-leather purse—clearly a dressing-up, night-on-the-town sort of accessory—the Christmas after the miniature Miss M was born. When I opened it, he told me that with the bag came a promise that the six-month-old baby I was still breastfeeding wouldn't stop us from going out and having a social life and doing things together, just the two of us, baby-free. When I finished blubbering, I showered him with a teary gratitude that was fueled by sheer postpartum desperation. A new baby makes you think you will never see a swanky cocktail or your Little Black Dress ever again, and here was the bountiful Mr. B promising me riches in the form of escape from dirty diapers and baby spit. What's more: He followed through on his promise and has in the years since given me many a fabulous night out on the town. Sorry, my dears. He's all mine, and I'm totally keeping him.

When at long last I gave in and joined my speedy better half at the racetrack, Mr. B's beneficent gift-giving followed suit. The Christmas immediately following my very first excursions to the racetrack featured a fleecy jacket from the enterprising marketing forces behind the Mini Cooper. Not only did Mr. B remember how cold I'd been during a chilly snap in upstate New York in August, but he also chose a jacket that with its red-and-white motif matched my beloved tiny car. Since my style usually leans more toward the feminine and funky—there is in fact a tie-dyed blue suede jacket with a huge fake fur collar in my closet—and I wear it, too—Mr. B's gift seemed to say, *Welcome to the club, Track Girl. You are only as aerodynamic as you look.* There were some other track-related gifts, of course. Nothing says love like a seat belt lock (and you know you are seriously hooked if you recognize it for what it is and are actually thrilled to get it). I got the sense that the man in my life had been waiting for years for the opportunity to buy me car parts under the guise of unabashed romanticism. How many men can shop for automotive accessories and truthfully say they are doing it for their wives? The only equivalent I can think of would be if your husband decided to transition to a female and you could go shoe shopping for her. But I'm not sure if this would have quite the same effect on the state of the marital romance.

IT WAS LATER the next spring when the full-blown nature of my addiction became clear, and all I could think about and talk about was the next opportunity to drive at the track, that Mr. B floored me with the most outrageous gift any girl has gotten since Charles offered Diana the kingdom. He decided that I should have my own dedicated track car. The Mini, he thought, should be preserved as my practical daily driver and commuter car. Any further modifications would begin to compromise its comfort and practicality for the street. His own track car, he felt, was too powerful and specialized for a novice like me. I did not put up much of a fuss on this point, not only because I didn't want to shoot myself in the foot on getting my own toy, but also because being responsible for his monstrous car felt like far too much of a burden—and frankly, it was so powerful it did scare me a bit.

The virtual shopping that we wallowed in during the weeks after the fateful decision was made was as filled with as much anticipation, cooing, and clucking as was the furnishing of the nursery when the embryonic Miss M was still cooking in the maternal Crock Pot. Although it is true that the generosity of Mr. B knows, apparently, no bounds, it should also be noted that he had in the past fantasized about the Lotus for himself, and this would be a guilt-free way of indulging that fantasy. "The Lotus is my wife's car," he could say with at least as much pride of ownership as claiming it for himself—maybe more, since he could also bask in the outrageous indulgence of the act. Moreover, it was understood that though this would be "my" car, like the child in a contested custody situation, Mr. B would retain visitation rights.

Perhaps most importantly of all, the acquisition of the Lotus satisfied—at least temporarily—the rapacious, lurking dark side of the outwardly disciplined and conservative fellow I married. My Mr. B is a one-woman man, and I truly do appreciate how lucky this makes me. He is a loving, faithful, unfailingly loyal husband, a doting father, a model son and son-in-law, and an all-around good guy. But he is a car slut. He has the worst roving eye I have ever seen when it comes to cars. On the upside, whenever we are walking down the street and his head snaps around so fast I fear whiplash, it is always a car he's undressing with his eyes, not a woman. He's always lusting after the next vehicle, and I long ago learned that once he starts to talk about a new car, and the evil gleam enters his eyes, I may as well sit back, relax, and let nature take its course. I am philosophical about this faithless whoring side of my spouse. As long as the new model in his life has four wheels and a turbocharger, I am unlikely to lose my position as Wife Number One. Maybe it's just pragmatism on his part: A new car will always cost a whole lot less than an equitable division of property and alimony. And I might just take the Lotus with me.

Lotus is a relatively obscure British marque that was founded shortly after World War II by a fellow named Colin Chapman, who believed that the way to build sports cars was the way Mies van der Rohe designed buildings: Less is more. Instead of increasing horsepower and adding more gear, the Lotus philosophy has always been about reduction—the less there is, the less the car weighs, the faster and more efficiently it can go. Probably the most famous Lotus of all time was the Esprit that turned into a submarine in the 1977 James Bond adventure *The Spy Who Loved Me*. With the possible exception of Chitty-Chitty Bang-Bang, the Lotus-submarine has to be the best movie car ever. More recently, Lotus scored a big hit with the Elise model introduced in 1995. It would be a perfect car for a Bond babe: the boot (it's British, so you don't say *trunk*) is only just spacious enough to stow a semi-automatic and a bikini—no more. The Elise is so small, so nimble, so responsive, that it was an immediate success with track enthusiasts. No one actually knows the origin of the name Lotus, which is ordinarily a type of aquatic plant, but my personal theory is that it is an acronym for Leave Off The Unnecessary Stuff. Of course, it might just as easily be Loud, Ornery, Truculent, Undersized and Speedy, so take your pick.

BEFORE SIGNING THE pink slip on the little yellow Elise we had test-driven, we decided that I should also visit her nearest potential competitor, a hot orange Lotus Exige (a very slightly different model with a stupid name that Mr. B simply can't pronounce, usually coming out as ex-CHEESE) at a used-car dealership on the far outskirts of Philadelphia. The Lotus is an unusual car whose only excuse for existence is as a weekend or track toy; only a few hundred are exported from the U.K. to the U.S. annually. Our first dealership experience was rather what one would expect—the dealer was a dedicated Lotus outlet, with both used and new Lotuses, and it was a place about the love of exotic and vintage cars. The building itself was a well preserved Art Deco–era garage, and the attentive and knowledge-able salesman, recognizing members of his own tribe, took Mr. B and me through the garage bays to see the vintage Aston Martins that were cur-rently receiving tender, loving restoration work there.

The Exige, however, was awaiting my inspection in a very different sort of place. This was a used car dealership in Bucks County, Pennsyl-vania, in a town called Feasterville, on a stretch of strip like that of any other strip in American exurbia, home to multiple car dealerships and the variety of businesses whose very existence I've always questioned. Who actually goes into these places advertising sleep sofas, vacuums, custom embroidery, or lash extensions? I found the lot, which was affiliated with an Isuzu dealership, and pulled up in front of the tiniest showroom I had ever seen. I knew I had arrived in the right place because I was greeted at the lot by a dancing inflatable—one of those twenty-foot high figures made out of nylon tubes through which air is forced at irregular intervals, causing them alternately to inflate and collapse as if afflicted by some de-generative nerve disease.

The suburban New Jersey landscape where I live is the native habitat of the decorative lawn inflatable. As all the furred and feathered wildlife has retreated well out of reach of the Home Depots and Toys "R" Us-es and other predatory retailers, the ripstop nylon inflatable has made significant inroads into the manicured lawn terrain. Their mating season seems to be between mid-October through January, when they proliferate explosively, and then, just as suddenly, they disappear as the new year arrives. Snoopies with pumpkins and Santa Clauses riding Harley Davidsons puff up like garish mushrooms on lawns across the New York metropolitan area. Personally I am most fascinated by a rarer subset, the snow globe inflatable with what appears to be actual snow falling inside. This is a mechanism that fascinates and delights me to no end; how *do* they do it?

There clearly exists some kind of inflatables pecking order, because you never see the dancing ones on residential lawns. They are a strictly commercial breed, and their natural habitat seems to be the used-car dealership. There these poor creatures flail their boneless arms through the air to entice us to enter the lot, and they give themselves hernias as they bob up and down, begging us to buy. They do their Saint Vitus Dance only at used-car dealerships, too, not the new-car ones. Even if the used-car place is affiliated with the new-car place, as was the case in Feasterville, the inflatable does the macarena only in front of the motley assortment of previously owned vehicles. The perfect, high gloss of new cars, the neat rows of identical models, that special, enticing fragrance—maybe it's all so brain-befogging that the dancing guy would only distract us.

At the lot in Feasterville I only had eyes for the Lotus, though. The dancing guy whooped it up outside with nary a glance from me. There in the concrete-block box with two glass sides was the Lotus, a throbbing hot orange, poised like an exotic butterfly in a terrarium. I prowled and poked and prodded, much to the bemusement of the salesman, who had never seen a Lotus before, had no idea what to do with it, and was clearly reveling in the novelty of a woman's interest in such an outrageously racy car.

"You probably don't get a lot of these here," I commented, in an effort to make friendly conversation.

"Nope," he said, "we have a deal with a local business that we'll take their used cars in lots, without refusals, and that's how we ended up with this. We put it here in the showroom mainly because it will attract the attention of people passing by on the highway and bring business in."

In fact, the dealer had propped its rear hatch up and opened the doors so that it resembled a tropical bird displaying its plumage during mating season. I could just imagine all the like-minded car sluts out there attracted to its pheromone output, preening and buzzing all around her and hoping to be chosen as her fortunate new mate.

In the end, the yellow Elise we had initially test-driven stole our hearts. She was in better condition, with far fewer miles, and I decided I was just not quite ready for a car with no rear window whatsoever—a dismaying feature of the fast-backed Exige. The day we drove back to the dealership and picked up my new companion in high-speed insanity was one I spent in utter dissociative euphoria. Could this possibly be small-town, nearsighted me, mother of one, professor of many, brownie-baker extraordinaire? How could I possibly have reached a point in my life in which I could, would, and did come into possession of the most extravagant, outrageous, ridiculously useless vehicle—next to the Oscar Mayer Wienermobile—it was possible to own? Not a blingy diamond tennis bracelet, not a Gucci bag, not an expensive coat made from small furry rodents, yet without a doubt this topped the charts as The Best Booty Ever. And it receives the designation not because it was expensive (though it weren't cheap neither), and not because it was glamorous (though it decidedly was that), but because like the mountain bike and the little black patent-leather purse, it represented Mr. B's implicit message to me: *Track Girl, I want you to join me. Let's motor off into the blue-smoked haze of the sweet asphalt sunset together.*

Toss me the keys, baby, lemme grab my helmet, and awaaaaay we go!

CHAPTER EIGHTEEN

I Am My Own Reality Star

W ithout question, the day the Lotus entered my life was a day that had a profoundly transformative effect on the way I live and interact with the general public. It was a completely unintentional side effect, one I could never have anticipated and which did not at all factor into the decision to purchase my racy little accessory. It was the day I went from Norma Jean to Marilyn. Not that I dyed my reddish-brown pixie cut platinum, nor did I begin enjoying wardrobe malfunctions over subway grates, but I did enter into an entirely new relationship with the public at large—at least on the nation's highways and in parking lots and gas stations.

Here's a typical scenario:

> Somewhere in the low, tree-covered mountains of northern Pennsylvania between Scranton and Binghamton, I have pulled off I-81 for a spot of automotive and human refueling at a roadside gas station and convenience mart. After suckling the Lotus with her premium formula, I pull her up to the shop so I can visit the ladies' room and grab a diet soda. Full tank, empty bladder: worlds better than empty tank, full bladder.

Sometimes it's the little things. As I stroll toward the automatic doors, I am approached by a bear of a man whose appearance, if I encountered him alone on a darkened street, would make me reach for my can of mace—if I actually carried one. He's heavyset but not fat, wearing a black Harley-Davidson T-shirt with the sleeves torn off, exposing his great tattooed biceps, and he has a shaved head with a bandana tied on top. But it's still daylight, there are plenty of people around, and I have a feeling I already know what this is about anyway, so I refrain from running away screaming, and instead pause when he addresses me very gently with, "Excuse me, ma'am, but can I ask you a kinda funny question?"

"Sure," I say, and catch myself before offering *shoot*, thinking it just possible he might take it literally. I settle for, "Go ahead."

"Would you mind," he asks, "if I took a picture of your car?"

Uh-huh: Just as I thought. Another victim has fallen for the devastating adorableness of my little yellow car.

"No problem," I tell him, "you go ahead while I go on in and get myself a soda."

"I gotta go get my camera," he informs me, suddenly as eager as a boy.

"Okay, take as many pictures as you like, and I'll just be inside," I reply as I head in. With the (non-) danger averted, my bladder is asserting its presence more urgently than before. I take care of business and return to the parking area to find the big man still circling the car.

He spots me and says, "My son's totally not gonna believe this, so I had to take some pictures so I could show him."

A loony impulse grabs me and I think, *Hell, why not?* "How tall are you?" I ask.

"Six-one," he replies.

I bend down, unlock the door, swing it open, and gesture inside. "You'll fit, then. Why don't you climb on in, give me your camera, and I'll take some pictures of you behind the wheel?"

"*No WAY!*" he enthuses. "Really?"

"Sure, go on and get in," I say.

"Oh man," he exclaims, "my son's gonna shit bricks!"

Harley-Davidson maneuvered himself into my tiny car—no mean feat for someone of his height and bulk—and I snapped some pix of him grinning hugely behind the wheel. We parted on excellent terms, he with a story and digital proof to tell his son and his friends, and I with a little warm glow of satisfaction pulsating in my breast. How often is it, really, that you get the opportunity to make a total stranger so happy?

I'M NOT BY nature a super-gregarious person or a huge spotlight-seeker. I've lived most of my life in quiet obscurity, and I've never been especially envious of celebrities who are recognized everywhere they go. It's with a mental shudder that I imagine not being able to run to the grocery store in sweatpants or enjoy a quiet, romantic dinner in a restaurant without being accosted by total strangers who think they know you or own a piece of you because they see you every Thursday night on their favorite TV program. Even the occasional random sighting by a former student in the mall—"*hey, professor!*"—is something I find a bit disconcerting. Because I've taught some very large classes, they'll know me when I won't know them, and I understand a little the jarring effect of being recognized and approached out of the blue in a public situation where you think you are anonymous.

But I'm by no means unfriendly, either, and I'd had a little experience with cars as conversation-starters from driving my Mini. The Mini is an extroverted little car to begin with, and my red-and-white version is probably the most eye-catching color combination. I have from time to time been approached by people in parking lots as I entered or exited my little go-kart.

"How do you like your Mini?" they want to know.

"Love your car! So cute!" they exclaim.

"Wish I could drive one," they lament, "but I've got kids."

And of course I respond that I love the car, it's a lot of fun, and it holds way more than you'd think—two kids and a week's worth of groceries are all possible to fit inside. I usually leave these encounters feeling gratified that I have been a goodwill ambassador for the cause of small cars, and basking ever so slightly in the pleasurable warmth of a stranger's approval for my taste in vehicles.

These genial parking-lot exchanges left me completely unprepared, however, for the highly public experience of owning an exotic, sunshine-yellow, cartoonishly smiley-faced sports car like the Lotus. I bought it because I had been seduced by its telepathic responsiveness and its Fred-Astaire nimbleness of foot. When I made the fateful decision, all I thought about was how great it would be to let it wale at the track. Of course I thought it was cute—who wouldn't? It looks like something right out of Japanese anime, and it has so much personality that it wouldn't surprise me in the least if it started to talk to me tomorrow.

Hey girl, it would say, tongue lolling and tail wagging, *let's go for a drive and collect some speeding tickets!*

But I'd had no idea that ownership of the Lotus came with an implicit contract with the public at large, an agreement on my behalf to enter into the public domain. When you are pregnant, everyone feels free to comment on your expanding belly; when you go out with a baby or a puppy, it is virtually a commandment that passersby must stop you to coo and to pet and to chat about the miniaturized version of the perfectly ordinary human being or dog your charge will turn into. Like puppies and babies, flashy little sports cars are practically public property, and the experience of driving about in one is not dissimilar from being a (very) minor celebrity. Everyone feels they own a little piece of you. It is not entirely unpleasant, but it is also not for the shy.

Even when I was young enough to get away with it, I wasn't the big-haired, big-bosomed, short-skirted type, so I never before in my life garnered masculine attention when I walked down the street. Drive through a town in a yellow Lotus, though, and all the little boys' eyes are on you. I was at first taken aback when they all started waving and shouting and throwing me thumbs-ups. But their joy is contagious, and it seems ungenerous not to respond, so I have gotten used to keeping my thumbs near the horn so I can give a little *hey-there-and-back-at-you* toot. Big boys and small ogle you on the highway, but it's far less troubling than getting wolf whistles on the street, I think. I've never actually had a wolf-whistle aimed at me, except once from a parrot in a zoo. One little boy had his mom pull into the passing lane alongside me on the highway so that he could snap pictures of me on the go with his cell phone. I wave, I smile, I pose—as much as one does while behind the wheel and humming along at (or slightly above) highway speeds. Is this what it's like to be stalked by paparazzi?

At an intersection, waiting to enter a highway in southern Maryland, a truck full of landscapers pulled up to my left. The guys on the passenger side had their windows rolled down and started waving and making peculiar gestures at me. They were flapping their hands in the air as if to say *sit* to a dog. Accustomed by this time to friendly waves but puzzled by the peculiar gestures they kept making—did they want me to let them pull in front when the light turned green?—I rolled down my window and gave them a quizzical gesture and look.

"*Push it down,*" they yelled, "*push it down!*"

A little light glimmered in the dim recesses of the brain, and I finally realized they wanted me to rev the engine while I was idling at the light. I gave the accelerator a tentative little nudge. *Grrrribbit-pup-pup-pup* sang my car happily.

That was a pretty nice sound, I thought: cute but with a slightly menacing edge to it.

"*Aww, c'mon,*" they protested, "*you can do better than that!*"

Okay, okay, I thought, I guess it's not actually illegal to make a lot of noise at a stoplight. Is it? I let 'er rip, pressing the accelerator pedal briefly down to the floor once or twice.

FWHOOOM-poppa-loppa-loppa-FWHOOOM-FWHOOOM she hollered, gratifyingly enough.

"*AwwRIGHT!!*" came the approving response from the truck next to me. I don't ordinarily seek the approval of men in pickup trucks, but their happiness with my noise gave me such delight that I grinned for miles at the encounter. It was like signing an autograph, I guessed—give so little, please so much.

NOT EVERY ENCOUNTER with the admiring public has been an unalloyed pleasure. Without exception, everyone loves the car. But the interactions can be a little sobering, too. While paying for my gas in an upstate New York, small-town gas station, I spoke with the young woman behind the cash register. Dumpling-shaped and with a rebellious complexion, the girl battled with her looks by taking the screw-you-Maybelline route: black nail polish, tattoos, nose ring, lip piercing, and quite possibly the most extreme skunk-dyed hair job I have ever seen. From coiffure alone she looked like Pepé LePew's girlfriend.

"Is that your car?" she wanted to know.

I acknowledged that it was.

"Someday," she said, "I'm gonna have a car like that."

My heart squeezed a little, and I said the only thing I possibly could under the circumstances:

"I hope you do." And she just might. When I was her age, it would never even have occurred to me in my wildest fantasies that I could ever drive such a car.

MOSTLY, THOUGH, IT'S terrific fun to be the girl in the Lotus. There are few enough of them exported to the United States that even at a track-driving event they are relatively uncommon. On the East Coast, they don't have their own club, so I drive as I did before with my Mini, mostly with the BMW and Porsche clubs. Parked in the paddock with all the other cars, even against racy Porsches the Lotus stands out with its canary color, its tiny size, and its hyperactive styling. In the ample downtime a club Driver's Ed event allows, men are regularly roaming around the paddock, comparing and assessing the goods on offer like sex addicts in Amsterdam. The Lotus is always a popular stop on the paddock tour, and I have gotten to be an expert on reciting my lovely girl's stats to her admiring fans.

The one thing they all want to know, though, is: Will I fit? The car is so small its rooftop reaches only to the leggy Mr. B's belly button, and when you are inside and driving around town, you are eyeball-to-hubcap with some of the larger pickup trucks and SUVs on the road. Part of the stiffness of the car's body also comes from its peculiar entry design. It has a very high sill, so getting into the car is a tricky process involving levering yourself in and not a little bit of athleticism. Lubrication might help.

Certainly if I can allow the kerchiefed stranger at the rest stop to climb into my car, I can let the boys in the paddock give it a try. One particularly fine day at Watkins Glen had me parked fairly close to the garages and in an area with a number of enthusiastic fellow near-beginners. One of them approached me, friend in tow, and asked the by-now familiar Funny Question: "Can I try to get into your car?"

Feeling royal and benevolent, like a princess about to bestow a lace hankie on an admiring suitor, I stepped aside and made the sweeping *entrez-vous* gesture. He managed the maneuver, mightily pleased with himself, and his friend snapped a photo. As with so many things in this life, like cheating on your taxes, your wife, or at cards, the Lotus is a whole

in the paddock at the track

lot easier to get into than it is to get back out of again. But with a little
inelegant rocking and shoving, and a few old-man-getting-out-of-his-La-
Z-Boy grunts, he ejected himself from the car.

I asked his friend, "You want to try, too?"

The invitation proved to be—as I knew it would—irresistible. This
activity had not gone unnoticed in the surrounding paddock area, and
first one, then another, would-be suitors ambled nonchalantly over. Soon
I had a little queue of men lined up, all wanting to see if they, too, could
fit in the tiny Lotus. I preened a little at all the attention, but I tried not
to let my head get too swelled. I knew it was not even remotely about my
own magnetic personality and rockin' bod, but my sexy little car. If I
vamped it up in a tube top and micromini, I would be unlikely to cause
them to line up in this manner—unless, perhaps, I was also willing to
grant free entry. Oh, well: Over forty, you can live vicariously through
the sex appeal of your car, so long as you are able to shed the muumuu
of the minivan.

BEING THE MOST Popular Girl in the Paddock and the subject of roadside worship has been a strange new role for me and has caused me to consider the nature of celebrity in a whole new light. Recently I pulled out of the confines of the racetrack in my attention-grabbing car, and I happened to be following a newly made friend with a Porsche in a nearly identical shade of yield-sign yellow. As we motored into town, a couple of bicyclists approached on the other side of the road. Upon seeing us, the lead cyclist sat up on his bike and gave us the classic salaam gesture: All hail, rajahs and ranees of the road, we are not worthy. And it struck me: All this adulation, as soothing to the ego as it is, has absolutely nothing to do with any particular virtue or talent of my own. Like a TV reality star, my tiny little piece of fame is completely unearned. I can enjoy it, but I certainly better not get used to it, because if you take away my shiny automotive accessory, I quickly melt back into the anonymity of the crowd.

That's okay with me. It means that, unlike real celebrities, I get to pick up and discard my public notoriety at will. But what the adventures in the flashy little sports car have taught me is to enjoy the starring role I have in my own life. I figure I have a reality life, and if it's not entertaining then I am the only one who can change the channel. Introduce a little adventure, a little flash, a little departure from the normal run of everyday life and suddenly you are in the midst of your own actually unscripted reality show. I mean, who needs *The Amazing Race* if in fact you are in the middle of a real one (even if there's neither audience nor stopwatch)?

Autographs, anyone?

CHAPTER NINETEEN

W.W.C.D.D.
(What Would Cameron Diaz Do?
Or, the Fossil Fuel Dilemma)

WARNING: Do not read the following if you are especially sensitive about the environment, drive a Prius, or care about penguins. For I have some appalling math that will make the ecologically-minded reader shudder with horror and quiver with fierce indignation. Here—as I bow my head in shame—are the figures:

90 (MILES PER HOUR): roughly average speed during a typical racetrack driving session

25 (MINUTES): the length of a typical racetrack driving session

37 (MILES): distance covered in 25 minutes at 90 miles per hour

4.5 (GALLONS): gas wantonly guzzled in 25 minutes at 90 miles per hour

8 (MILES PER GALLON): fuel efficiency of vehicle while on racetrack

Yep, that's right: I get about eight miles per gallon, and often less, in my high-strung and deeply thirsty little hellhound while I am piloting it about the track. You dump a truly appalling amount of gasoline into your engine when you ram that accelerator pedal down to the floor and push the tachometer right up to the redline every time you pull out of a corner. Forgive me, Cameron, for I have sinned.

It poses an honest-to-God dilemma for the thinky person who adores the sport of high-performance driving but regrets the flagrant violation of modern-day morals as set by the environmental evangelists. In a world where celebrities endorse cruelty-free cosmetics, vegan shoes, and holier-than-thou hybrid cars, the moral authority of the sports car enthusiast is tenuous at best. How can one possibly justify deliberately purchasing a criminally thirsty car whose sole aim is to consume as much fossil fuel as possible while going absolutely nowhere at great speed? I have to admit to pangs of guilt that plague me with every visit I make to the pump with my greedy little gas-sucker. It's a small tank that needs to be refilled twice on a typical day at the track. As my darling little Lotus gleefully slurps up gallon after gallon of high-octane fuel, I do indeed wrestle with my conscience about the yeti-sized carbon footprint I am creating.

I am not a religious person, and I don't believe that either God or Santa Claus or even Cameron Diaz is keeping close tabs on whether I've been bad or good. What I have to deal with on a daily basis is much worse, for I report to myself. I possess a finely tuned moral sense and am cursed with an excruciatingly sensitive conscience. I am possibly the world's worst liar and have on more than one occasion been the person who points out to the waiter that I have been *under*charged for my meal. Once, an entire bottle of wine got left off the bill, and even when the waiter maintained that, since it was his error, he would let the accounting stand, I made him go back and put the booze on the bill. I absolutely can't help but ponder the moral repercussions of every significant choice I make, and that means I die a little death every time I fill up the tank at the racetrack.

As an art historian, I have always admired the clear-cut vision of the moral universe of the church in medieval European times. Good and evil, sin and redemption, and Heaven and Hell all got a lot of airtime in medieval art, and the message was straightforward: Lie, cheat, or steal—give in to pride, envy, wrath, sloth, gluttony, or (everyone's favorite) lust—and you will go to Hell, where demons torment you with pitchforks and hot spikes and razor-sharp teeth for all eternity. At the end of your life, there will be a reckoning. Your little soul will be placed on God's balance beam, and while the angels will try to help by lifting you up, the demons will have a jolly old time stomping on the other side to weigh you down.

THINGS HAVE CHANGED a bit since then, and it seems to me that the question of eternal damnation has gotten a bit more complicated in the past thousand years or so. We're still pretty much against killing and stealing (though try telling that to the big banks), but we've gotten a whole lot looser on stuff like sloth, gluttony, and lust: Witness the cable lineup, the Super Size Value Meal, and Tiger Woods. And the entire Kardashian universe is clearly based on a potent if soul-compromising combination of pride, envy, and a pinch of wrath thrown in for good measure.

So what's left for the sinners? Just what do you have to do to get yourself thrown into the fiery pits of hell today? Other than vote Republican.

Today a far, far worse evil is to sin against the environment. Moral condemnation and hot spikes up the ass are reserved for the rainforest-clearing, sludge-dumping, factory-farming manufacturers of Styrofoam coffee cups and Hummers.

Old sin: taking the Lord's name in vain. New sin: imported raspberries in January.

Old sin: worshipping false idols. New sin: letting your car idle at the curb.

Old sin: hitting the bottle. New sin: plastic bottles.

Our new moral universe is one in which your carbon footprint is your measure of saintliness. Which brings me to the struggle between my moral conscience and my love of an activity whose foundation is the wanton consumption of nonrenewable energy sources. How can I possibly rationalize a basically indefensible hobby, environmentally speaking? The first answer to that is to respond with what Mr. B inelegantly refers to as the *fuckits*: As in, I am a decent, moral, upstanding person who spends the great preponderance of her time caring for others—her child, her husband, her dog, her friends, her family, her students. Dammit, I deserve to have some fun where I can find it, and if this is what gives me my jollies a few weekends out of the year, then well, you know. I would actually *like* to be able to dismiss the question so easily, but I am not constitutionally capable of shutting down my moral conscience at that point.

The second approach is to look back at the medieval system of checks and balances, and place my environmental sins and good deeds on the scales of the Final Judgment:

Good Girl

- I turn off the water while brushing my teeth. This despite the fact that I really, really like hearing it run while I foam at the mouth.

- I recycle *everything*—paper, cardboard, plastic, metal; I turn old T-shirts into rags.

- I am maniacal about turning off lights.

- I installed some of those awful fluorescents in my house, even though I hate how dim they are when you first turn them on and how you have to wait forever for them to warm up. Yecch.

- I run a small, fuel-efficient car to work and around town. Love my Mini.

- I use a refillable aluminum water bottle.

- I bring bags to the grocery store. Except when I forget them in the back of the car.

- I buy organic. Well, mostly.

- I patronize my local farmer's market, and when I go, I walk.

- I mostly read my news online.

- I recycle toner cartridges even though it's a pain in the ass.

Bad Girl

- Sometimes I get a terrible hankering for strawberries out of season. I give in.

- I have to buy the Sunday *Times* in paper form because it contains the crossword puzzle. The rest is disposable.

- I leave my computer on all the time. So sue me.

- There are times when I stand under the hot water and let it pound on my shoulders, and it feels so good I can't turn it off.

- I have been known to sneak a small battery in the trash.

- When we order wine, it comes in massive Styrofoam packaging.

- And, bad, bad, bad: I am depleting nonrenewable resources, spewing pollutants in the air, and wantonly contributing to global warming about eighteen days a year when I take my car and run it around the racetrack.

Is the good stuff enough to weigh against the bad? Can I purchase absolution for my sins at the racetrack by doing enough Hail Marys in the form of the Holy Trinity of Reduce, Reuse, and Recycle? I have a sneaking suspicion that this is all pure rationalization and that ultimately, there really is no defense for me and my fellow automotive sinners. Simply put, if I didn't do it, I wouldn't be contributing that extra little bit to the destruction of the planet. As a result, I will likely be damned to the lower levels of the environmentalists' hell, where I will be consigned to an eternity of sorting through comingled garbage while standing ankle-deep in the seeping carcinogenic toxins of the Love Canal. I probably deserve it.

There is, however, the possible salvation of the Greater Good defense, which has the potential to keep me and my cohort from eternal damnation. Think of the world of high fashion. The couture houses in Paris and Milan and London and New York produce astoundingly expensive and outrageously glamorous clothing for a minute clientele with bottomless pockets. Most of the rest of us, however, wouldn't know what to do with a Christian Lacroix or Versace gown if it dropped into our dresser drawers of its own volition and came accompanied by all the right accessories. Wear it to the next PTA meeting? To T.G.I. Friday's for a night out with the girls? Yet without a doubt, our closets are filled with the highly-filtered stylistic innovations these haute-couture designers experiment with in their rarified ateliers. It's the trickle-down effect that starts on the runways and ends up in our closets via Banana Republic or H&M. Sometimes when I see what is hanging on the racks at Macy's or walking about the streets of New Jersey I wonder about the actual benefit this fashion-based trickle-down system is bringing us—why, oh why, can't leggings and UGGs die the quiet death they so richly deserve?—but the point is that major innovation happens at the very expensive high end, and then those innovations are adapted for both user- and wallet-friendly mass consumption.

It works this way in the automotive world, too, only one can legitimately argue that some of the benefits, unlike those of fashion, are very real. Professional racing is a living laboratory for the automobile manufacturers and related industries like tires. Big, big money is spent to make Formula One or Indy cars faster, more efficient, and even safer. It's a give-and-take system with the big auto manufacturers, but, for a potent example: The rearview mirror was actually a development from racing. Where would all the strangler movies be without that invention? You only have to look at the death rates of professional race-car drivers since the fifties or sixties to see that racecars have gotten much, much safer. I've witnessed this personally more than once at the track, where I have seen cars get pretty much trashed, but their drivers emerge intact and unharmed.

It's not just safety, but also automotive technology that sees improvements develop in the world of professional racing. Despite the fact that pro racers are going nowhere at very high speeds and consuming tremendous amounts of fuel while doing so, it is still to their benefit to do all this as efficiently as possible. The less fuel you consume, the less time you waste at pit stops. Take, for example, the turbocharger. The technology emerged first for aircraft engines, but it was applied and refined for racecars before it hit the larger market. It was especially important during the oil crisis of the 1970s, when racing teams were actually given limits to the amount of gasoline they could use. The turbocharger allowed the engine to get more power out of less gasoline. There is also a fair amount of experimentation and development in materials and coatings, and especially tires, in which the racing milieu is a living laboratory for the automotive industry. Moreover, today pretty much all racing series have "green" competitions associated with them. Window dressing? Perhaps; but someday, some of that technology may filter down to the ordinary driver.

SO IN ADDITION to the sheer entertainment value of professional racing (and somehow I don't think the environmental argument holds much water with the millions of NASCAR enthusiasts out there), we the practical sedan and minivan drivers of the world benefit from all the experimenting that goes on at the top tier of the racing world. Those of us who drive for sport on occasional weekends at the racetrack aren't exactly creating the next great automotive innovation, but we are the willing guinea pigs and a small cog in the system that gets such developments from a Formula One Ferrari to your garage in suburbia. I don't have the chutzpah to pat myself on the back and say that by driving at the track I am doing you a service, but maybe it's not entirely as sinful as it looks at first glance. Perhaps there's hope of my joining the lesser angels after all.

On the other hand, heaven may have to wait. For in addition to the damning charge of wreaking environmental havoc, one might also be prompted to add the sin of elitism. In a soured economy, do I feel guilty owning and driving a flashy little exotic sports car? You betcha. I can trot out all kinds of qualifiers by insisting that it's multiples less than, say, a Ferrari, and that we found it used for about what you'd pay for a new (loaded) Accord, but the bottom line is that it's a great luxury and has the potential to make me look like a let-them-drive-Porsches Marie Antoinette. There's a certain home truth in this, but before you haul out the guillotine, consider that it's a hobby that is no more elitist than any that requires an expensive initial outlay. Certainly it was many multiples less than the beach house that many Jerseyites shell out for (and which, for us, this habit replaces). Most golf memberships cost several times what my car did. A fully outfitted sailboat, powerboat, or RV: ditto. Even a nice pair of his-and-hers Harley-Davidsons will set you back a pretty penny. So you make your choices and you find your passion and you pursue it as far as you can afford it.

NOR IS RACECAR driving as elitist as it may at first sound. The kinds of cars and the kinds of people you find at the racetrack are as variable as any cross-section of Americana. At the low end there are young guys with Subarus or VW Golfs and there are older guys who are trying things out in the family sedan or wagon. These are the cars they drive every day, and they are just out to have a little fun with them. Having a dedicated racing car needn't be all that expensive, either. I have seen a guy with a beat-up old Honda Civic completely stripped out and playing with the big boys in their Porsches and doing a little humiliating in it, too. There's a pair of guys I encounter from time to time who come in nearly identical white Ford Taurus SHOs. The cars may look a little dorky, but these guys rock. BMW 2002 models date back to the seventies and are beloved of the track-driving purists who strip them out and bounce them around the track like pinballs. You can buy one for about $7,000. There is an entire entry-level racing series for stock Miatas, which may not have a lot of power but are cheap and fun and highly maneuverable. There are doctors and lawyers aplenty, but there are also landscapers and contractors, and they all happily mix in their mutual love of the internal combustion engine.

Among them all there's plenty of wry amusement, as well as moaning and groaning, at the expense of the hobby. Many of the drivers like to joke about sponsorship—we are all self-sponsored, of course—and make up imaginary racing teams for them to belong to. My personal favorite is the group that calls themselves *Duct Tape Racing* in honor of that much-beloved staple of the paddock. Herewith, a brief tribute to that essential of American life, dedicated to my father-in-law, who believes that there are few problems in life that cannot be solved by that magical silver strip:

ODE TO DUCT TAPE
(for Walt)

Duct tape is great
Duct tape is good
Duct tape keeps us
From coming unglued.

Duct tape is silver
Duct tape is sticky
Duct tape solves all
From simple to tricky.

Duct tape in rolls
Is simple and handy
Duct tape is better
Than beer—no, than candy.

Duct tape for holes
Duct tape for cracks
Duct tape for parts
That hang off the back.

Duct tape's a wonder
Duct tape cures warts
Duct tape fixes seams
When you rip your shorts.

Duct tape for yards
Duct tape for miles
Duct tape the whole earth
And see how it smiles.

Duct tape is great
Duct tape is true
Duct tape is love
From Home Depot to you.

Duct tape is a perfect symbol of the self-sufficiency and ingenuity of most of the types who populate the racetrack. Yes, there's money there, but for the most part it is not especially elitist. There are exceptions. Occasionally someone will show up in a beautiful new Aston Martin to see what it can do, or someone will arrive in a riotous orange Lamborghini. Members of the Ferrari Club have their cars hauled to the track in enclosed semis, and they come with mechanical support to service their cars. Their ceramic brake rotors run about ten large (yes: I do mean ten *thousand* dollars) for a complete set, and their luncheons are catered, with tablecloths and centerpieces (true: sunflowers).

But they are the elite outliers. We the scrappier and much cooler racers who drive our own cars to the track and make do with the fried chicken tenders at the concession stand tend to sneer at the overt decadence of these types and know in our hearts that they aren't really the true drivers. They simply have more money than talent. Or so we'd like to think. Of course, give us several million dollars to spend any way we want and then come back and ask us how we feel about having our cars trucked in and our lunches catered.

There's another trickle-down effect to be found in this, as well, that has to do not with technology but with the simple question of financial trickle-down. Noisy and smelly racetracks are not exactly in high demand as neighbors. They can't be located in areas with pricey real estate anyway, since they require far too much of it. One of the newest tracks to open in the Northeast is in depressed southern New Jersey, an area too far away to benefit from the ripple-effect of the economies of New York or Philadelphia. There's no question that this new track has brought jobs and an influx of money to the post-industrial town of Millville—when we come, we get a hotel room, we eat out, and we rely on employees at the track to keep us safe (the flaggers, the ambulance and tow-truck drivers) and to supply us with gas, food, and toilet paper in the restrooms. It's not super-glam, but it siphons metropolitan money to an area desperately in need of it. So far, all the residents of the town have treated us with the greatest cordiality, admiring the fancy cars with good humor and not a trace of (overt) resentment. We try in return to be the best guests we can and parade through town at a grandmotherly tempo.

So, the question still hangs in the air: Am I going to hell? Can I possibly compensate for the flagrant abuse of fossil fuel, and driving around in a showy car, by being an otherwise model citizen? I do realize that such moral questions are really the by-products of enormous privilege anyway. But I vow to continue to sort and recycle, turn off lights and turn down thermostats, and be a nice person generally to everyone I meet. And if all of that isn't enough, I'll go back to the far simpler philosophy of embracing the *fuckits*. The demons always looked like they were having a whole lot more fun anyway.

CHAPTER TWENTY

Both Feet In

With a nearly full season of driving under my belt, I realize with a mixture of pride and consternation that I have gotten faster. *Lots* faster. I've learned many things, both about myself and about driving, and the result is that I keep pushing harder and harder at both the limits of my car's ability to adhere to the road and my physical capacity to control it. As I left the ranks of the beginners and began to progress through the intermediate-level driving groups, what began as a bashful, gaze-averting relationship with that tall, dark, devastating stranger known as Danger turned into full-blown, eyelash-batting, booty-shaking flirtation.

Hey, big boy, you want a piece of *me*?

At some point you really have to ask: Why would an otherwise sane, safety-conscious mother, who eats plenty of fiber and slathers on sunscreen in an effort to thwart skin cancer and premature wrinkles, actively court danger in the form of a pursuit that stands a reasonably high chance of death and destruction? Why on earth would I wedge a helmet on my head—and, okay, let's be realistic here, how much good will a helmet really do you in a fiery crash at a hundred miles an hour?—strap myself securely into a two-thousand-pound death machine, and go hurtling

driving the carousel

around corners that have sent far more accomplished drivers than myself careening into the tire wall? Why not take up golf, for heaven's sake? Nobody dies in golf.

I don't believe in fate, or that things happen for a reason. As far as I can tell, they just happen. A friend's child is diagnosed with leukemia. Mr. B's client bends to tie his shoe and keels over, dead of a brain aneurism. One minute you're fine, and the next there's an airplane in your living room.

ONE NIGHT IN mid-July 2009, in the small town of Nachterstedt, Germany, a portion of a long-abandoned mine collapsed, and two houses were swept into its depths hundreds of feet below. Three people lost their lives in that freak occurrence. These were three ordinary people who one night ate their dinner, brushed their teeth, put on their pajamas, and climbed into bed with the assumption that in the morning they would climb back out of bed, pour themselves a cup of coffee, and get on with the sorts of chores that make up all of our daily lives. But instead of that, while they were in their beds, the earth opened up and swallowed their house whole. What were the chances of that? In the immortal words of Monty Python: Nobody expects the Spanish Inquisition. I, for one, don't live in fear of the earth opening up underneath me and swallowing me up while I sleep— and yet it's actually happened. You can look it up.

On the other I hand, I do sometimes have nightmares of my darling Miss M, the light of my life, meeting with a violent end as I watch helplessly, or the staunch Mr. B inexplicably disappearing from my life. We all know—whatever forces we ascribe to their occurrence—that bad things happen, for no apparent reason. If you lived constantly in fear of what could happen at any moment—you step in front of a bus, or someone loses control of their car, or you trip and fall just so—then you'd be utterly, permanently paralyzed. But by entering into the sport of high-performance driving, I'm deliberately putting myself in harm's way, aren't I? Scary things sometimes happen at the racetrack, and they certainly have given me some new things to think about in terms of my own mortality. I've never been tempted to bungee jump or skydive before, and I've always dreamed of living to a ripe old age, side-by-side in matching rocking chairs with a snaggle-toothed Mr. B. Am I being brave, or simply stupid, by voluntarily undertaking a patently dangerous sport?

IN THE NORTHEAST, the driving season begins around April first and ends around November first. It is dictated by the chance of water turning from soggy and inconvenient to icy and lethal. Cold is the track driver's enemy. Even if there is not actually snow or ice on the track surface, cold asphalt and cold tires have a great deal less grip than their hot and sticky counterparts. Less grip is simply another way of saying: slicker than Elvis's pompadour. Mr. B and I eked out one last precious driving weekend from the season by going in early November last year. We arrived at the paddock the evening before to drop off his car and change his wheels, so he wouldn't have to do it the next morning. It was already pitch black, and my fingernails turned blue as I held the flashlight for him to see what he was doing. Teeth chattering in the cold, I once again marveled at the masochistic things we do for love.

The next morning, I woke to find my car covered with a beautiful lacy carapace of ice that glittered in the brittle sunshine. My instructor that morning was a lovely, soft-spoken man, a chiropractor who bore a disconcerting likeness to Kevin Spacey, whose understated, creepy performance in *The Usual Suspects* makes him one of my all-time favorite actors. And he's a born New Jerseyan—from South Orange!—so he's got that going for him, too. Not-Kevin advised great caution during our first session out on the track, but he didn't really need to: Driving felt more like ice skating, and I exercised delicate fingertip care with my turns, not wishing to be among the many that morning to slingshot themselves right off the track. In fact, the second session of the morning lasted all of about seven minutes, black-flagged after someone flung himself off the track and had to be pulled out of the rough with a tow truck. By midday, though, the sun was shining strongly, the asphalt was warming up, and it was shaping up to be a nice day for the last drive of the season. I was looking forward to the first afternoon session, waiting for my turn to come up after lunch, when it became clear that an unfortunate incident had occurred on the track. It was serious enough to clear the track, and all activity halted as the situation was dealt with. Someone in the instructors' run group had misjudged Turn One and had managed to pull a 180 and slam the driver's side of the car into the concrete barrier. We waited and watched as first the ambulance, then the fire truck, and finally the tow truck scurried to the site of the incident.

All activity on the track came to a leaden halt as the driver of the car had to be taken to the hospital; without an ambulance present, the sessions could not continue, so we waited, patient and rather subdued, for the ambulance to return. In the meantime, the members of the club dealt with the sadly crumpled vehicle. Club-based driving events are populated by a relatively small and dedicated group of people. Everyone gets to know everybody else, and many of the guys have known each other not just for years but also for decades. No matter what you need—a quick repair, a quart of oil, a tire to limp home on, a lifesaving bottle of beer—someone is bound to help you out. They are all there out of pure love for the sport, and they all know that what someone else needs today, you may need tomorrow. So like platelets rushing to coagulate around a wound, half a dozen of them pitched in to get the car loaded and secured onto a volunteered trailer (the driver hadn't used one) and drive it to a nearby garage. With nothing else to do and morbidly curious about the damage, I ambled over to the hive of activity to suss out the situation. As I drew close, I experienced a jolt of recognition that hit me with a near-physical impact: The vehicle in question was the formerly pristine Porsche of my own instructor.

"Oh, no!" I lamented. "Is he okay?" I wanted to know.

Fortunately, it turned out, he'd suffered nothing worse than a broken arm. Bad enough, if you are a chiropractor, but not life-threatening. Still, it was sobering. He and I had been having a good time, chatting about how I could carry more speed—ironically, we'd even discussed the rookie mistake at Turn One that it appears he ended up making himself—and then, next thing I knew, he was out of the game and in the hospital, his car a total write-off.

IN ONE SENSE, of course, this can happen to anybody at any time and in any place: That is the nature of accidents. If we'd planned for them, then they wouldn't be accidents, would they? At the same time, we do everything we can to try to avoid death and destruction. We wear seat belts, install carbon monoxide detectors, make our kids wear helmets, look both ways, hold hands. Even superstitions die hard, and I know plenty of rational, highly educated people who hedge their bets with Murphy's Law and a refusal to make optimistic predictions. Of those rituals of protection, some are pragmatic, and many are wishful thinking. We cling to them like talismans, and they give us the comfort we need to feel safe enough to carry on.

But short of encasing our entire bodies in bubble wrap and never leaving the safety of the bomb shelter, we have to encounter risk anyway. Life itself is a risk. We can only minimize it. We take calculated risks based on the knowledge we have and then we do the things that we have to do—commute to work, chop the chicken, put up highly flammable Christmas trees—and then the things that we love to do. So we go motor-cycling, bungee jumping, skydiving, rock climbing, skiing, kayaking—even though it's dangerous.

DRIVING AT THE track is not, in many ways, as dangerous as it sounds. Everybody is going in the same direction, mostly at the same rate of (admittedly hell-bent-for-leather) speed. No one is talking on a cell phone; no one is texting. And while I am on the subject: Just who are these morons who text while behind the wheel? They belong in the same category as suicide bombers: criminally solipsistic, self-deluded, colossally ignorant homicidal maniacs. I could rummage through my mental thesaurus all day long and still not come up with rhetoric scathing enough. They deserve to have their tiny brains pulled out through their nostrils. And that, as Forrest Gump put it with such finality, is all I have to say about that. But back to the track, where there are no steaming lattes or Egg McMuffins in the drivers' hands, no screaming babies in the back, no sat-nav, no talk radio, no little old ladies and Mack trucks gunning for each other in the merge lane.

At the track, everybody's equipment has been triple-checked—once by a mechanic, once by the owner, once by the crew in the tech line—and everybody has safety on the brain. The helmets, the neck braces, the fire extinguishers, the six-point harnesses: Even if you never rely on any of this equipment to save your life, the very employment of these devices keeps safety foremost in your mind at all times. The strict adherence to track etiquette, principally the rules about passing, means that drivers are always communicating with one another while in proximity to each other on the track. Above all, when you are driving on the track, you are focused on one thing, and one thing only, and that is the driving you are doing. If civilian drivers paid one tenth of the amount of attention to what they're doing on the streets that track drivers do on the track, the world would be a much, much safer place. And I say that with the guilty conscience of a self-confessed, but largely reformed, distracted driver myself.

Add to all these circumstances the flaggers. They are the unsung heroes of the track driving world, underpaid yeoman workers on whose attention and good judgment we are staking our lives. The layout of a racetrack is planned as strategically as a medieval fort. Watchtowers are stationed around the perimeter such that every flagger has a sightline that at a minimum overlaps with the nearest one on either side of him, and every inch of the track is visible to at least one pair of watchful eyes. From their observation posts, the flaggers—also called corner workers— watch what is happening on the track, communicating with the drivers via colored flags and with each other via walkie-talkies. They start out our sessions with the *green-means-go-go-go* flag, and they end our sessions with the *time's up, dude* checkered flag of lore. Let me tell you: Even if you've never won a thing, having the checkered flag waved at you is still a total kick in the pants. They wave the yellow flag for caution (and no passing), and the black flag to clear the track if conditions are too dangerous to continue. The very serious and seldom used red flag brings everyone to a halt. The black flag with an orange circle in the middle, affectionately termed the *meatball*, is pointed at individuals and means there is a problem with the equipment and the driver must come to the pit to check it out or fix it.

The flaggers are the ones who enforce the passing rules, throwing the dreaded blue flag with the diagonal yellow stripe that officially means *fast-moving vehicle approaching from behind*, but which everybody really knows to mean *move over, asshole, you're holding up traffic*. They can black-flag an individual who takes a pass without being given the point-by: *naughty, naughty boy*. They look out for problems on the track, waving the red-and-yellow vertically-striped flag that designates *debris on the road surface,* and which can in practice mean anything from *someone dumped oil on the track* to *there's a groundhog with a death wish on the side of the road.* At one particular track, Mother Nature runs so much interference—deer, turtles, wild turkeys—that a club member proposed, in all seriousness, the introduction of a wildlife flag. I believe it was to have an image of Elmer Fudd on it.

What this system means is that while you are engaged in rocketing around the track, guardian angels are watching over you at all times, ready to tell you when something goes wrong. I've often thought just how marvelous it would be if we had flaggers for driving in real life. You'd be cruising through the park at twilight, and—*fwhup*—just in time, a flagger would whip out the striped debris flag to let you know that a herd of kamikaze deer was up ahead, just waiting to hurl themselves in front of your car. Or you'd be humming along in fast-moving, bumper-to-bumper traffic on the interstate, and a flagger would throw the red emergency halt flag in time to stop you just before you rear-end the driver ahead of you. How many insurance headaches would that solve? Or—best of all—someone would wave the blue-and-yellow passing flag at that cretin who is driving in the left-hand lane at a snail's pace and holding up all the rest of us who actually want to get somewhere. Damn, where are the flaggers when you need them?

Or how about if there were flaggers for the rest of our lives? You take out your razor, about to shave, and a flagger whips out the meatball (faulty equipment) flag to let you know that the razor is too dull and you'll cut yourself if you insist on using it anyway. And just before you step on that invisible icy patch on the sidewalk in your stilettos, heading for a tailbone-shattering, panty-baring fall, a flagger warns you with the debris flag and you manage to save your tender behind. Or you're dithering about asking for a promotion at work, and a flagger gives you the passing flag to let you know that the ambitious guy or gal in the cubicle next door is about to jump in there and get to your boss ahead of you. How many of us wish there'd been a *bad boyfriend/bad girlfriend* warning flag before we headed into a particularly dangerous stretch on the road of life? I think there ought to be flags for all the hazards of life: *Warning: Tax Audit Ahead* and *Ill-Tempered Mother-in-Law* and *Elderly Sushi* would all be really useful things to get a heads-up on.

Still, no matter how many precautions you put into place, in life or on the racetrack, mishaps are bound to occur. On the streets I've seen people fling themselves at guard rails and introduce themselves gracelessly to cars parked on the side of the road (*crunch*). I once witnessed a car flip end-over-end on the highway, and this past summer on our vacation in Scotland we watched a car misjudge a pass, clip a lorry, and spin over 360 degrees, just missing the unguarded edge that dove into a lake. Breathtaking. At the track, I've watched a guy crawl out of his sunroof after his car ended up perched on its side, and in addition to quite a lot of minor body-panel remodeling, I've seen a couple of cars get completely trashed. Fortunately, the only human injury I've encountered was my unlucky instructor's broken arm, and in a decade of such driving, Mr. B has only seen one other broken limb (not his own) to add to the tally. Not bad, given how anarchical it appears to the uninitiated.

AT SOME POINT or other you will inevitably experience your own moment of mortality behind the wheel of a car out on the nation's highways and byways. If you drive long enough, you will have a near miss—or a hit. Everyone has a story to tell: the truck that almost couldn't stop, the guy who veered into your lane, the icy patch or the standing water that caught you by surprise. Mostly we come out unscathed, sometimes we have to get on the horn with our insurance agents, but always it's an upsetting moment, because it's the moment in which the illusion of control reveals itself to be nothing more than just that: an illusion.

ONE OF THE reasons I find I love the track-driving experience so much is the feeling of mastery, of control I get when I'm behind the wheel and the car is obeying my every command. It's a heady sensation you cannot experience within the tamer confines of everyday driving. But as hard as I try, and as much of my brainpower and focus as I put into it, I'm still human and I still make mistakes. I've done it on the streets, and it was stunningly frightening and revelatory when it happened to me on the track.

All of the practical, daily-driving types of cars I had ever driven have been front-wheel drive. The front end of the car does the pulling, and this means that the tail end does the following, with the logical end result that the car pretty predictably does what you want it to do as you go in and out of turns. Almost all serious sports cars, on the contrary, are rear-wheel drive, which quite literally puts the car(t) in front of the horses—all two, or three, or four hundred of them. The back end pushes the front end around, and sometimes this means that the tail end wants to get to the front faster than the front end does. Translation: spin. This is something I found out the hard way as I worked on the transition from front-wheel to rear-wheel drive at the track with my Lotus.

What happened was a classic mistake: I approached a ninety-degree turn at high speed. I braked, I turned, but as I was in the middle of the turn, I felt the rear end wiggle a little bit. I got spooked, I lifted off the accelerator, and this meant that even more force was transferred away from the rear end of the car, causing it to wing away around to the front. The end result was that I executed a full 360-degree spin, ending up facing the same direction I started out in, not even leaving the surface of the track. This is such a common occurrence that it has a variety of descriptive names—trailing-throttle oversteer or snap oversteer are used most often. It's comforting to know my screwup was a textbook one.

If this description sounds overly technical and dry, that's because it's an accurate description of what happened to the car. Now let's back the reel up and replay it in slo-mo to create an accurate description of what happened to the driver. For whatever reason, this particular turn looked extra intimidating to me. I was taking it with caution, leaving lots of extra room. My instructor was encouraging me to carry more speed through it, and this is what I was trying to do. I braked when he wanted me to, turned where he said to turn, but then I felt that scary little wobble in my hind-quarters and purely of its own volition my foot lifted off the gas. I could feel the momentum of the tail of the car pull the front around, but I was powerless to do anything to correct it any more.

Time froze. I clutched. My chest felt like a great black hole. In a ter-rifying moment, my mind went numb with the realization: *There is abso-lutely nothing I can do.* Did my life flash before my eyes? Not quite, but the rest of the world certainly did. It is a bizarre and disorienting experience to be behind the windshield of a car that is executing a spin. The landscape whirls around, playing like a cinematic dolly shot before your eyes.

In the land of high-performance driving, in the books and in the classroom, you are taught a little mantra:

If you start to spin,
Put both feet in.

The charming rhyme's message is simple and prescriptive. Once you have irretrievably entered the spin (it's possible to correct and save yourself at the wobbly point, but once the end comes fully loose, there's no turning back), the only thing you can do, and must do, is put your left foot on the clutch pedal and your right foot on the brake: Both Feet In. Depressing the clutch releases the engine from powering the car and prevents it from stalling out once you've come to a stop—and, well, braking is what you do when you want to stop. Duh.

I'd like to say I remembered this instructive little poem in my time of need, and that I calmly and authoritatively depressed the clutch and brake pedals as exhorted by the couplet. But I did not.

"*BothfeetinBOTHFEETIN!*" my instructor hollered, and I unthinkingly obeyed.

It was all over, of course, in a matter of about two to three seconds, and there I was, marooned at a standstill on the track as my fellow drivers roared on past me, all of us mercifully unscathed.

As the car settled to a stop and I realized that everyone was okay, the first thing I did was resume breathing. And how. Gulping for breath, my heart hammering in my chest, my whole body shaking with the adrenaline dump, I tried to regain control over my body and my head.

"What do I do now?" I asked, and my instructor pointed to the flagger, my guardian angel, who signaled when it was safe to re-enter the flow of traffic. Numbly and on autopilot I completed the circuit of the track, pitting in at the exit to discuss the incident with my instructor and the club personnel. While spins are not uncommon, they are serious enough that most clubs require you to report them to their event managers. One spin earns you a *tsk-tsk-tsk*, but a second spin implies that you are not in control, and you may be asked to sit out the rest of the day or even leave for the weekend. I was so freaked out I didn't want to go back on the track, and as it happened the session was at a close anyway.

I pulled into the paddock and climbed out of the car, still breathless and shaky from what felt like a near-death experience. Although everyone else looked upon the occurrence as not an especially big deal and all a part of the learning process—just about everyone spins out at one time or another—it was a first for me, and at that moment I wasn't sure if I ever wanted to go back out there again. As my mind played and replayed the terrifying moment when I lost control, my self-preservation instincts rebelled at the very notion of subjecting myself to such potential danger again. *You blithering idiot,* I chided myself, *you could well and truly die out there. You're not some young stallion hopped up on testosterone and needing to prove what a stud he is. You're a grown-up, middle-aged wife and mother who's supposed to be pretty smart. Stay out of it, stay safe, walk away from this thing while you still have viable legs to walk on. Besides, who would make sure Miss M clipped her toenails if you're not around?*

But even as the part of my brain dedicated to sunscreen and seat belts fretted and seethed, another part interrupted and said: *No, okay, I don't want to die, but I do want to live—and I mean really* live*—live without regrets, live to the fullest extent possible, and this crazy lunatic thing makes me feel whoop-a-loop alive.* I have never in my life felt as vibrantly, tinglingly, scarily alive as when I stare down death in the form of a high-speed turn and come out of it intact at the other end—a tiny life-affirming triumph each and every time. No way, dammit, am I stopping now. And it is one of those moments in life—stupid or no—that I am proudest of: that I got back into the car the next time my turn came up, and I went back out there and looked into that black abyss, held my breath, and jumped. That turn still scared the flaming crap out of me, and I treated it with great respect and trepidation, but still, I did it, and I kept on doing it, and as of now, I'm still at it.

Take that, Grim Reaper, and eat your cold dead heart out.

That night, it happened, there was a banquet, sponsored by a generous car dealership hoping to endear itself to a presold crowd that chews through cars like other people chew through antacid tablets (cash bar, though: They're not stupid). In the cocktail hour I found a table with a few empty chairs and began to chat and make some new acquaintances. At one point I allowed that I had experienced my first spin that afternoon. That was *you?* came repeated choruses from the delighted gentlemen at the table. I reddened as I realized that everyone there had either witnessed my moment of ignominy or had passed it along as a juicy little tidbit of gleeful gossip. Truth: Men *love* to gossip. It just has to be gossip that interests them. The track is a very small place indeed, and those who are not driving with you are often watching from the sidelines—and I had executed my spin in a very visible place. In a bright yellow Lotus at a Porsche event. I may as well have had a neon sign blinking I Spun Out Today over my head.

"*You* were the one who did the pirouette?" one marveled.

"It looked so elegant, so dainty, and you came to a perfect stop right there on the track where you started from. You handled it well," another one complimented. "If you're going to spin, that's the way to do it."

As if, I thought, *I'd had any control over that.*

"Be honest," said another, "how brown were your shorts?" (Notice he didn't say *panties.*)

That was when I started to feel a little better. As everyone at the table began sharing spin stories, it started to feel more like a rite of passage. It was as scary to every single one of them as it had been for me, but now we shared a bond of the battlefield, and this gave me an oddly comforting sense of camaraderie.

And I thought, too, about the moment that comes when you have to put Both Feet In. It's a moment that comes to us all sometime in our lives. It's the moment when you have to acknowledge you've just lost control, and there's nothing more you can do. You realize you have no other choice but to give in to the spin, and put both feet in—surrender to the inevitable, hold your breath, and let the car, or life, take you where it's jolly well going to go. And then when it's over, you stop, you assess, you catch your breath, and you just keep on going.

Life is for living. Strap on your helmet, fasten your seat belt, and go.

CHAPTER TWENTY-ONE

Mistress of My Domain

On the eve of my first anniversary at the racetrack, I realized I'd come a long way, baby. Sure, I'd acquired a whole new set of skills, and I could drive pretty fast. But that's far from all. I'd stared down death and deep-fried food and won on both counts. I'd become a master of the torque wrench. I'd eaten snails, slurped on a pickle-juice snow cone, and drunk moonshine. I'd been chased by a police officer and overtaken a flame-spitting Porsche Turbo. I'd found a new role model. I'd discovered Flow. I'd located my Inner Testicles. I'd even envisioned an entirely new career for myself. Not bad for a year behind the wheel. But there was one thing I still hadn't done, and that was drive all by myself, alone.

I pride myself on being a spunky, independent sort of gal. I'd like to think I take after my mother. The first person in her extended family to go to university, my German mother won a Fulbright scholarship to study English in the United States. Hailing from a tiny farming town where her mother still kept chickens, made pickles from heaven, and boiled her linens, my own mother was a real aberration. None of her family had ever traveled further afield than Denmark, and here was my petite mother-to-be, the intrepid Fräulein, packing her bags and heading off to the land of cowboys and chewing gum. (Most German's ideas about America at the time were informed by a wildly popular series of Westerns by the German author Karl May, who never actually traveled further west in the U.S. than Buffalo. That and the American GIs' well-known passion for Juicy Fruit.) My grandparents' darkest fears came to horrifying fruition (*ach du lieber Gott*) when my mother met and married my *Amerikanischen* father. Ordinarily phlegmatic and practical in the extreme, my German Oma suffered a nervous breakdown when she discovered she'd lost her daughter to the Yanks across the great ocean.

The first magnanimous gesture of my life was being born almost Kewpie-doll cute: big blue eyes, white-blond hair, button nose—the whole package. My mother started bringing darling diapered me as a peace offering to her family as soon as I was able to travel. It was fortunate for everyone that I was adorable enough to win over my poor beleaguered Oma and Opa. Thus began an annual ritual of lengthy summer visits that inevitably resulted in my being clad in dirndls and

my first race car

my little brother in lederhosen in smiling pictures of the *Familien-gruppe*. Perhaps this is where I absorbed my affinity for fine German engineering—this despite the fact that neither of my grandparents ever owned a car or learned to drive. My Oma rode her bicycle to the town bakery every morning until she was eighty-five.

I crossed the Atlantic by myself (with, admittedly, the help of Lufthansa) at the precocious age of eight. It was the seventies and the Golden Age of Unaccompanied Minors. As chaperones I had glamorous stewardesses—who hadn't graduated to being flight attendants yet—and they took me to visit the pilot in the cockpit. I adored the exhilarating sense of adventure that felt to my childish self like the very essence of bravery and triumph. Oh boy, did I feel superior for going to Germany all by myself. I can still recall a flight in which little me was upgraded to first class and seated next to a big burly man with a fear of flying. I watched him white-knuckle the ends of the armrests during takeoff, and I can remember trying to reassure him that everything was going to be okay, while I privately wallowed in my worldly wisdom and greater brav-ery. They no longer seat adorable towheaded little girls next to big burly men. This is probably wise.

My mother still recalls the first time she handed me over at the air-port as a tremendously emotional moment. She was about to send me solo almost four thousand miles away, and there I was in my little travel out-fit, a tiny suitcase in one hand and a Winnie-the-Pooh in the other. She hugged me and kissed me and told me good-bye, and—here I have to trust her retelling, as I have no personal memory of this—I marched off with the stewardess with nary so much as a backward glance for my poor heartbro-ken parents. It was only decades later, when I became a parent myself, that I recognized that the courageous one in this situation was not little me but, of course, my mother who was able to let go.

Since then I've never been afraid to go anywhere alone. As soon as I had my own car, my staunch little Honda Civic hatchback, I traipsed all over the place in it—ferrying myself the three hundred miles to college and back home again, going on roadtrips to visit Mr. B at his college also three hundred miles away, and teaching summer school in Virginia after graduation. When Mr. B moved to New York City and I entered graduate school, it was without hesitation that I stormed the Cross-Bronx and Bruckner Expressways and the Triborough Bridge and FDR Drive to get to my honey's fourth-floor walk-up shoebox on Ninety-Third Street. I was never afraid to go head-to-head with a New York City cab driver or elbow my way across five lanes of traffic to make a turn. I still kind of relish doing battle in Manhattan traffic, just to be sure that I haven't lost my finely honed edge. Outta my way!

But for all my chin-jutting bravado and post-feminist independence, I have to confess to a near-paranoiac dislike of dining alone. Why is it that a woman who will cheerfully navigate (before sat-nav, I might add) the Verrazano-Narrows Bridge and the famously anarchical Brooklyn-Queens Expressway to get to a research library, or fly off to conferences in San Antonio or Chicago, would do anything rather than request a table for one at a restaurant? I will trawl the sidewalk stands, shop the convenience stores, hoard the energy bars, or simply starve—anything to keep from sitting down at a table alone. The prospect of sitting down and waiting to be served and eating a meal with a knife and fork, with no one to look at, no one to talk to, is so utterly off-putting and depressing to me that I'd rather have nothing at all.

If you are juggling dual careers, a house, and a child, and you want to get to the racetrack as often as you can, then sooner or later you will probably have to go it alone. For my first several excursions, of course I went in the company of my better half, who knew the ropes and served as mentor, cheerleader, mechanic, and therapist (or are not mechanic and therapist the very same thing?). But when the bug bit bad, I eventually decided to venture out alone. This in itself was not such a big leap for a girl who had flown across the Atlantic as an unaccompanied minor all those years ago.

And the nice men who populate these driving events are not averse to adopting the lone female driver. It is already a group with a strong sense of solidarity: The Few. The Speedy. The Motorheads.

In joining this elite corps, I knew I'd have compatriots galore. But the rare woman—especially an unaccompanied one—brings out their protective side. Because of that, I also knew I would never have to deal with any mechanical difficulties on my own. Really, it's adorable. These guys can barely keep their hands off of each other's equipment (make of that what you will). Give them a damsel in distress and they start competing for the honor of fixing whatever went wrong. I had my first taste of this asphalt chivalry when I showed up solo at an event and a fellow participant pointed out that I had my rear wheels swapped left to right—embarrassing, but not fatal.

"Oh, whoops," I said, "I don't have a jack with me—do you?"

"Sure," came the reply, "come park over by me; I'm with a guy who has his own shop."

Within moments of my arrival, three men had swarmed my car, and—*fwhup-fwippity-fwhip*—the wheels were changed in a blur of masculine competence while I stood by and buffed my manicure, metaphorically speaking.

Could I have changed the wheels myself, once in possession of the proper tools? Sure I could. I know how, and I wield a pretty mean torque wrench. More than one man at the track has commented on the—what is for them—sexiness of a woman who knows how to take care of her own machinery (yes, yes, go on and have fun with that one, too). But why deprive the men of their pleasure? They practically elbowed me out of the way to get to my cute little car. It was clear that my help was not wanted. I thanked them enthusiastically, and knew that by allowing them to take care of this little inconvenience for me, I had my set of pals for the remainder of the event. It is, fortunately, fairly easy to make casual friends at the racetrack.

It is much like being a new mother. As soon as you have a baby, you can make friends with any other mother on the face of the planet, because whoever or whatever else the other woman may be, you have that one deeply important thing in common with one another. I once watched a young mother in a park with a little boy who was licking a top-heavy ice cream cone.

"Be careful," she warned, "or your ice cream will fall off, and I'm not going to buy you another one."

Of course that is exactly what happened next, and the little boy promptly threw the expected tantrum.

"You stop that right now," she scolded, "or we will go home this very instant!"

Here's the thing: Her actual words were not uttered in English. She was speaking in Russian perhaps, or something similarly Slavic, and I don't understand any language spoken east of the Baltic. It didn't matter. She was speaking International Motherese, and I could follow every word, because I have uttered the same phrases in the same situation and with very likely the same intonation. The identical exchange was probably occurring on park benches all over the world at that very moment, and it doesn't matter if the language is Hindi or Japanese, because mothers are the same everywhere.

For many men, the spiritual glue is cars. For them, their cars are their babies, all the more lovable for not needing to be fed in the middle of the night. This is even more the case when you throw together a bunch of like-minded brand-loyal car nuts in one place, pour in a little motor oil, and stir. Display even the slightest interest in the baby of a proud automotive papa, and you have an instant compadre. I sense that they are even more delighted to pull out the wallet and show off the pictures if the interested party is a member of the gentler sex. A woman who will listen! I suspect that for most of them this is an enchanting novelty. All I need to do is sidle up to a car and ask its owner a question about it, and I will have a companion for lunch or dinner or my cousin's wedding, if I so choose.

Thus going alone to racetrack driving events was not, on the scale of things, such a big adventure. I suspect the gentlemen thought it was a little bit brave and rather cute—which is more or less how I felt. Not unlike the eight-year-old version of me marching off at the airport, I thought I was pretty nifty for going it alone at the track. And other than breakfast, which can quite easily consist of a granola bar eaten on the fly, I have never had to eat by myself. There was, however, another milestone of independency at the racetrack, the Holy Grail of the beginning student that still remained: driving solo.

NO MATTER WHAT organization you sign up with to learn how to pilot your car at high speeds, you begin with an instructor who sits next to you in the passenger seat and tells you what to do. Fortunately this is nothing like having your father-in-law as a passenger telling you which lane you should be occupying in order to take the exit that is still two miles down the road. My own grandmother was in the habit of manipulating the passenger-side sideview mirror so that she could see better out of it. Unlike excessively helpful fathers-in-law and misguided grandmothers, however, the racetrack driving instructor is a passenger whose presence you are fervently thankful for. Their first job is to keep you safe, and at the outset, they help you to sift through the tremendous mountain of information that constantly bombards you on the track. They quiz you on flags and point out the locations of the flaggers; they help you with track etiquette and guide you on when to pass and when to allow passing. Their knowledge of the track is extensive, and they will help you ascertain the correct line. Primarily, though, their purpose is to help you to become a better, smoother, more confident driver of your own car—the ultimate payoff for which is getting faster and faster.

Eventually, though, the day will come when you are ready to go it alone, to be master—or mistress—of your own domain. While it is true that in most areas of life, taking the lonely road is the recourse of the sexually frustrated, in the world of high-performance driving, it is a consummation to be devoutly desired. The contest in this arena is not how long you can hold out without a partner, but rather how quickly you can kick your instructor out of the car and fly solo. For men this seems to be a particularly attractive goal, as they are almost always champing at the bit to be able to lock themselves in their cars with their copies of *Road & Track* dancing in their heads if not actually before their eyes. Most of them just can't wait to be the masters of their own domain, pants up and flies zipped for a change.

I, on the other hand, wasn't so sure I wanted to be all by myself out there on the track. Despite being a confident driver and an intrepid traveler in the real world, I really liked having someone there in the passenger seat beside me, even once I was beyond needing to be told to watch the flaggers or where the apex was. Stories abound in paddock lore about students who run amok even under instructional supervision. One that came to me firsthand was about an instructor who, after a number of sessions of telling his student, "brake here; turn in now; give it gas" decided to stay quiet and let his student do the driving without the running commentary for a change. They arrived at the end of a long straight, and instead of braking and turning, the student just kept on going at full tilt, right off the track. Fortunately there was a great deal of open runoff, and no one was hurt. When the car finally came to a halt and the dust settled and the instructor swallowed his lungs back into his chest, he asked his student why he hadn't braked and turned at the appropriate time.

"Because," came the simple response, "you didn't tell me to."

I wasn't afraid that I would do anything quite so egregiously boneheaded, but the presence of a knowledgeable guide was always soothing, and I felt like I had so much to learn from these automotive Yodas that I was in no particular hurry to toss my instructors out of the car. I went on happily like this, bouncing from one instructor to the next in an asphalt variation of speed-dating for the entire first year of my on-track adventures. By the time I had reached the first anniversary of my initial terror-stricken voyage, I was certainly over the young Jedi jitters and was feeling somewhat more confident if not yet a certifiable Master of the Force. It was at this juncture that I had an instructor who decided that I was ready for my first solo drive.

This was at a standard two-day event, and our first day was spent together as he acquainted me with the track and learned where I stood as a student. It was on the second day that he popped the Big Question: "How would you like to be signed off to drive solo?"

This was the moment that every track rat dreamed of and trained for, and it arrived sooner than I had thought possible. "Sure," I said, "I'm game."

Whereas what I actually wanted to do was clutch the front of his long-sleeved instructor's T-shirt and beg him, "Please, *please* don't leave me!"

A man would never do that, so I restrained myself.

THE NEXT TIME we went out on the track, he took me through a very different set of paces than I had ever been through before. Ever since I had first started driving on the track, The Most Holy Line had been placed before me as my guiding light. Suddenly, my instructor wanted me to drive off The Line in what is brilliantly called Off-Line Driving. The Line is always the fastest and most efficient way to get through a turn, but circumstances are not always ideal, and sometimes you will need to enter a turn Off The Line if you are given a late pass—or if someone else takes one. Whether you can improvise while Off The Line and still come safely through a turn is an important test of your driving skills and a key component to determining whether it is safe to turn you loose without the talking head in the passenger seat next to you. I came through this key test well enough that my instructor took me to the next step: taking yet another instructor out for a ride.

This second instructor would not actually do any instructing, but would instead attempt to throw me off my game by having me do all sorts of things I would not normally do, especially Off The Line. If you recall the nerve-wracking ordeal of the stranger from the DMV climbing into your car when you were a teenager hoping to get your driver's license, then you will have some idea of what a lip-chewer this was. Some low-level bureaucrat with a clipboard has the power to determine whether you win the one thing you covet most in the world at that point in your life (besides maybe going to second base with the hot guy/girl who sits in front of you in Algebra). Being tested for solo status at the racetrack was at least as unnerving as that adolescent rite of passage. Would I measure up to his fly-boy standards? Would my mad skills dazzle him enough to persuade him I was capable of taking the wheel all by my lonesome? Or would I relive the ignominious experience of failing my driver's test the first time around as I had done when I was sixteen? I wouldn't know until well after those stressful laps, when the two instructors would put their heads together and decide whether or not I was worthy.

A little less than an hour later, my instructor approached me with a grin on his face and a checkered wristband dangling from his outstretched hand.

"Congratulations," he said to me as he dropped that desirable trinket into my waiting palm, "you did it. Here's your wristband." And to Mr. B, who was standing nearby, he said, "This one's gonna be a *star*."

If there has been a prouder moment in my life since the one when I walked out of my dissertation defense knowing that I was now in possession of a PhD and could fancy myself a "doctor," I can't recall it. My head, like the Grinch's heart, swelled to three times its normal size. I expected a band to strike up the national anthem, or at the very least a scratchy recording of Steppenwolf pounding out *Born to Be Wild*, but the handover was accomplished with no further ceremony. Never mind; it was as good as an Olympic medal as far as I was concerned.

O, say, can you see, by the xenon-tinged light,
What so proudly I've earned on the track while I'm speeding?

Whose bright red-and-white squares, in a pattern so bright,
Now adorn my own wrist, to drive solo I'm needing?
And the turbo's great roar, as o'er the asphalt we soar,
Gives proof to the foot that is pushed to the floor.
O say, does that wristband its powers still cast
O'er the land of the speed, and the home of the fast?

THERE WAS ONLY one session left to the two-day event when I filed into pit lane for my first independent drive. I proudly waggled my checkered bracelet at the guy examining wristbands as I waited on the hot grid. I was reminded of the excursion to the liquor store on the day of my twenty-first birthday, when I bought my very first legal bottle of $5.99 wine. At the checkout counter, I stood at the ready, driver's license in hand. I couldn't wait to thrust it in the face of the bored-looking cashier. *Lookit my ID, lookit, lookit, I'm a grown-up now. I can buy booze whenever I want.* The thrill of alcohol acquisition has since faded somewhat, and, sadly, no one has bothered to ask me for ID for many a long year now, but the moment when I showed my solo-driving checkered wristband in pit lane was at least as good as that long-ago day when I reached the age of majority.

I was as nervous as a virgin at a porn fest as I waited for the signal to go out onto the track. After what seemed like eons, the session at long last began. I gave my imaginary testicles one final squeeze, my lacy panties one last adjustment, and headed out for that beckoning ribbon of asphalt. As I swung into the initial series of esses and pressed the accelerator down, I felt a mad rush of exultation as the car responded to my urgings, and I knew that it was all up to me. I felt curiously light and gloriously free as I reveled in the sensation of being mistress of my own fate. It was as heady an experience as I have ever had. Those twenty minutes passed in a breathless blur of speed and exultation. After I exited the track and leaped out of my car in the paddock, I spiked the invisible football and did the little celebratory dance recognizable across the land as American Sign Language for *TOUCHDOWN!* With apologies to my fantastically satisfying partner in life, this was every bit as good as a knock-down, drag-out hoedown in bed.

Talk about autoeroticism.

AS IT DOES with go-go boots and goatees, history repeats itself in the next generation, and I bring the Divine and now multilingual Miss M to Germany each summer so that she may learn German in the sandbox as I did. Shortly after earning the coveted solo-driving wristband, I found myself all alone in Germany with some time to kill while Miss M was at a camp in the north German heath. I decided to make a pilgrimage to the mecca of automotive engineering, home to both Porsche and Mercedes-Benz: Stuttgart. I pointed my rental Opel southward on the legendary German Autobahn, vainly wishing for a little more horsepower so I could play World War I Flying Ace with the Bimmers on the highway. I checked myself into a downtown hotel on the edge of the kilometer-long pedestrian zone, and I wandered into the city center as the sun was beginning to go down. The sandwich I'd packed for my on-the-go lunch had long since departed my system, and my stomach was beginning to growl. I realized with desperation that I was going to have to figure out something to do about dinner.

Scheisse, I said to myself, translating that all-purpose four-letter cussword for poo into German, *now I'm going to have to eat by myself.* I supposed I'd stop by one of the street kiosks and pick up some *wurst* on a stick. I started looking at the glass-fronted cases, pondering what to order, when I reminded myself of my checkered wristband achievement.

No going the wussy way out, woman, I chided myself sternly. *If you can go solo at the racetrack, then you can't let yourself be intimidated by a table for one at a restaurant.*

It was a beautiful summer's evening, and I thought I could negotiate a compromise by claiming a table at a restaurant with tables placed outside with a view onto the *Schlossplatz* or Palace Square. I settled myself in and even ordered a drink to prolong the experience. The weather was soft and hazy and warm, the view of the fountains and palace was splendid, and the parade of people strolling through the pedestrian shopping zone was an endlessly shifting spectacle. I ordered a real meal and ate it with knife and fork while I watched the city lights glimmer into life as the twilight faded. Did I feel independent, strong, and empowered as I ate my solitary meal? Did I finally decide that dining solo is as liberating as going it alone on the racetrack? Have I conquered my intense and by all rational standards nonsensical dislike of dining alone?

Nope. Did it, still hate it.

LIFE IS LIKE that. Sometimes you're Wonder Woman, and sometimes you're Diana Prince. Sometimes you can hang with the Ferraris, and sometimes all you want is someone to share your flaming waffle with. For me, learning how to run with the wolves has changed everything—and nothing. I still live in New Jersey, in my pretty little suburb with my husband, my daughter, and my tiny fluffy dog. I put out my mixed recyclables on Thursdays and I make sure we never run out of vitamins, or fabric softener, or toilet paper. And I'm still not entirely sure just where my career is going. But sometimes, a few days a year, you'll find me with my helmet on and my stability control off, hurtling around the racetrack in search of that heady, elusive combination of abject terror and ferocious joy that feeds my soul and makes me—for a brief, splendid moment—a speeding superhero, lacy panties and all.

Acknowledgments

Thanks to Karl Benz, Henry Ford, Colin Chapman, and all the other people who made the internal combustion engine generally—and my little racy car specifically—possible. I love you guys.

And thank you to the many people who made this book a reality—to my agent, Barbara Braun, for taking a risk with a most unlikely candidate; to my editor at Seal, Krista Lyons, for reining me in when necessary; to Lenny Cassuto, for being my writerly mentor and midwife; to Sabine Eck, for being my favorite guinea pig; to Klaus "Bokeh" Schnitzer and Bill Heuberger for taking such fabulous pictures and making me look a whole lot racier than I really am; to Ike Nielsen and all his illustrious successors, for willingly stepping into the passenger seat and actually making me a whole lot racier than I formerly was; to Studio Yoga in Chatham, New Jersey, for helping me find my om (and it's not their fault if I didn't); and to Mom and Dad for (more or less) holding their tongues when I undertook this insane hobby in the first place.

But most of all, thanks to Mr. B, because of whom—everything; and to the Divine Miss M, for whom—everything.

© WILLIAM HENBERGER

About the Author

ngrid Steffensen was born and raised in Lewisburg, Pennsylvania, and attended the University of Virginia, Yale University, and the University of Delaware, where she earned a PhD in art history. She has taught art and architectural history at Princeton, Rutgers, NJIT, and Bryn Mawr, and she is the author of numerous articles and books on nineteenth- and twentieth-century art and architecture. Having discovered a passion for high-performance driving and a desire to write for a broader audience, she has embarked on a mission to convert more women to the joys of the high-G turn and the mysteries of the torque wrench. When she is not in the classroom nor at home in suburban New Jersey with her husband, daughter, and tiny dog, she may be found hurtling around the racetrack with her crash helmet on and her stability control off.

SELECTED TITLES FROM SEAL PRESS

For more than thirty years, Seal Press has published groundbreaking books. By women. For women.

Second Wind: One Woman's Midlife Quest to Run Seven Marathons on Seven Continents, by Cami Ostman. $16.95, 978-1-58005-307-5. The story of an unlikely athlete and an unlikely heroine: Cami Ostman, a woman edging toward midlife who decides to take on the challenge to run seven marathons on seven continents—and finds herself in the process.

Rocking the Pink: Finding Myself on the Other Side of Cancer, by Laura Roppé. $17.00, 978-1-58005-417-1. The funny, poignant, and inspirational memoir of a woman who took on breast cancer by channeling her inner rock star.

Pale Girl Speaks: A Year Uncovered, by Hillary Fogelson. $16.00, 978-1-58005-444-7. An edgy, funny memoir about a woman who became angry and self-absorbed when she was diagnosed with melanoma—until her father was diagnosed with the same skin cancer, and she had to learn to lead by example and let go of her fear.

Marrying George Clooney: Confessions from a Midlife Crisis, by Amy Ferris. $16.95, 978-1-58005-297-9. In this candid look at menopause, Amy Ferris chronicles every one of her funny, sad, hysterical, down and dirty, and raw to the bones insomnia-fueled stories.

Go Your Own Way: Women Travel the World Solo, edited by Faith Conlon, Ingrid Emerick & Christina Henry de Tessan. $15.95, 978-1-58005-199-6. Paying tribute to the empowerment of independent adventure and discovery, women recount the thrills of traveling solo, from Borneo and Senegal to Argentina, Paris, Japan, and more.

Kissing Outside the Lines: A True Story of Love and Race and Happily Ever After, by Diane Farr. $16.00, 978-1-58005-396-9. Actress and columnist Diane Farr's unapologetic, and often hilarious, look at the complexities of interracial/ethnic/religious/what-have-you love.

Find Seal Press Online

www.SealPress.com
www.Facebook.com/SealPress
Twitter: @SealPress